D1310198

JIM MANTHORPE has trekked in many of the world's mountainous regions from Patagonia to the Himalaya and Scandinavia to the Canadian Rockies. Since 1999 he has worked as a freelance travel writer, photographer and lecturer. He is the author of two other Trailblazer guidebooks, *Pembrokeshire Coast Path* and *Scottish Highlands – The Hillwalking Guide*. He has also researched and updated *West Highland Way, Cornwall Coast Path* and the *Coast to Coast Path* in the British Walking Guide series as well as *Trekking in Ladakh* and *Trekking in the Annapurna Region*.

Following stints at Stanfords Travel Books and Maps in London and on *The Scotsman* newspaper in Edinburgh he is now living on the west coast of Scotland in Knoydart, accessible only by boat. When not writing, he works as a ranger. He can be contacted at 💻 www.jimmanthorpe.com.

HENRY STEDMAN updated this third edition of *South Downs Way*. He's been writing guidebooks for about 15 years now and walking for even longer. Henry is the author of *Coast to Coast Path* and *Hadrian's Wall Path*, both also in Trailblazer's British Walking Guide series, as well as *Kilimanjaro*. When not walking the national trails of Britain, he can usually be found dragging suffering trekkers to the summit of Kilimanjaro. He loves his job.

The South Downs Way
First edition: 2004; this third edition 2009

Publisher
Trailblazer Publications
The Old Manse, Tower Rd, Hindhead, Surrey, GU26 6SU, UK
Fax (+44) 01428-607571; info@trailblazer-guides.com
www.trailblazer-guides.com

British Library Cataloguing in Publication Data
A catalogue record for this book is available from the British Library

ISBN 978-1-905864-18-8

© **Trailblazer 2004, 2007, 2009**
Text and maps

Editor: Anna Jacomb-Hood
Proof-reader: Nicky Slade
Layout: Anna Jacomb-Hood
Illustrations: © Nick Hill (pp52-4)
Photographs (flora): bee orchid © John Curtin
all others © Bryn Thomas
Photos opp p32 & p144 (bottom): © Jim Manthorpe
Cover photograph and all other photographs: © Henry Stedman
Cartography: Nick Hill
Index: Jane Thomas & Anna Jacomb-Hood

The maps in this guide were prepared from out-of-Crown-
copyright Ordnance Survey maps amended and updated by Trailblazer.

Warning: **hiking and cliff walking can be dangerous**
Please read the notes on when to go (pp20-3) and outdoor safety and health (pp63-6).
Every effort has been made by the author and publisher to ensure that the information
contained herein is as accurate and up to date as possible. However, they are unable
to accept responsibility for any inconvenience, loss or injury sustained by anyone
as a result of the advice and information given in this guide.

Printed on chlorine-free paper by
D2Print (☎ +65-6295 5598), Singapore

South Downs
WAY

WINCHESTER TO EASTBOURNE
planning, places to stay, places to eat,
includes 60 large-scale walking maps

JIM MANTHORPE

THIRD EDITION RESEARCHED AND UPDATED BY

HENRY STEDMAN

TRAILBLAZER PUBLICATIONS

For Mum and Dad

Acknowledgements

From Jim: I would like to thank everyone at Trailblazer for all their hard work in putting this third edition together. I'm particularly grateful to Henry Stedman for updating all the information and to Nick Hill for his usual diligence with the maps and for his work on the previous edition. Thanks also go to Anna Jacomb-Hood for pulling everything together in her usual indefatigable way and, as always, to Bryn Thomas for giving me such a wonderful opportunity. Finally, thanks to everyone who has written in with comments and updates, including Laurie Wedd, Laura Redfield, Charlie Davies-Gilbert and, in particular, thanks to Bill Jenman.

From Henry: Just a quick thank you to Paula Coyne and Tam Lush for their company on bits and pieces of the trail – lovely days indeed; to Jim for letting me loose on his work, Nick Hill for clearly doing a cracking job on the last edition, to Anna for editing, to Roderick Leslie for checking the birds text in the flora and fauna section. And as ever, to Bryn, for keeping me busy. I do appreciate it. Thanks.

A request

The author and publisher have tried to ensure that this guide is as accurate and up to date as possible. However, things change even on this well-worn route. If you notice any changes or omissions that should be included in the next edition of this guide, please write to Trailblazer (address on p2) or email us at 🖳 info@trailblazer-guides.com. A free copy of the next edition will be sent to persons making a significant contribution.

Updated information will shortly be available on:
🖳 **www.trailblazer-guides.com**

Front cover: On the cliffs known as the Seven Sisters, looking east to Birling Gap.
© Henry Stedman

CONTENTS

PART 4: ROUTE GUIDE AND MAPS

Using this guide

APPENDICES:

INDEX

INTRODUCTION

The South Downs are a 100-mile (160km) line of chalk hills stretching from the historic city of Winchester, in Hampshire, across Sussex to the Pevensey Levels by Eastbourne. For centuries travellers and traders have used the spine of the Downs as a route from one village to the next.

Today that route is still used by walkers, outdoor enthusiasts and others who simply need to escape from box-like offices in congested towns and cities. London, Brighton, Southampton and other urban areas are all within an hour or two of the South Downs, making these beautiful windswept hills an important recreational area for the millions who live in the region.

A traverse from one end to the other following the national South Downs Way trail is a great way of experiencing this beautiful landscape with its mixture of rolling hills, steep hanging woodland and windswept fields of corn. Add to this the incredible number of pretty Sussex and Hampshire villages with their friendly old pubs, thatched cottages and gardens bursting with blooms of foxgloves and hollyhocks and one begins to understand the appeal of the Downs as a walking destination.

The South Downs Way begins in the cathedral city of Winchester from where it heads across rolling hills and the Meon Valley with its lazy, reed-fringed chalk-bed river and charming villages. At Butser Hill the Way reaches the highest point of the Downs with views as far as the Isle of Wight and, in the other direction, the North Downs. Continuing along the top of the ridge the Way passes through ancient stands of mixed woodland, past the Roman villa at Bignor and on towards the sandstone cottages of Amberley. Close by is the fascinating town of Arundel with its grand cathedral and even grander castle rising above the trees on the banks of the River Arun. Then it is on to Chanctonbury Ring with its fine views across the Weald of Sussex. The next stretch climbs past the deep valley of Devil's Dyke and over Ditchling Beacon to Lewes with its crooked old timber-framed buildings and the famous Harvey's Brewery.

Finally, the path reaches the narrow little lanes of Alfriston with more historic pubs than one has any right to expect in such a small village. The walk's grand finale includes the meandering Cuckmere River and the roller-coaster Seven Sisters chalk cliffs – before reaching the final great viewpoint of Beachy Head, overlooking the seaside town of Eastbourne.

Walking the South Downs Way can easily be fitted into a week's holiday but you should allow more time for excursions to the many nearby places of interest such as Arundel, Lewes and Winchester itself ... not to mention the lure of all those enchanting village pubs that are bound to make the trip rather longer than intended!

About this book

This guidebook contains all the information you need; the hard work has been done for you so you can plan your trip from home without the usual pile of books, maps, guides and tourist brochures. It includes:

● All standards of accommodation from campsites to luxurious guesthouses
● Walking companies if you want an organised tour
● A number of suggested itineraries for all types of walkers
● Answers to all your questions: when to go, degree of difficulty, what to pack and the approximate cost of the whole walking holiday

When you're all packed and ready to go, there's detailed information to get you to and from the South Downs Way with over 60 detailed maps (1:20,000) and village plans to help you find your way along it. The route guide section includes:

● Walking times in both directions
● Reviews of campsites, bunkhouses, hostels, B&Bs, guesthouses and hotels
● Cafés, pubs, teashops, takeaways, restaurants and shops for buying supplies
● Rail, bus and taxi information for all the villages and towns along the path
● Street maps of the main towns and villages: Winchester; Cheriton; East Meon; Petersfield; Arundel; Storrington; Steyning, Bramber & Upper Beeding; Ditchling; Lewes; Alfriston; Meads Village, and Eastbourne
● Historical, cultural and geographical background information

Minimum impact for maximum insight

Nature's peace will flow into you as the sunshine flows into trees. The winds will blow their freshness into you and storms their energy, while cares will drop off like autumn leaves.
John Muir (one of the world's earliest and most influential environmentalists, born in 1838)

It is no surprise that, since the time of John Muir, walkers and adventurers have been concerned about the natural environment; this book seeks to continue that tradition. There is a detailed, illustrated chapter on wildlife and conservation as well as a chapter devoted to minimum impact walking with ideas on how we can broaden that ethos.

By developing a deeper ecological awareness through a better understanding of nature and by supporting rural economies, local businesses, sensitive forms of transport and low-impact methods of farming and land-use we can all do our bit for a brighter future. There can be few activities as 'environmentally friendly' as walking.

Break clear away, once in awhile, and climb a mountain or spend a week in the woods. Wash your spirit clean.   **John Muir**

About the South Downs Way

HISTORY

There has been a long-distance route running along the top of the South Downs for far longer than walking has been considered a leisure activity. The well-drained chalk hilltops high above the densely forested boggy clay below were perfect for human habitation and were certainly in use as far back as the Stone Age.

From this time onwards a complex series of trackways and paths developed across the land and it is believed that by the Bronze Age there was an established trade route along the South Downs. All along the crest of the Downs escarpment there is evidence of Iron Age hill-forts and tumuli (ancient burial grounds), many of them very well preserved, particularly the Old Winchester hill-fort site in Hampshire.

In more recent times the land was cleared and enclosed, and the flat hilltops were put under the plough. Although this process erased many of the lesser tracks the most significant of them remained; the one which ran east–west along the edge of the escarpment.

It was not until 1972, amid rapidly growing public interest in walking, that the Countryside Commission designated the eighty miles from Eastbourne to the Sussex–Hampshire border the first long-distance bridleway in the UK. Later, the final section through Hampshire was added bringing the length of the South Downs Way to one hundred miles and bringing it to a spectacular halt in the historic city of Winchester. Today the route is growing in popularity with walkers, cyclists and horse-riders alike, all of whom tend to mingle with ease.

❏ Geology

To understand how the South Downs reached their present-day form one also needs to consider the geology of the whole of South-East England which is made up of three bands of rock and sediment, the deepest layer being sandstone, the one above clay and the top layer chalk. Through time these three layers were pushed up, probably due to tectonic plate movements, with Africa nudging into Europe. Through the ensuing millennia the soft chalk was eroded through weathering, exposing first the clay and then the more resistant sandstone. The North and South Downs are all that remains of the chalk that lies over the deeper clay and sandstone layers. They are still being eroded today.

One interesting feature of the Downs is the lack of streams. Chalk (see box p55) is highly permeable so streams flow only very briefly during periods of very heavy rainfall. It is worth remembering this when walking on a hot day.

HOW DIFFICULT IS THE SOUTH DOWNS WAY?

The South Downs Way has to rank as one of the most accessible and easiest of Britain's long-distance paths. Those on foot will find the path usually follows wide, well-drained tracks in keeping with its designation as a long-distance bridleway, catering for cyclists and horse-riders as well as walkers. If anything walkers may, on occasion, crave a few more lightly trodden paths since the route always sticks to the well-beaten track.

This one-hundred-mile walk can be conveniently divided into sections starting and stopping at any of the numerous little villages that sit at the foot of the escarpment or in a fold in the hills.

Route finding

There is very little opportunity to get lost along the Way. It would be an easy route to follow even without the waymark posts, which are usually marked with the National Trail 'acorn' symbol. Posts are often also marked with a blue chevron but bear in mind that these are not exclusively related to the South Downs Way: they also indicate other footpaths.

Nevertheless, it is hard to go astray. Should you find yourself erring from the path the chances are a fence on one side or the steep Downs escarpment on the other will deflect you back in the right direction. In addition there are usually other walkers around, both on and off the official route, so getting lost is nothing to get worried about. Someone will be able to steer you on the right course.

GPS WAYPOINTS

If you have a handheld **GPS receiver** you will be able to take advantage of the waypoints marked on the maps, and listed in the appendix on p178 of this book.

Essentially a GPS will calculate your position on the earth using a number of satellites and this will be accurate to a few metres. You might wonder that if this is possible, what is the point of taking paper maps and a compass with you. The answer is that if the batteries go flat, or the machine malfunctions, you'll be left with only your sense of direction. Depending on how good that is, you might, or might not, be left wondering exactly where you are.

Having said this, it is **by no means compulsory** that you use a GPS in conjunction with this guide and you should be able to get by with simply the signposts on the trail and the maps in this book. However, a GPS can be useful if for some reason you do get lost, or if you decide to explore off the trail and can't find your way back. It can also prove handy if you find yourself on the trail after dark when you can't see further than your torch beam.

If you do decide to use a GPS unit in conjunction with this book don't feel you need to be ticking off every waypoint as you reach it; you'll soon get bored and should get by without turning on your GPS for most of the trail. But if at any point you are **unsure of your position**, or wonder which way you should be headed, your GPS can give a quick and reassuring answer.

You can either manually key the nearest presumed waypoint from the list in this book into your unit as and when the need arises. Or, much less laboriously and with less margin for keystroke error, download the complete list (but not the descriptions) for free as a GPS-readable file from the Trailblazer website. You'll need the right cable and adequate memory in your unit (typically the ability to store 500 waypoints or more). This file, as well as instructions on how to interpret an OS grid reference, can be found in the updates section of the South Downs Way text on the Trailblazer website (🖳 www.trailblazer-guides.com).

HOW LONG DO YOU NEED?

Walkers will find that the whole route can be tackled over the course of a week but it is well worth taking a couple of extra days to enjoy the beautiful downland villages that are passed along the Way. It is also worth taking time to explore the former capital of Saxon England, Winchester, a historic town with a beautiful cathedral. At the other end of the walk Eastbourne, to be polite, is possibly a little less interesting but will keep those who like to sit on a windy seafront happy for hours.

Practical information for the walker

ACCOMMODATION

The South Downs lie in a populous area so there are plenty of villages and towns within easy reach of the Way, most of which offer accommodation for the walker. However, the Way generally follows the high ground along the top of the South Downs escarpment while the villages lie at the foot of the hills. This tends to leave the walker with a small detour to reach a bed at the end of each day. Bear this in mind when calculating times and distances from the maps in Part 4. As a general rule it is a good idea to allow an extra hour each day for the walk to and from your accommodation.

Camping

Unfortunately, there is little to no opportunity for wild camping on the South Downs so campers will have to rely on organised campsites of which there are few. Refer to the itinerary chart for campers on p26 to organise a schedule. Most of these campsites charge from £5 per camper. Some of the more complex, organised sites have showers and washing facilities while others are merely a place to pitch a tent in the grass.

It is difficult to arrange a camping trip along the length of the Downs without being forced into more solid accommodation for one or two nights. Those who have the urge to camp in greater isolation where there is no recognised site may find it worthwhile asking a landowner for permission to set up camp.

Those who do camp will certainly appreciate the experience: the pampered comforts of a bed and breakfast are outweighed by the chance to sleep under the stars and be woken by the sun, should it happen to be showing.

Hostels and camping barns

There are just four youth hostels within easy reach of the Way and all are between Arundel and Alfriston. However, two new hostels should be open in East Sussex, in Lewes and Eastbourne, by 2010.

Despite the name, anybody of any age can join the YHA. This can be done at any hostel or by contacting the **Youth Hostels Association of England and Wales** (☎ 01629-592700, 🖳 www.yha.org.uk). The cost of a year's membership is £15.95 per year (£9.95 for anyone under 26). Having secured your membership, youth hostels are easy to book, either online or by ringing each individual hostel separately.

Each hostel has a drying room, shower and a fully equipped kitchen. Telscombe (see p146) is self-catering only but both it and Truleigh Hill (see p132) have a shop selling basic groceries. The others offer breakfast, a packed lunch and an evening meal. The Arundel hostel has good entertainment facilities as well as internet access; Alfriston also has the latter.

There is an **independent hostel** located near East Meon called Wetherdown Hostel (p85) and two **camping barns**: the first, which is run by the National Trust, is near Bignor Hill and has the charming name of Gumber Bothy (p107); the other is at the Foxhole Campsite near Exceat (p160).

Bed and breakfast

Some B&Bs can be quite luxurious and come at a price but in our experience all the Downs walker really wants is a warm bed and a hot bath. For this reason most of the B&Bs listed in this guide are recommended because of their usefulness to the walker and convenience to the Way, not for how many stars the tourist board has awarded them.

Bed and breakfast owners are often proud to boast that all rooms are **en suite**. This enthusiasm for private facilities has led proprietors to squeeze a cramped shower and loo cubicle into the last spare corner of the bedroom. Not having an en suite room is sometimes preferable as you may get sole use of a bathroom across the corridor and a hot bath is just what you need after a day's walking – and you will also probably save a few pounds.

You may find it hard to find establishments with **single** rooms. **Twin** rooms and **double** rooms are often confused but a twin room usually comprises two single beds which can either be pushed together for a couple or kept separate. A double room has one double bed. **Family** rooms are for three or more people and usually consist of a double bed and a single or three single beds.

Most B&Bs do of course provide a hefty cooked **breakfast** as part of the rate though some now also offer a lighter continental-style breakfast. Some also provide a packed lunch or an evening meal but you will need to give them advance warning and there will be an extra charge. Most B&Bs, however, are close enough to a pub or restaurant but if not the owner may give you a lift to and from the nearest eating place.

Rates B&Bs in this guide vary from around £40 for two sharing a room and for the most basic accommodation to over £70 for the most luxurious, en suite

❑ **Booking accommodation**

You should always book your accommodation because of the competition for beds in summer and the distinct possibility that the place is closed in winter. It is often possible to book online but if not phone the establishment. When booking check the rate and facilities and always let the owner know if you need to cancel so that they can free the bed for someone else. You may be asked to pay a deposit, usually 25-50%.

If you are having problems finding accommodation most tourist information centres (see p34) provide a booking service. The majority charge for this and take a 10% deposit towards the cost of the first night's accommodation, though the deposit is then deducted from the bill. Information about accommodation registered with tourist information centres in Sussex is available on ⌨ www.enjoysussex.info and about Hampshire is on ⌨ www.visit-hampshire.co.uk.

places. Most charge around £50 per room. Remember that many places do not have single rooms and deduct between £5 and £15 for single occupancy of a double or twin room. Prices can be less during the winter months and if you are on a budget you could always ask to go without breakfast which will usually result in a lower price.

Guesthouses, hotels, pubs and inns

Guesthouses are usually more sophisticated than bed and breakfasts, offering evening meals and a lounge for guests; rates are around £30-40 per person.

Pubs and inns offer bed and breakfast of a medium to high standard and have the added advantage, of course, of having a bar downstairs, so it's not far to stagger back to bed. However, the noise from tipsy punters below your room might prove a nuisance if you want an early night. Prices usually range from £30 per person per night.

Hotels are usually aimed more at the motoring tourist rather than the muddy walker and the price (£40-50 per person) is likely to put off the budget traveller. A few hotels have been included in the trail guide for those feeling they deserve at least one night of luxury during their trip.

FOOD AND DRINK

Breakfast and lunch

If staying in a B&B, guesthouse or hotel you'll be served a full cooked breakfast which may be more than you are used to. Ask for a lighter continental breakfast if you can't stand so much food first thing in the morning; alternatively, ask to have a packed lunch instead of breakfast, particularly if you are planning an early start. Many B&Bs and youth hostels can also provide you with a packed lunch at an additional cost.

Alternatively, breakfast and packed lunches can be bought and made yourself. There are some great cafés and bakeries along the Way which can supply both and if you are lucky you will be in town on the day of a farmers' market (see box p15); they are great places to pick up fresh food and try something from the local area. Remember that certain stretches of the walk are devoid of places to eat so check the information in Part 4 so you don't go hungry.

Evening meals

The **pubs** that grace the pretty flint villages of the Downs rank as some of the most authentic country inns in England. Many of them date from the 14th or 15th centuries and have fascinating histories. Food can vary from cheap traditional bar food to high-quality cuisine served in a pub restaurant. For the serious 'connoisseur' drinker the best thing about the downland pub is the range of real ales on offer (see box below).

While evening meals in the villages are often limited to whatever the local pub is serving, some of the larger towns such as Winchester, Eastbourne,

---

❏ LOCAL FOOD AND DRINK

Food

Food in Hampshire and Sussex is varied and tasty. Local farm produce concentrates on beef and pork but there is also a variety of local cheeses and other dairy products. Look out for traditional English dishes such as steak and ale pie, shepherd's pie and ploughman's lunch which can all be found on pub menus.

Fruit farms are a common sight in the south. Most of them invite people to '**pick your own**'. That is not an invitation to get off their land and pick your own elsewhere but to help yourself to their strawberries, raspberries, blueberries and other fruit growing in the fields. Once you have picked enough, you take the fruit to be weighed and paid for.

Hampshire has also long been well-known for its **watercress** beds, particularly around Warnford, Overton and Hurstbourne Priors. The large-scale propagation of watercress in these areas dates back to the 19th century and is much aided by alkaline water provided by the chalky streams of Hampshire. Some of the original watercress beds are still used today.

Cream teas can be ordered in many of the cafés along the South Downs Way. Partaking in this quintessentially English activity is usually done in the mid-afternoon and involves a pot of tea accompanied by scones, clotted cream and jam.

Drink

There's a plethora of local breweries for the real-ale connoisseur to get excited about. Probably the most famous Sussex brewery, and certainly the oldest, is **Harvey's** of Lewes which dates from 1790. Beers to look out for include their Sussex Best and Armada Ales while in September they release their seasonal Southdown Harvest Ale which they proudly describe as the 'taste of the South Downs'.

There are also several newer local breweries. Of particular interest are **Rectory Ales** of Plumpton Green, a tiny brewery set up in 1996 by the rector of Plumpton to raise funds for the local parish, a once-common tradition. Their most popular brews are Rector's Pleasure (4%) and Rector's Revenge (5%). On tap at the The Five Bells at Buriton is real ale from **Ballard's Brewery**, which was founded on a farm near Petersfield in 1980. Finally, there is the **Gribble Brewery** from Chichester whose ales deserve awards not just for flavour but for decorating beer pumps with some of the quirkiest names. Look out for Pig's Ear and the dangerously named Plucking Pheasant but go steady on the Winter Wobbler which, at 7.2%, is probably one of the most dangerous concoctions ever to drip from a beer tap.

PLANNING YOUR WALK

❏ Farmers' markets

Farmers' markets are held in a number of towns and villages throughout Hampshire and Sussex. These give local farmers a chance to showcase their produce and give consumers the opportunity to purchase locally grown stuff in the knowledge that they are helping not just the local economy but the environment too. Buying local produce helps cut down on the wasteful long-distance carriage of food both nationally and internationally – plus, of course, the food is much fresher; see p56 for more details.

To find out more about farmers' markets near the South Downs Way check out the websites 💻 www.farmersmarkets.net, 💻 www.hampshirefarmersmarkets.co.uk and 💻 www.ruralsussex.org.uk; the latter usually has a useful downloadable pdf file with details of all the farmers' markets in Sussex.

The following farmers' markets are all close to the South Downs Way:
- **Winchester** The biggest of its kind in the United Kingdom. Held on Middle Brook St on the first and third Sunday of the month
- **Petersfield** On the first Saturday every month (Mar to Dec) in Market Square
- **Midhurst** In Capron House car park on the fourth Saturday of every other month starting in January
- **Arundel** In Market Square on the third Saturday of every month
- **Pulborough** In the village hall on the last Saturday of every month from February to November (Pulborough is just one stop on the train from Amberley)
- **Steyning** In the main car park off the High St on the first Saturday of every month
- **Lewes** On Lower High St by the river on the first Saturday of the month.

Petersfield and Midhurst are home to some quality **restaurants** with specialities ranging from fish to Italian fare. Those on a budget, or walkers who stumble into town late in the evening, will find a number of late-night **takeaway** joints offering everything from kebabs and pizzas to Indian and Chinese and, of course, traditional fish and chips.

Self-catering supplies

If you are camping, fuel for the stove and other equipment is an important consideration. Supplies can be found at any of the outdoor shops in Winchester and Eastbourne, whilst en route there are outdoor shops in Petersfield, Lewes and Arundel. Check Part 4 for more detailed information about these shops.

Drinking water

Depending on the weather you will need to drink as much as four litres of water a day. If you're feeling lethargic it may well be that you haven't drunk enough, even if you're not feeling particularly thirsty.

Although drinking directly from streams and rivers can be tempting, it is not a good idea. Streams that cross the path tend to have flowed across farmland where you can be pretty sure any number of farm animals have relieved themselves. Combined with the probable presence of farm pesticides and other delights, it is best to avoid drinking from these streams. Drinking-water taps are marked on the route maps. Where these are thin on the ground you can usually ask a friendly shopkeeper or pub barman to fill your bottle or pouch for you – from the tap, of course.

MONEY

While Eastbourne and Winchester at each end of the Way have plenty of banks and cash dispensers (also known as ATMs or cashpoints), the villages in between do not. Bear in mind that some of these ATMs charge up to £1.50 per withdrawal. However, if you find yourself without a penny on the Way it is only a short detour to some of the larger towns; banks with cash dispensers can be found in Petersfield, Midhurst, Arundel, Storrington, Steyning, Lewes and Meads Village. Nevertheless, it is worth having more cash than you think you might need since small local shops will require you to pay in cash, as will most B&Bs, camping barns and campsites, though they will probably all accept a cheque if you have a debit card. Shops that do take cards, such as supermarkets, will sometimes advance cash against a debit card (a transaction known as 'cashback') as long as you buy something for at least £5 at the same time. **Travellers' cheques** can be cashed only at banks, foreign exchanges and some large hotels.

Several banks in Britain now have agreements with the Post Office allowing customers to make cash withdrawals (with a debit card and PIN number or by cheque with a debit card) and deposits at branches throughout the country. As there are several post offices along the Way this is a very useful facility for the walker. For further information contact your bank or call the Post Office's helpline (☎ 08457-223344).

See also p33 for information about money.

OTHER SERVICES

Most villages and all the towns have at least one public **telephone**, a small **shop** and a **post office**. Post offices can be used for receiving mail – if you know where you are going to be from day to day – or for sending unnecessary equipment home which may be weighing you down. In Part 4 mention is given to other services that may be of use to the walker such as **banks**, **cash machines**, **outdoor equipment shops**, **laundrettes**, **internet access**, **pharmacies** and **tourist information centres** which can be used for finding and booking accommodation among other things.

WALKING COMPANIES AND BAGGAGE CARRIERS

There are a number of holiday companies who will arrange all your accommodation and baggage transport for you. Some of the best are listed below.
● **Footprints of Sussex** (☎ 01903-813381, 🖳 www.footprintsofsussex.co.uk) Does seven- to nine-night self-guided holidays along the Way (£415-565 per person); the price includes B&Bs and transport to and from the start of each day's walk. They also organise an annual 'supported' rather than guided 9-day South Downs Way walk (🖳 www.southdownsway.com).
● **ExploreBritain** (☎ 01740-650900, 🖳 www.xplorebritain.com) Runs numerous walking holidays across Britain. They offer a wide selection of self-guided

trips with luggage transfer and accommodation in inns on the South Downs from two-night excursions around Eastbourne and Alfriston (from £222) to trips covering the whole length of the Way. An eight-night trip from Eastbourne to Winchester starts at £640 while a more sedate twelve-night trip starts at £854.
● **Sherpa Walking Holidays** (☎ 020-8577 2717, 🖳 www.sherpa-walking-holidays.co.uk) Offers eight-day and ten-day self-guided inn to inn walks from Eastbourne to Winchester covering 9-11 miles per day. The cost is £537 per person for eight days and £632 for ten days, with a single supplement of £170-224.
● **Sherpa Van Project** (☎ 01609-883731, 🖳 www.sherpavan.com) Sherpa Van offers an accommodation-booking service for the South Downs Way but currently not a luggage-transfer service.
● **Contours Walking Holidays** (☎ 017684-80451, 🖳 www.contours.co.uk) Has a variety of South Downs packages including short three-night sections from £195 to the whole trek for between £425 and £665.
● **HF Holidays** (☎ 020-8732 1220, 🖳 www.hfholidays.co.uk) This long-established company runs at least one guided walk along the length of the trail (Winchester to Eastbourne) in summer; prices from £919.

MOUNTAIN BIKING

The South Downs Way is perfect for cyclists. It is Britain's first long-distance bridleway so it is specifically geared to horse-riders, cyclists and walkers. The entire route can be followed on two wheels on wide tracks which are, on the whole, well drained, with only a few very steep sections either side of the major river valleys.

TAKING DOGS ALONG THE WAY

Dogs are allowed on the South Downs but should be kept on a lead whenever there are sheep around. Considering the Downs is a prime sheep-farming area this is most of the time and it is worth remembering that farmers are perfectly within their rights to shoot any dog they believe to be worrying their sheep; see box p62.

Dog excrement should always be cleaned up to prevent it from being transferred to the soles of walkers' boots.

DISABLED ACCESS

Many of the councils are taking steps to improve access to the Sussex and Hampshire countryside but, unfortunately, some parts of the South Downs Way are still quite inaccessible to disabled people.

Nevertheless, there are stretches of the Way that can be followed quite easily, particularly where roads provide direct access to the top of the hills such as at **Ditchling Beacon** (see p134). Here there are gates designed for wheelchair users and there are also plenty of benches at intervals along the path to the west of Ditchling Beacon. **Devil's Dyke** (see p128) is another good spot where access is relatively easy and the path not too rough.

The **Seven Sisters Country Park** (see box p160) has good facilities for the disabled both in the park and at the visitor centre and access to the beach at Cuckmere Haven is quite straightforward. Disabled Ramblers (🖳 www.disabledramblers.co.uk) occasionally organise rambles around Beachy Head.

Further west the easiest stretches of the Way can be found to the west of **Bignor Hill** (see p107), where there is a car park near the top, and on **Harting Down** (see p94) which has a relatively long stretch of gentle, level pathways. Finally, **Queen Elizabeth Country Park** (see p90) has a maze of wide, level tracks and easy access.

Budgeting

The amount of money you take with you depends on where you plan to stay and how you're going to eat. If you camp and cook your expenses can be low but most people prefer to have at least some of their meals cooked for them and even the hardiest camper may be tempted into a B&B when the rain is falling.

❏ **Information for foreign visitors**

● **Currency** The British pound (£) comes in notes of £100, £50, £20, £10 and £5, and coins of £2 and £1. The pound is divided into 100 pence (usually referred to as 'p', pronounced pee) which comes in silver coins of 50p, 20p, 10p and 5p and copper coins of 2p and 1p.

● **Rates of exchange** Up-to-date exchange rates can be found at 🖳 www.xe.com/ucc.

● **Business hours** Most **shops** and main **post offices** are open at least from Monday to Friday 9am-5pm and Saturday 9am-12.30pm. Many choose longer hours and some open on Sundays as well. However, some also close early one day a week, often on Wednesday or Thursday. **Banks** are usually open 10am-4pm Monday to Friday. New licensing laws came into effect in November 2005. Since then **pub** opening hours have become more flexible so each pub may have different opening hours. However, most pubs on the South Downs Way continue to open between 11am and 11pm and some still close in the afternoon, usually about 3-6pm.

● **National (bank) holidays** Most businesses are shut on 1 January, Good Friday (March/April), Easter Monday (March/April), the first and last Monday in May, the last Monday in August, 25 December and 26 December.

● **School holidays** School holiday periods in England are generally as follows: a one-week break late October, two weeks around Christmas and the New Year, a week mid-February, two weeks around Easter, one week around the end of May/early June and six weeks from late July to early September.

● **Travel insurance** The European Health Insurance Card (EHIC) entitles EU nationals (on production of the EHIC card) to necessary medical treatment under the UK's National Health Service while on a temporary visit here. However, this is not a substitute for proper medical cover on your travel insurance for unforeseen bills and for getting you home should that be necessary. Also consider cover for loss and theft of personal belongings, especially if you are camping or staying in hostels, as there will be times when you'll have to leave your luggage unattended.

PLANNING YOUR WALK

CAMPING

It is possible to survive on as little as £10 per person per day by camping at the cheapest sites and cooking all your own food. However, it is always best to take more than you think necessary to cover those inevitable luxuries like a warm bed after a day walking in the pouring rain. If you like to treat yourself to a pint at the end of the day remember that one costing less than £2.50 is a rare thing in the south of England. Bearing this in mind it is worth counting on £15 per day.

CAMPING BARNS AND HOSTELS

The **camping barn** called Gumber Bothy will set you back a mere £8 per night while the youth hostels along the route all cost £13.95 (under 18s £10.50), making this accommodation a bargain. Rooms are surprisingly good for such a budget price.

   Hostels usually have a self-catering kitchen allowing you to survive on cheap food from the supermarket or local shop. However, if you want to make use of their meals expect to pay about £4.50 for breakfast, £4-5.10 for a packed lunch and £6.50-9 for an evening meal. Now and then, however, you

---

● **Smoking** A ban on smoking in public places came into force in July 2007. The ban relates not only to pubs and restaurants, but also to B&Bs, hostels and hotels. These latter have the right to designate one or more bedrooms where the occupants can smoke, but the ban will be in force in all enclosed areas open to the public – even if they are in a private home such as a B&B. Should you be foolhardy enough to light up in a no-smoking area, which includes pretty well any indoor public place, you could be fined £50, but it's the owners of the premises who suffer most if they fail to stop you, with a potential fine of £2500.

● **Weights and measures** In 2007 the European Commission announced they would no longer attempt to ban the pint or the mile: milk can be sold in pints, as can beer in pubs, and road distances will continue to be given in miles. Most food is now sold in metric weights (g and kg) but the imperial weights of pounds (lb) and ounces (oz) can also be displayed. However, the population remains split between those who are happy with centigrade, kilograms and metres and those who still use fahrenheit, pounds, and feet and inches.

● **Time** During the winter, the whole of Britain is on Greenwich Meantime (GMT). The clocks move forward one hour on the last Sunday in March, remaining on British Summer Time (BST) until the last Sunday in October.

● **Telephone** The international access code for Britain is +44, followed by the area code minus the first 0, and then the number you require. Within Britain, to call a number with the same code as the phone you are calling from, the code can be omitted: dial the number only. It is cheaper to phone at weekends, and after 6pm and before 8am on weekdays. If you're using a mobile phone that is registered overseas, consider buying a local SIM card to keep costs down. See also p32 for details about using a public phone.

● **Emergency services** For police, ambulance, fire or coastguard dial ☎ 999, or the EU standard number (☎ 112).

may prefer to eat out which would add to your daily expenditure. To cover the cost of a night in a hostel, the occasional bar meal and drink count on at least £23 per person per day. If you are planning on eating out most nights this figure is likely to be nearer £25-30 per day.

B&Bs

B&B rates can be as little as £20 per person per night but are usually nearer £25-30 per person for two sharing a room (most places add a single occupancy supplement of £5-10). Breakfast is, of course, almost always included in the total cost but if an evening meal is offered you will be charged an extra £10-15 for it. If you decide to treat yourself to pub meals, beer and other goodies you will probably need around £40-60 per person per day.

EXTRAS

Don't forget all those little things that secretly push up your daily bill – postcards, stamps, beer, ice-cream, buses here, buses there, more beer and getting back to Winchester at the end of your walk. All these extras will probably add up to between £50 and £100.

When to go

The south-east of England has probably the best climate in a country maligned for its fickle weather. By best climate I mean not too much rain and more hours of sunshine than other parts of the UK. The route can be followed at any time of year but clearly the chances of enjoying good weather do depend on the season.

SEASONS

Spring

A typical spring is one of sunshine and showers. From March to May a day walking on the Downs may involve getting drenched in a short sudden shower only to be dried off by warm sunshine a few minutes later. However, the weather can vary enormously from year to year, sometimes with weeks of pleasantly warm sunny weather and in other years days of grey drizzle. In general this is a great time to be on the Downs. Walker numbers are low and the snowdrops, bluebells and primroses decorate the bare woodland floors.

Summer

It can get surprisingly hot and sunny in the summer but again the weather can vary from one year to the next. Always be prepared for wet weather but also be confident of enjoying some balmy summer days too. Occasionally it can be a touch too hot for walking. This can be a problem as there is not much water on the Downs so bring plenty of full bottles. Visitor numbers are high at this time of year, as one would expect, so it can be a little difficult to enjoy a solitary day on the Way. The hills can look quite colourful in summer with wild flowers in bloom in the meadows, red poppies among the corn and fields of bright yellow oil-seed rape. Hay-fever sufferers may not agree that this is such a good thing. However, everyone seems to be in a good mood and the pubs are brimming with all sorts of folk, from fellow walkers to country gents. The big advantage of walking in the summer is that it remains light until well after nine in the evening so there is never any rush to finish a day's walk.

Autumn

Autumn is probably the season when one can reliably expect to be rained on. The weather tends to be characterised by low-pressure systems rolling in from the Atlantic one after another, bringing with them prolonged spells of rain, mist and strong winds. On the positive side those who enjoy a bit of peace and quiet will find very few fellow walkers out and about at this time of year so you can enjoy the raw elements alone.

Furthermore, it is not all rain and wind. Sometimes the weather can surprise you with a day of frost and cold sunshine that can make a day on the Way a real treat. It's important to remember that some businesses shorten their opening hours at this time of year or even close all together.

Winter

Southern England does not experience as many cold snowy winters as it used to some ten to twenty years ago. Winter these days is usually relatively mild with wet weather and occasional spells of colder, dry weather. Any snow that does fall is usually during the months of January and February. It is more likely the further east you go since it is the south-east corner that gets caught by the snow showers that roll in from the North Sea, when the wind is from the north or east. Many walkers will appreciate winter walking for the wilder weather it offers and the days of lonely walking along the high windswept crest of the Downs. The best days are the cold, frosty days when the air is clear and the views stretch for miles.

Bear in mind that in winter many businesses, particularly in the more remote villages, are closed. It is always wise to call a guesthouse or pub before turning up expecting a bed or dinner.

TEMPERATURE

Generally, temperatures are comfortable year-round. In winter, warmer clothes will be needed as the temperature drops towards and, on occasion, just below freezing. Summer is usually pleasantly warm with temperatures around 16°C to 23°C but temperatures as high as the low thirties

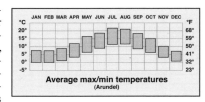

Average max/min temperatures
(Arundel)

Celsius do occur on at least a few days during July or August which can make walking on exposed sections of the Way uncomfortable.

RAINFALL

The weather in England is affected mostly by the weather systems that come from the south-west. These are usually low-pressure systems that contain a lot of rain. Rain can and does fall in any month of the year but dry weather is usually more likely in the early summer.

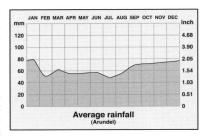

Average rainfall
(Arundel)

DAYLIGHT HOURS

If walking in autumn, winter and early spring, you must take account of how far you can walk in the available light. Also bear in mind that you will get a further 30-45 minutes of usable light before and after sunrise and sunset depending on the weather.

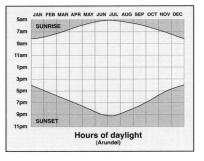

Hours of daylight
(Arundel)

FESTIVALS AND EVENTS

A number of festivals take place in Hampshire and Sussex during the summer, offering everything from live music to fruity beer and comedy. Some of the best events to look out for are:

May
● **Winchester Mayfest** (🖳 www.winmayfest.co.uk) Well-known international folk, jazz and blues acts perform at venues across the city. One weekend in mid-May.
● **Charleston Festival** (☎ 01323-811626, 🖳 www.charleston.org.uk) This festival is held in Charleston Manor (see p150) in the last week or two of May. Arts and literature abound.

June/July
● **Winchester Hat Festival** (☎ 01962-849841, 🖳 www.hatfair.co.uk) Originally a buskers' festival, now a celebration of streets arts and community; all events are free but contributions are welcome – hence the name Hat Festival, as performers can pass around a hat for donations after their show. Held the first weekend of July.

● **Goodwood Festival of Speed** (☎ 01243-755055, 🖥 www.goodwood.co.uk) If you are in the area early July and fancy a change of speed visit this celebration of the history of motor sport; see box p94. Horse racing takes place here between May and October.

● **Winchester Festival** (🖥 www.winchesterfestival.co.uk) A two-week festival in mid-July which includes classical and choir music in the cathedral, folk music in the pubs, dancing in the street, photographic and art exhibitions, comedy events and plenty more.

July/August
● **Lewes Guitar Festival** (🖥 www.lewesguitarfestival.co.uk) Held in the last week of July/first week of August with guitarists from around the world.

● **Arundel Festival** (🖥 www.arundelfestival.co.uk) takes place over the last ten days of August and is held in the castle's grounds. There is music for everyone – folk, rock and classical – as well as plays (Shakespeare) and comedy.

November
● **Lewes Bonfire Celebrations** (🖥 www.lewesbonfirecouncil.org.uk)   The largest bonfire-night celebrations in the country, held on 5 November each year, unless it is a Sunday. However, the organisers prefer non-residents to stay away on this occasion as it is always so crowded.

Itineraries

This guidebook has not been divided up into rigid daily stages. Instead, it's structured to make it easy for you to plan your own itinerary. The South Downs Way can be tackled in any number of ways, the most challenging of which is to do it all in one go. This requires about one week. Others may prefer to walk it over a series of short breaks, coming back year after year to do a bit more. Some choose to walk only the best bits.

To help you plan your walk the **planning map** (see opposite the inside back cover) and the **table of town and village facilities** (pp24-5) give a rundown on the essential information you will need regarding accommodation possibilities and services. Alternatively, you could follow one of the **suggested itineraries** (see pp26-7) which are based on preferred type of accommodation and walking speed. There is also a list of recommended **day and weekend walks** (see p28) which cover the best of the path, all of which are well served by public transport. The **public transport map** is on p39.

Once you have an idea of your approach turn to **Part 4** for detailed information on accommodation, places to eat, and other services in each village and town on the route. Also in Part 4 you will find route descriptions to accompany the detailed trail maps.

TOWN AND

Place name (Places in brackets are a short walk off the SDW)	Distance from previous place approx miles/km	Cash machine (ATM)/ Bank	Post Office	Tourist Information Centre/Point (TIC)/(TIP)
Winchester	0	✔	✔	TIC
Chilcomb	2/3.5			
(Cheriton)	4.5/7(+1.5)		✔	
Exton	5.5/9			
(East Meon)	5/8(+1)		✔	
(Buriton)	7.5/12(+0.5)			
(Petersfield)	(+2)	✔	✔	TIC
(South Harting)	3.5/5.5(+0.5)		✔	
(Cocking)	7/11(+0.5)		✔	
(Heyshott)	2/3(+0.5)			
(Graffham)	1.5/2.5(+1)		✔	
(Sutton & Bignor)	4/6.5(+1)			
(Bury & W Burton)	2.5/4(+1)		✔	
Houghton Bridge	1/1.5			
Amberley	1.5/2.5		✔	
(Arundel)	(+4)	✔	✔	TIC
(Storrington)	3/4.5(+1.5)	✔	✔	TIP
(Washington)	3/4.5(+0.5)		✔	
(Steyning, Bramber & Upper Beeding)	6/9.5(+1)	✔	✔	TIP
(Fulking)	4.5/7.5(+0.5)			
(Poynings)	2/3(+0.5)			
Pyecombe	2/3			
(Clayton)	1/2(+0.5)			
(Ditchling)	1.5/2(+1.5)		✔	
(Plumpton)	2/3(+0.5)			
(Lewes)	1/1.5(+3)	✔	✔	TIC
(Kingston-nr-Lewes)	5/8(+1)			
Rodmell & Southease	4/6			
(West Firle)	3.5/5.5(+1)		✔	
(Alciston & Berwick)	2.5/4(+1)			
Alfriston	2/3		✔	
Litlington	1/2			
Exceat/Seven Sisters	1.5/2.5			TIC
Birling Gap	4/6			
Beachy Head	3/4.5			
Meads Village	1.5/2.5	✔	✔	
Alternative (inland) route from Alfriston				
(Milton Street)	1/2(+0.5)			
(Wilmington)	(+1)			
Jevington	2.5/4			
Eastbourne	4/6	✔	✔	TIC

Total distance 100 miles/162km (via Seven Sisters), 97.5miles/158km (via Jevington)

VILLAGE FACILITIES

Eating Place ✔ = one; ✔✔= two ✔✔✔= three+	Food Store	Campsite	Hostel YHA or H (Ind Hostel) camping barn (CB)	B&B-style accommodation ✔= one, ✔✔= two ✔✔✔= three+	Place name (Places in brackets are a short walk off the SDW)
✔✔✔	✔			✔✔✔	**Winchester**
	✔¹			✔	**Chilcomb**
✔	✔			✔✔	**(Cheriton)**
✔		✔²		✔²	**Exton**
✔✔	✔	✔	H³	✔✔	**(East Meon)**
✔				✔✔	**(Buriton)**
✔✔✔	✔			✔✔	**(Petersfield)**
✔✔	✔			✔✔✔	**(South Harting)**
✔	✔			✔✔✔	**(Cocking)**
✔				✔✔	**(Heyshott)**
✔✔	✔	✔		✔	**(Graffham)**
✔		✔⁴	CB⁴	✔	**(Sutton & Bignor)**
✔				✔	**(Bury & W Burton)**
✔✔✔				✔✔	**Houghton Bridge**
✔✔	✔			✔✔	**Amberley**
✔✔✔	✔		YHA	✔✔✔	**(Arundel)**
✔✔✔	✔			✔✔	**(Storrington)**
✔	✔	✔		✔	**(Washington)**
✔✔✔	✔	✔	YHA⁵	✔✔✔	**(Steyning, Bramber & Upper Beeding)**
✔					**(Fulking)**
✔✔				✔✔	**(Poynings)**
✔				✔	**Pyecombe**
✔				✔✔	**(Clayton)**
✔✔	✔			✔✔	**(Ditchling)**
✔		✔			**(Plumpton)**
✔✔✔	✔			✔✔✔	**(Lewes)**
✔				✔✔	**(Kingston-nr-Lewes)**
✔			YHA¹	✔	**Rodmell & Southease**
✔	✔				**(West Firle)**
✔✔				✔	**(Alciston & Berwick)**
✔✔✔	✔	✔	YHA	✔✔✔	**Alfriston**
✔✔					**Litlington**
✔✔		✔	CB	✔	**Exceat/Seven Sisters**
✔				✔✔	**Birling Gap**
✔					**Beachy Head**
✔✔✔	✔			✔	**Meads Village**
					Alternative (inland) route from Alfriston
✔					**(Milton Street)**
				✔	**(Wilmington)**
✔✔		✔		✔✔✔	**Jevington**
✔✔✔	✔			✔✔✔	**Eastbourne**

¹ 30- to 45-minute walk from village; ² one mile from village; ³ two miles from village;
⁴ at Gumber Bothy 10-20 mins from SDW; ⁵ at Truleigh Hill on SDW

PLANNING YOUR WALK

WHICH DIRECTION?

There are many criteria that will determine in which direction to tackle the Way. It always seems a good idea to finish a walk with something that was worth walking towards. With this in mind Winchester is a far more attractive place to finish in than Eastbourne. Thus, east to west seems a good choice of direction. However, the scenery improves towards the eastern end and what finer place to conclude the walk than by the sea and on top of the white cliffs of the Seven Sisters and Beachy Head. Another factor is the prevailing wind which normally comes from the south-west. Having the wind at your back is a great help so this would also suggest starting at Winchester and finishing at Eastbourne.

Although the maps in Part 4 are arranged in a west to east direction, times for walking in both directions are always given so that the book can be used back to front.

SUGGESTED ITINERARIES

The itineraries below are based on different accommodation types – B&Bs, hostels/camping barns and campsites, with each one divided into three categories of walking speed. They really are only suggestions and all of them can be easily adapted by using the more detailed information on accommodation found in Part 4. Don't forget to add your travelling time from/to your accommodation both before and after the walk.

	CAMPING					
	Relaxed pace		**Medium pace**		**Fast pace**	
Night	**Place**	**Approx distance** miles/km	**Place**	**Approx distance** miles/km	**Place**	**Approx distance** miles/km
0	Winchester*		Winchester*		Winchester*	
1	Cheriton	8/13	Exton	12/19.5	East Meon	18/29
2	Exton	7/11	Sth Harting*	16.5/26.5	Cocking*	19.5/31.5
3	East Meon	6/9.5	Bignor	16/25.5	Washington	18.5/29.5
4	Sth Harting*	12.5/20	Washington	12.5/20	Plumpton	20/32
5	Cocking*	8/13	Pyecombe	15/24	Alfriston	18.5/29.5
6	Bignor	9/14.5	Rodmell*	14/22.5	Eastbourne*	12.5/20
7	Washington	12.5/20	Alfriston	8/13		
8	Steyning	7.5/12	Eastbourne*	12.5/20		
9	Pyecombe	9.5/15				
10	Plumpton	5/8				
11	Rodmell*	10.5/17				
12	Alfriston	8/13				
13	Exceat	2.5/4				
14	Eastbourne*	10/16				

* There are no campsites at places marked with an asterisk but alternative accommodation is available

STAYING IN HOSTELS/CAMPING BARNS

	Relaxed pace		Medium pace		Fast pace	
Night	Place	Approx distance miles/km	Place	Approx distance miles/km	Place	Approx distance miles/km
0	Winchester*		Winchester*		Winchester*	
1	Cheriton*	8/13	Cheriton*	8/13	East Meon	18/29
2	East Meon	13/20	East Meon	13/20	Buriton*	9/14.5
3	Buriton*	9/14.5	Sth Harting*	12.5/20	Bignor	19.5/31.5
4	Cocking*	11.5/18.5	Bignor	16/25.5	Truleigh Hill	20/32
5	Bignor	9/14.5	Truleigh Hill	20/32	Rodmell	21/33.5
6	Washington*	12.5/20	Ditchling*	10.5/17	Eastbourne*	20.5/33
7	Truleigh Hill	8.5/13.5	Rodmell	13.5/21.5		
8	Ditchling*	10.5/17	Exceat	10.5/17		
9	Kingston*	10/16	Eastbourne*	10/16		
10	Rodmell	5/8				
11	Alfriston	8/13				
12	Eastbourne*	12.5/20				

* No hostels/camping barns at places marked; alternative accommodation available

STAYING IN B&BS

	Relaxed pace		Medium pace		Fast pace	
Night	Place	Approx distance miles/km	Place	Approx distance miles/km	Place	Approx distance miles/km
0	Winchester		Winchester		Winchester	
1	Cheriton	8/13	Cheriton	8/13	Exton	12/19.5
2	Exton	7/11	East Meon	13/20	South Harting	16.5/26.5
3	East Meon	6/9.5	South Harting	12.5/20	Amberley	20/32
4	Buriton	8.5/13.5	Heyshott	10/16	Pyecombe	20.5/33
5	Elstead	6.5/10.5	Amberley	11/17.5	Kingston	11/17.5
6	Graffham	9/14.5	Steyning	13/21	Alfriston	13/21
7	Amberley	9.5/15	Kingston	20/32	Eastbourne	12.5/20
8	Steyning	13/21	Alfriston	13/21		
9	Pyecombe	9.5/15	Eastbourne	12.5/20		
10	Kingston	11.5/18.5				
11	Rodmell	5/8				
12	Alfriston	8/13				
13	Eastbourne	12.5/20				

SIDE TRIP TO MOUNT CABURN

The only part of the South Downs that is not covered by the South Downs Way is the isolated hill near Lewes known rather grandly as Mount Caburn. It is something of an anomaly, being the only part of the Downs separated from the

❏ HIGHLIGHTS – THE BEST DAY AND WEEKEND WALKS

There is nothing quite like taking on a long-distance path in one go but sometimes the time needed is just not available. The following list suggests a number of day and weekend walks covering the best of the South Downs Way, most of which are easily accessible using public transport (see pp38-40). Many walkers come back weeks, months or even years later to walk sections of the path they have missed. Fitter walkers will find that many of the weekend walks suggested here can be completed in a day.

Day walks

● **Exton to Buriton** 12 miles/19.5km (see pp80-90) The best of the East Hampshire downland, passing over Old Winchester Hill and its magnificent hill-fort remains and Butser Hill, the highest hill on the Downs, with magnificent views over the Meon Valley and Queen Elizabeth Country Park.

● **Amberley to Steyning** 13 miles/21km (see pp117-26) Starting in one of the prettiest villages on the Way and ending in one of the most beautiful towns, this walk provides extensive views from the spine of the Downs, taking in the famous local landmark of Chanctonbury Ring.

● **Devil's Dyke to Ditchling Beacon** 5 miles/8km (see pp128-37) Possibly the most spectacular dry valley on the Downs, Devil's Dyke is the magnificent starting point of this short section that continues by climbing over the isolated Newtimber Hill before ending at the beauty spot of Ditchling Beacon.

● **Kingston-near-Lewes to Southease** 5 miles/8km (see pp146-51) One of the quieter stretches of the Downs with fine views of Mount Caburn on the other side of the Ouse Valley and a little bit of literary history to be had at Rodmell, home of the late Virginia Woolf.

● **Exceat to Eastbourne Pier (via Cuckmere Haven)** 9 miles/14.5km (see pp158-69) Arguably the finest day of walking anywhere between Winchester and Eastbourne, following the rollercoaster tops of the Seven Sisters chalk cliffs to the high point of Beachy Head high above Eastbourne.

● **Alfriston to Eastbourne Pier (via Jevington)** 10 miles/16km (see pp167-76) Not as spectacular as the coastal route to Eastbourne but equally enjoyable, encompassing the beautiful Cuckmere Valley, the ramshackle timber-framed houses of Alfriston and the curious Long Man of Wilmington chalk figure.

Weekend walks

● **Buriton to Amberley** 23½ miles/38km (see pp90-112) Stopping off in either Cocking or Midhurst for the night, this section takes in the fine wooded sections close to Buriton and the airy Harting Down on the first day, followed by Bignor Hill with its Roman Road, Stane Street, on the second day.

● **Amberley to Pyecombe** 20½ miles/33km (see pp112-34) Extensive views and the curious, enchanted Chanctonbury Ring are the highlights of the first day with a wide choice of places to stay in historic Steyning or Bramber with its castle. The second day follows the open top of the Downs all the way to the impressive valley of Devil's Dyke.

Eastbourne circular walk via Alfriston and Cuckmere Haven

If there is one section of the Downs that should be seen before any other it is this wonderful circular walk. Beginning and ending in Eastbourne, the walk combines the coastal and inland routes of the SDW. You'll pass through the beautiful villages of Jevington, Alfriston, Litlington and West Dean as well as walking the entire coastal section from Cuckmere Haven to Eastbourne. This is possibly the most spectacular walking that can be found anywhere in South-East England.

main spine of chalk hills. The hill's unique position makes it an excellent vantage point for admiring the rest of the Downs stretched out to the south, as well as the Ouse Valley and the county town of Lewes. The top of the hill is a National Nature Reserve renowned for its butterflies as well as its paragliders.

The hill is best approached from the village of Glynde where there is a train station. From the train station Mount Caburn (152m/498ft) looms above. Head towards the hill by walking up the road for five minutes. Just past the old village smithy (blacksmith), which is still being used, is a junction that marks the centre of Glynde village. Turn left and look for the stile in the hedgerow opposite the village shop. The path to the top of Mount Caburn follows the obvious route through the fields from the stile and takes about 30-45 minutes. The return is by the same route or via a path further to the north which drops through a small copse to emerge on the lane north of Glynde village.

What to take

Deciding how much to take with you can be a difficult decision. Experienced walkers know that you really should take only the bare essentials but at the same time you need to ensure you have all the equipment necessary to make the trip safe and comfortable.

KEEP IT LIGHT

Carrying a heavy rucksack really can ruin your enjoyment of a good walk and can also slow you down a great deal, turning an easy seven-mile day into an interminable slog. Be ruthless when you pack and leave behind all those little home comforts that you tell yourself don't weigh that much really. Always pack the essentials, of course, but try to leave behind anything that you think might 'come in handy' but probably won't. This advice is even more pertinent to campers who have the added weight of camping equipment to carry.

HOW TO CARRY IT

The size of the **rucksack** you should take depends on where you are planning to stay and how you are planning to eat. If you are camping and cooking for yourself you will probably need a 65- to 75-litre rucksack which can hold the tent, sleeping bag, cooking equipment and food. Make sure your rucksack has a stiffened back and can be adjusted to fit your own back comfortably. This will make carrying the weight much easier.

Rucksacks are decorated with seemingly pointless straps but if you adjust them correctly it can make a big difference to your personal comfort while walking. Make sure the hip belt and chest belt (if there is one) are fastened tightly as this helps distribute the weight: most of it should be carried on the hips.

When packing the rucksack make sure you have all the things you are likely to need during the day near the top or in the side pockets. This includes a map, water bottle, packed lunch, waterproofs and this guidebook (of course!).

Consider taking a small **bum bag** or **day pack** for your camera, guidebook and other essentials.

If you are staying in bunkhouses and hostels you probably won't need to carry a sleeping bag or camping stove. All the youth hostels provide bedding and have cooking facilities. Some of the independent hostels, however, may not have such facilities so check with them beforehand. A 40- to 60-litre rucksack should be sufficient.

If you have gone for the B&B option you will probably find a 30- to 40-litre daypack is more than enough to carry your lunch, warm- and wet-weather clothes, camera and guidebook.

A good habit to get into is always to put things in the same place in your rucksack and memorise where they are. There is nothing more annoying than pulling everything out of your pack to find that lost banana when you're starving or that camera when there is a butterfly basking briefly on a rock ten feet away from you. It's also a good idea to keep everything in **canoe bags**, **waterproof rucksack liners** or strong plastic bags (or binliners). If you don't it's bound to rain.

FOOTWEAR

Boots

Your boots are the single most important item of gear that can affect the enjoyment of your hike. In summer you could get by with a light pair of trail shoes if you're carrying only a small pack, although this is an invitation for wet, cold feet if there is any rain and they don't offer much support for your ankles. Some of the terrain can be quite rough and wet so a pair of good walking boots is a safer bet. They must fit well and be properly broken in: it is no good discovering that your boots are slowly murdering your feet two days into a one-week walk.

Socks

The traditional wearing of a thin liner sock under a thicker wool sock is no longer necessary if you choose a high-quality sock specially designed for walking. A high proportion of natural fibres makes them much more comfortable. Three pairs are ample.

Extra footwear

Some walkers like to have a second pair of shoes to wear when not on the trail. Trainers, sport sandals or flip flops are all suitable as long as they are light.

CLOTHES

Experienced walkers will know the importance of wearing the right clothes. Always expect the worst weather even if the forecast is good. Modern technology in outdoor attire can seem baffling but it basically comes down to the old multi-layer system: a base layer to transport sweat away from your skin; a mid-layer to keep you warm; and an outer layer or 'shell' to protect you from the rain.

Base layer
Cotton absorbs sweat, trapping it next to the skin which will chill you rapidly when you stop exercising. A thin lightweight **thermal top** made from a synthetic material is better as it draws moisture away, keeping you dry. It will be cool if worn on its own in hot weather and warm when worn under other clothes in cooler conditions. A spare would be sensible. You may also like to bring a **shirt** or top for wearing in the evening.

Mid-layers
In the summer a woollen jumper or mid-weight polyester **fleece** will suffice. For the rest of the year you will need an extra layer to keep you warm. Both wool and fleece, unlike cotton, have the ability to stay reasonably warm when wet.

Outer layer
A decent **waterproof jacket** is essential year-round and will be much more comfortable (but also more expensive) if it's also 'breathable' to prevent the build up of condensation on the inside. This layer can also be worn to keep the wind off.

Leg wear
Whatever you wear on your legs it should be light, quick-drying and not restricting. Many British walkers find **polyester tracksuit bottoms** comfortable. Poly-cotton or microfibre trousers are excellent. Denim jeans should never be worn; if they get wet they become heavy, cold and bind to your legs. A pair of **shorts** is nice to have on sunny days. Thermal **longjohns** or thick tights are cosy if you're camping but are probably unnecessary even in winter. **Waterproof trousers** are necessary most of the year. In summer a pair of windproof and quick-drying trousers is useful in showery weather. **Gaiters** are not really necessary but may come in useful in wet weather when the vegetation around your legs is dripping wet.

Underwear
One or two changes of what you normally wear is fine.

Other clothes
A **warm hat** and **gloves** should always be kept in your rucksack; you never know when you might need them. In summer you should also carry a **sun hat** with you, preferably one which covers the back of your neck. Another useful piece of summer equipment is a **swimsuit**.

TOILETRIES

Take only the minimum: a small bar of **soap** (unless staying in B&Bs) in a plastic container which can also be used instead of shaving cream and for washing clothes; a tiny tube of **toothpaste** and a **toothbrush**; and one roll of **loo paper** in a plastic bag. If you are planning to defecate outdoors you will also need a **lighter** for burning the paper and a lightweight **trowel** for burying the evidence (see p58 for further tips). A **towel** (if camping or staying in a hostel), **razor**, **deodorant**, **tampons/sanitary towels** and a high-factor **sunscreen** should cover most needs.

FIRST-AID KIT

Medical facilities in Britain are excellent so you need only take a small kit to cover common problems and emergencies.

A basic kit will contain a pack of **aspirin** or **paracetamol** for treating mild to moderate pain and fever; **plasters/Band Aids** for minor cuts; '**moleskin**', '**Compeed**' or '**Second skin**' for blisters; a **bandage** for holding dressings, splints or limbs in place and for supporting a sprained ankle; an **elastic knee support** for a weak knee; a small selection of different sized **sterile dressings** for wounds; **porous adhesive tape**; **antiseptic wipes**; **antiseptic cream**; **safety pins**; **tweezers** and a small pair of **scissors**. Pack the kit in a waterproof container.

GENERAL ITEMS
Essential
The following should be in everyone's rucksack: a **water bottle/pouch** (holding at least one litre); a **torch** (flashlight) with spare bulb and batteries in case you end up walking after dark; **emergency food** which your body can quickly convert into energy; a **penknife**; a **watch** with an alarm; and a **bag** for packing out any rubbish you accumulate. A **whistle** is also worth taking. It can fit in a pocket and although you are very unlikely to need it you may be grateful of it in the unlikely event of an emergency (see p63).

Useful
Many would list a **camera** as essential but it can be liberating to travel without one once in a while; a **notebook** can be a more accurate way of recording your impressions. Other items include a **book** to pass the time on train journeys; a pair of **sunglasses** in summer; **binoculars** for observing wildlife; a **walking stick** or pole to take the strain off your knees and a **vacuum flask** for carrying hot drinks. Although the path is easy to follow a 'Silva' type **compass** is a good idea.

A **mobile phone** is useful, especially as reception is generally good. Even so, make sure you always have the wherewithal to call from a public phone box in case you have no signal at the crucial moment. Calls to the emergency services (☎ 999, or ☎ 112 from a mobile) are free of charge, but those urgent calls to book a night's accommodation can catch you out. Calls cost a minimum of 40p, but increasingly you will need a credit, debit, BT or prepaid card instead. (Insert the card then follow the instructions.)

(Opposite): A hot summer's day and classic South Downs rolling landscape: the view towards Truleigh Hill (see p130).

SLEEPING BAG

A sleeping bag is necessary only if you are camping. Clearly you won't need one if you are staying in bed and breakfasts and the same is true if you are planning on using hostels. Campers should find that a two- to three-season bag will cope but obviously in winter a warmer bag is a good idea. On hot summer nights you could get away with a one-season bag.

CAMPING GEAR

Campers need a decent **tent** (or bivvy bag if you enjoy travelling light) that's able to withstand wet and windy weather; a **sleeping mat**; a **stove** and **fuel** (there is special mention in Part 4 of which shops stock fuel); a **mug**; a **spoon**; a wire/plastic **scrubber** for washing up; and a pan or pot. One pot is fine for two people; some pots come with a lid that can be used as a plate or frying pan.

MONEY

There are not many banks along the Way so you will have to carry most of your money as **cash**. A **debit/credit card** is the easiest way to withdraw money either from banks or cash machines and can be used to pay in most larger shops, restaurants and hotels. A **cheque book** is very useful for walkers with accounts in British banks as a cheque will often be accepted where a card is not.

MAPS

The hand-drawn maps in this book cover the trail at a scale of 1:20,000 – plenty of detail and information to keep you on the right track. However, if you have plans to explore further afield it is wise to arm yourself with a *South Downs Way Map* (Harvey Maps, £11.95, 🖳 www.harveymaps.co.uk) at a scale of 1:40,000, or Ordnance Survey maps (☎ 0845-605 0505, 🖳 www.ordnance survey.gov.uk). Relevant sheets include OS Landranger maps (pink cover) at a scale of 1:50,000, Nos 185, 197, 198 and 199 (£6.99 each) or OS Explorer Maps (orange cover) at 1:25,000 Nos 119, 120, 121, 122, 123 and 132 (£7.99 each).

Enthusiastic map buyers can reduce the often considerable expense of purchasing them: members of the **Ramblers' Association** (see box p34) can borrow up to 10 maps for a period of six weeks at 50p per map from their library (or £1 for the weatherproof version).

RECOMMENDED READING

Many bookshops and most of the tourist information centres along the South Downs Way stock all or at least some of the following books.

(Opposite) Top: The Way takes you through, or close by, numerous pretty English villages such as Southease (see p150) with their thatched cottages, village greens and ancient churches. **Bottom**: A wonderfully tranquil track near Graffham.

Walking guidebooks

For a guide to some of the lesser-known walks on the Downs try Ben Perkins' *Pub Walks in the South Downs* (£6.95). An excellent read recounting one person's experience of his walk is *The South Downs Way* (£7.99) by Martin King.

Flora and fauna field guides

The best guidebook specifically aimed at the wildlife of the region is *Downland Wildlife – A Naturalist's Year in the North & South Downs* by John S Burton, published by Phillips. However, it is out print and only available from special-

---

❏ SOURCES OF FURTHER INFORMATION

Tourist Information Centres
Tourist Information Centres (TICs) are based in towns throughout Britain and provide all manner of locally specific information and an accommodation-booking service.

The following TICs lie on or near the Way: **Winchester** (☎ 01962-840500, 🖥 www .visitwinchester.co.uk); **Petersfield** (☎ 01730-268829); **Midhurst** (☎ 01730-817322, 🖥 www.visitmidhurst.com or for further details on the wider area look at 🖥 www .visitchichester.org); **Arundel** (☎ 01903-882268, 🖥 www.sussexbythesea.com); **Lewes** (☎ 01273-483448, 🖥 lewes.tic@lewes.gov.uk); **Eastbourne** (☎ 0871-663 0031, 🖥 www.eastbourne.com).

In addition there are a number of visitor centres such as the ones at Queen Elizabeth Country Park (see p90) and Seven Sisters Country Park (see box p160).
● **Tourism South East** This regional tourist board (🖥 www.southeastengland.uk .com) is responsible for the official tourist information centres. Their website has a wealth of information regarding accommodation, things to see and do, and they can keep you informed about upcoming festivals and events.
● **Society of Sussex Downsmen** Supported entirely by donations and subscriptions, this society (🖥 www.sussexdownsmen.org.uk) has been around since 1923, helping to protect and conserve the Downs which they have divided into 12 distinct areas, each of which is under the care of a volunteer district officer. Their main responsibility is to peruse all planning applications that may affect the Downs. They also arrange a programme of strolls and walks, on and around the Downs, throughout the year.

Organisations for walkers
● **Backpackers' Club** (🖥 www.backpackersclub.co.uk) A club aimed at people who are involved or interested in lightweight camping through walking, cycling, skiing, canoeing etc. The club produces a quarterly magazine, provides members with a comprehensive advisory and information service on all aspects of backpacking, organises weekend trips and also publishes a farm pitch directory. Membership is £12 per year.
● **Long Distance Walkers' Association** (🖥 www.ldwa.org.uk) An association for people with the common interest of long-distance walking. Membership includes a journal three times per year giving details of challenge events and local group walks as well as articles on the subject. Information on over 500 long-distance paths is presented in the LDWA's *Long Distance Walkers' Handbook*. Membership is £13 per year.
● **Ramblers' Association** (🖥 www.ramblers.org.uk) The long-established Ramblers' Association looks after the interests of walkers throughout Britain. They publish a large amount of useful information including their annual *handbook* (free for members, £5.99 for non-members), a full directory of services for walkers. Membership costs £27 per year for an individual and £36 for joint membership.

ist/second-hand booksellers. For a more general guide there are plenty of books to choose from including the *Collins Bird Guide* (£16.99, or £25 for the hardback version) by Lars Svensson et al. A good field guide is the *New Birdwatcher's Pocket Guide to Britain and Europe* (£9.99) by Peter Hayman and Rob Hume: it is packed with illustrations of 430 European bird species. The RSPB's *Pocket Guide to British Birds* (£4.99, Simon Harrap and David Nurney) is also recommended. Birds are identified by their plumage and song.

One of the best field guides to British flora is *The Wildflowers of Britain and Ireland* (£16.99) by Marjorie Blamey et al.

The Field Studies Council (☎ 0845-345 4071, 💻 www.field-studies-council .org) publishes a series of identification guides in the form of laminated sheets (£2.50-3.75 each) showing commonly found birds, trees, flowers etc.

Getting to and from the South Downs Way

It could not be easier to reach the South Downs from London as there are numerous road and rail links not just to Winchester and Eastbourne, the start and finish of the walk, but to many other points along the Way. Most parts of

---

❏ **Getting to Britain**

● **By air** The nearest international airport to Winchester is Southampton Airport on the south coast. The main international carrier flying here is the low-cost airline Flybe (💻 www.flybe.com) which serves mainly French and Spanish cities. The alternative would be to fly to London's Gatwick or Heathrow airports, both of which serve destinations worldwide. Low-cost carriers using Gatwick include Flybe (as above), easyJet (💻 www.easyjet.com), Thomson Fly (💻 www.thomsonfly.com) and Ryanair (💻 www.ryanair.com). Between these four, all main European cities are served. Flights from destinations outside Europe mostly go to Heathrow Airport.

● **From Europe by train** Eurostar (💻 www.eurostar.com) operates a high-speed passenger service via the Channel Tunnel between Paris/Brussels and London. The Eurostar terminal in London is at St Pancras International station: some services also stop at Ashford International. For information about the various rail services to Britain from the continent contact Rail Europe (💻 www.raileurope.com).

● **From Europe by coach** Eurolines (💻 www.eurolines.com) have a huge network of long-distance coach services connecting over 500 cities in 25 European countries to London. However, these tickets often don't work out that much cheaper than flying the same route with a budget airline which is also far quicker.

● **From Europe by car** Eurotunnel (💻 www.eurotunnel.com) operates a shuttle **train** service for vehicles via the Channel Tunnel between Calais and Folkestone, taking an hour between the motorway in France and the motorway in England.

There are many **ferry** routes between France (Caen, Cherbourg, St Malo, Dunkerque and Calais) and the south coast ports of England such as Dover, Newhaven, Poole and Portsmouth. There are also services from Bilbao, Spain, to Portsmouth. Look at 💻 www.ferrysavers.com or 💻 www.directferries.com for a full list of companies and services.

the South Downs Way are no more than 1¹/₂-2 hours from the capital. Access from other parts of Britain often involves going via London but there are rail services to the south coast via Reading.

From the continent there are air links to London and Southampton, rail links to Ashford International and London as well as ferry routes between various ports in France and Southampton, Portsmouth and Newhaven. The rail line running across the south coast goes from Dover to Ashford International, then to Hastings and along the coast to Eastbourne and Brighton.

NATIONAL TRANSPORT

By rail
The two main rail operators for services to locations along the South Downs are Southern Railway and SouthWest Trains. Winchester is also a stop on the Cross Country route between Bournemouth and Manchester. See box below and map p39 for contact and service details. Timetables, ticket and fare information can be found on their websites, and it is also possible to buy tickets online. Alternatively, timetable and fare information can be found at **National Rail**

❏ USEFUL RAIL SERVICES

Southern Trains (☎ 0845-127 2920, 🖥 www.southernrailway.com)
(Note all services to/from London Victoria stop at Gatwick Airport)
● London Victoria to Arundel via Pulborough, Mon-Sat 2/hr, Sun 1/hr (stops at
  Amberley daily, 1/hr)
● London Victoria to Brighton, daily 2-3/hr
● London Victoria to Eastbourne via Lewes, Mon-Sat 2/hr, Sun 1/hr
● London Victoria to Eastbourne via Plumpton (and Lewes), daily 6-7/day but
  mostly in the mornings and evenings
● Ashford International to Brighton via Hastings, Eastbourne, Polegate and Lewes,
  daily 1/hr
● Portsmouth to Chichester, Mon-Sat 2/hr, Sun 1/hr
● Chichester to Brighton via Worthing, Mon-Sat 2/hr, Sun 1/hr
● Arundel to Chichester (change at Barnham), Mon-Sat 2/hr, Sun 1/hr
● Brighton to Seaford via Lewes and Newhaven, daily 2/hr (stops at Southease 1/hr)
● Brighton to Eastbourne via Lewes, daily 2/hr (stops at Berwick and Glynde 1/hr)
● Brighton to Hassocks, Mon-Sat 1-4/hr, Sun 1/hr
● Eastbourne to Lewes, Mon-Sat 2-3/hr, Sun 2/hr

SouthWest Trains (☎ 0845-600 0650, 🖥 www.southwesttrains.co.uk)
● London Waterloo to Winchester, Mon-Sat 4/hr, Sun 2/hr
● Southampton to Winchester, daily 2-3/hr
● Bournemouth to Winchester, daily 3/hr
● Weymouth to Winchester, daily 1/hr
● Portsmouth to Winchester, Mon-Sat 1/hr, Sun (change at Fratton) 1/hr
● London Waterloo to Petersfield, daily 2/hr
● Portsmouth to Petersfield, Mon-Sat 3/hr, Sun 2/hr

Cross Country Trains (☎ 0844 811 0124, 🖥 www.crosscountrytrains.co.uk)
● Bournemouth to Manchester Piccadilly via Winchester, daily 1/hr

PLANNING YOUR WALK

❑ USEFUL COACH SERVICES

National Express (☎ 0871-781 8181, 🖳 www.nationalexpress.com)
Note: not all stops are listed – contact National Express for full details.

SH032   London Victoria Coach Station (VCS) to Portsmouth via Heathrow Airport,
Basingstoke, **Winchester**, Southampton and Fareham, 5/day

SH030   London VCS to Southsea via Guildford, Hindhead, Liphook, Rake,
Petersfield & Portsmouth, 4/day

SH027   London VCS to Chichester via Gatwick Airport, Crawley, Horsham, Findon,
Worthing, Goring-by-sea, Rustington, Littlehampton, & Bognor Regis,
1/day

SH025   London VCS to Brighton via Gatwick Airport & Hickstead, daily 1/hr plus
1/day continues to **Eastbourne** via Rottingdean, Saltdean, Peacehaven,
Newhaven & Seaford

SH024   London VCS to Hastings via East Grinstead, Uckfield, Polegate,
Eastbourne, Pevensey Bay, Bexhill, & St Leonards, 2/day

NX315   Helston to **Eastbourne** via Falmouth, Truro, Plymouth, Exeter, Bridport,
Dorchester, Weymouth, Poole, Bournemouth, Southampton, Portsmouth,
Chichester, **Arundel**, Worthing, Brighton, Newhaven & Seaford, 1/day

Megabus (☎ 0900-160 0900, 🖳 www.megabus.com/uk)
London to Bournemouth via **Winchester** and Southampton, 1/day
Leeds to Portsmouth via **Winchester**, 1/day (not all stops listed)

Enquiries (☎ 08457-484950; 🖳 www.nationalrail.co.uk). Another useful site
is 🖳 www.the trainline.com with timetables, fares and an online ticket-purchasing
facility. Trains from London Waterloo stop at Winchester and Petersfield and from
London Victoria there are regular trains to Amberley, Arundel, Hassocks,
Brighton, Lewes, Newhaven, Seaford, Falmer, Southease and Eastbourne.

If you think you may want to book a taxi for when you arrive details of
companies are given in Part 4. Alternatively, visit 🖳 www.traintaxi.co.uk for
details of taxi companies operating at rail stations throughout England. It is also
often possible to book train tickets that include bus travel to your ultimate destination: enquire when you book your train ticket or look at Plus Bus's website
(🖳 www.plusbus.info).

By coach

Coach travel is generally cheaper but takes longer than the train. **National
Express** is the principal coach (long-distance bus) operator in Britain and has
services to a number of destinations on or near the Way. **Megabus** operates a
more limited network but offers cheaper fares. For details of both companies'
services see box above and map p39.

By car

The south of England is overrun with dual carriageways and bypasses so there is
no shortage of 'A' roads to follow down to the Downs. On holiday weekends,
however, be prepared for long tailbacks as everyone heads for the coast. There are
main roads from London passing through Winchester, Petersfield, Cocking,
Amberley and Arundel, Washington, Pyecombe, Lewes, Brighton and Eastbourne.

PLANNING YOUR WALK

By air

Although there are local airports, such as the one at Shoreham, the easiest way to fly to the South-East from other corners of England is to get a flight to Gatwick or Southampton. However, this really is not the best choice of transport. The train is cheaper, less polluting and can carry the walker directly to various points on the Downs. See 🖳 www.chooseclimate.org for the true costs of flying.

LOCAL TRANSPORT

Hampshire, West Sussex and East Sussex all have excellent local transport networks which make planning linear day and weekend walks easy. There is generally a very good bus service and in places such as Lewes, Seaford and Eastbourne the train can be used to plan useful start and finish points.

The public transport map opposite summarises all the useful routes and gives an indication of frequency of service in both directions and which bus company to contact for more detailed timetable information.

The tourist information centres along the Downs can provide, free of charge, a comprehensive local transport timetable for their particular region.

❏ LOCAL BUS SERVICES

Brighton & Hove Buses (☎ 01273-886200, 🖳 www.buses.co.uk)

2a	Rottingdean to Steyning via Woodingdean, Brighton, Hove, Shoreham, Upper Beeding & Bramber, daily 1/hr
12	Brighton to Eastbourne via Rottingdean, Newhaven, Seaford, Exceat (Seven Sisters CP) & East Dean, daily 4/hr
12a	Brighton to Eastbourne via Rottingdean, Newhaven, Seaford, Exceat (Seven Sisters CP), East Dean, Birling Gap & Beachy Head, Mon-Sat 2/hr
20	Brighton to Steyning via Hove, Shoreham, Bramber & Upper Beeding, Mon-Sat 2/day
28	Brighton to Lewes, Mon-Sat 2/hr, Sun 6/day
29/29a	Brighton to Tunbridge Wells via Lewes, Ringmer & Uckfield, Mon-Sat 2/hr, Sun 6/day
77	Brighton to Devil's Dyke, Apr-Sep Sat, Sun & bank holidays plus Jul & Aug daily, 1-2/hr
79	Brighton to Ditchling Beacon, Apr-Sep, Sat, Sun & bank holidays 1/hr, Oct-Mar Sun & bank holidays 1/hr

Brijan Tours (☎ 01489-788138, 🖳 www.brijantours.com)

17	Bishops Waltham to Petersfield via Swanmore, Droxford, Corhampton (for Exton), Warnford, West Meon, East Meon & Stroud, Mon-Sat 4/day

Compass Travel (☎ 01903-690025, 🖳 www.compass-travel.co.uk)(see also p112)

23	Worthing to Horsham via Washington, Sun 6/day (see also Metrobus)
74	Ashington to Horsham via Storrington, Mon-Sat 6/day
85	Chichester to Pulborough via Arundel and Bury, Mon-Sat 2/day
99	Chichester to Petworth via Goodwood, Graffham, Sutton & Bignor, Mon-Sat 4/day but only stops if prebooked (☎ 01903-264776)
100	Burgess Hill to Pulborough via Henfield, Upper Beeding, Bramber, Steyning Washington & Storrington, Mon-Sat 1/hr, Sun 5/day (cont'd on p40)

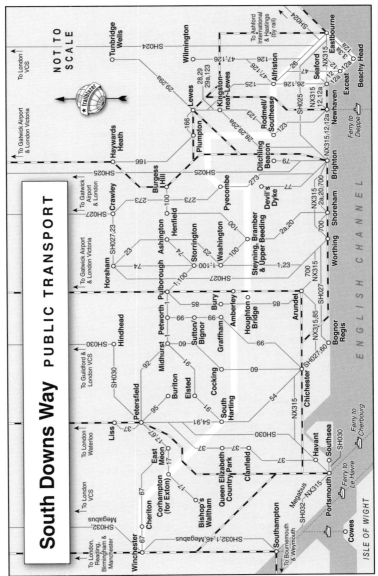

South Downs Way **PUBLIC TRANSPORT**

❑ LOCAL BUS SERVICES (cont'd from p38)

Countryliner (☎ 01483-506919, 🖳 www.countryliner-coaches.co.uk)

54   Petersfield to Chichester via South Harting, Uppark House & Compton, Mon-Sat 5/day

91   Midhurst to Petersfield via Elsted & South Harting, Mon-Sat 6/day

92   Midhurst to Petersfield, Mon-Sat 3-5/day

95   Buriton to Buriton circular route via Petersfield & Steep, Mon-Sat 8/day

125 Lewes to Alfriston via Glynde, Firle, Selmeston & Berwick (Drusillas), Mon-Sat 5/day

166 Lewes to Haywards Heath via Plumpton, Mon-Sat 6-7/day

Cuckmere Community Bus (☎ 01323-870920, 🖳 www.cuckmerebus.freeuk.com)

26   Seaford to Eastbourne via Alfriston, Sun & Bank hols 3-4/day

47   Cuckmere Valley Rambler: Berwick Station circular route via Drusillas Zoo Park, Alfriston, Seven Sisters Country Park/Exceat and Wilmington, Easter to Oct Sat, Sun & public hols 1/hr, Oct-Easter Sat, Sun & public hols 2/day

Note: They also operate some limited-frequency services, driven by volunteers. These include: 40 (Berwick to Seaford via Drusillas, Wilmington, Lullington, Litlington, Charleston, Wesdean & Exceat, Tue & Fri 1/day); 42 (Berwick to Hailsham circular route via Alciston & Alfriston, Wed 2/day, Fri 1-2/day; 44 (Berwick to Eastbourne via Polegate & Langney, Mon 1/day, Tue 1/day, Thur 2-3/day: note the routes vary so check in advance). In rural areas these services pick up and drop down wherever it is safe

Eastbourne Buses (☎ 01323-416416, 🖳 www.eastbournebuses.co.uk)

3/3A Foot of Beachy Head to Eastbourne via Meads Village, Mon-Sat 1/hr from Meads village plus 1/hr from Beachy Head, Sun 1/hr from Beachy Head

Metrobus (☎ 01293-449191, 🖳 www.metrobus.co.uk)

23   Crawley to Worthing via Horsham, Ashington & Washington, Mon-Sat 9/day, Sunday service operated by Compass (see box p38)

273 Brighton to Crawley via Pyecombe, Mon-Fri 8/day, Sat 4/day

Renown Coaches (☎ 01424-210744, 🖳 www.renowncoaches.co.uk)

123 Lewes to Newhaven via Kingston, Rodmell & Southease, Mon-Fri 10/day, Sat 5/day

126 Eastbourne to Seaford via Wilmington, Drusillas & Alfriston, Mon-Sat 4-5/day

bluestar (☎ 023-8061 8233, 🖳 www.bluestarbus.co.uk)

1   Winchester to Southampton, Mon-Sat 3/hr, Sun 2/hr

Stagecoach (☎ 0845-121 0190 for Hampshire, ☎ 0845-121 0170 for Sussex, 🖳 www .stagecoachbus.com/south)

1   Midhurst to Worthing via Petworth, Pulborough, Storrington & Washington, Mon-Sat 1/hr, Sun 7/day

37   Havant to Liss via Waterlooville, Horndean, Clanfield, Queen Elizabeth Country Park, Petersfield & Sheet, Mon-Sat 1/hr

46   Southampton to Winchester, Mon-Sat 5-7 day

60   Bognor Regis to Midhurst via Chichester, West Dean, Singleton & Cocking, Mon-Sat 2/hr, Sun 1/hr

67   Winchester to Petersfield via Cheriton, Bramdean, West Meon & East Meon, Mon-Sat 1/hr

700 Arundel to Brighton via Littlehampton, Goring, Worthing, Shoreham, Hove & Brighton, Mon-Sat 2/hr

Conservation of the South Downs

Ever since the Industrial Revolution and the rapid development over the last 200 years the English countryside has been put under a great deal of strain. The South Downs were once wooded hills, home to wolves, wild boar and other species that have long since left the English countryside. The need to feed an increasing population led to much of the countryside being cleared and ploughed. The result of this is the landscape we see today, although the traditional patchwork pattern of fields and hedgerows has been replaced in some parts of the Downs by much larger fields, the hedgerows having been torn out.

The South Downs is, then, a man-made landscape: even the woodland has been coppiced and the meadows at one time or another ploughed. This is not necessarily a bad thing, however. The resulting habitat is a rare one that provides an essential niche for endangered species, most notably the butterflies for which the Downs are famous.

Although the Downs, positioned in a populous corner of England, continue to be put under pressure from road and housing projects, the increasing awareness of the value of our natural (or perhaps semi-natural) heritage has resulted in greater efforts in the conservation of the Downs. There are a number of groups, on both a local and national scale and on both a voluntary and government basis, who help protect the species, habitats and buildings of the Downs. They also help visitors to get the most out of their trip to the countryside whilst at the same time trying to ease the pressure that the increase in tourist numbers brings.

If and when the Downs are eventually granted National Park status (see p42) the effort to conserve the area should become less of a struggle due to the increased environmental protection and financial benefits that the National Park designation brings.

GOVERNMENT AGENCIES AND SCHEMES

Natural England

In October 2006 the Countryside Agency, English Nature and the Rural Development Service merged to become Natural England (see box p44). This was due to the National Environment and Rural Communities Bill which became law on 30 March 2006. The official responsibilities of Natural England are to 'enhance biodiversity and our landscapes and wildlife in rural, urban, coastal and marine areas; promote access, recreation and public well-being, and contribute to the way natural resources are managed'. Natural England is a single body responsible for identifying, establishing and managing: National

Parks, Areas of Outstanding Natural Beauty, National Nature Reserves, Sites of Special Scientific Interest, and Special Areas of Conservation.

The highest level of landscape protection is the designation of land as a **National Park** which recognises the national importance of an area in terms of landscape, biodiversity and as a recreational resource. This designation does not signify national ownership and they are not uninhabited wildernesses, making conservation a knife-edged balance between protecting the environment and the rights and livelihoods of those living in the park.

At the time of writing there were eight National Parks in England (plus the Norfolk and Suffolk Broads which has equivalent status) but no part of the South Downs was inside any of the parks; see box below. Until the South Downs become a National Park it will remain protected within two pieces of land that are designated **Areas of Outstanding Natural Beauty** (AONB), the second highest level of protection.

The western end of the path is in the 383km square **East Hampshire AONB** that was created in 1962 and lies within the County Council boundaries of Hampshire. This land is maintained by **Hampshire County Council**. The eastern part of the trail is included in the 983km square **Sussex Downs AONB** that was created in 1966 and lies within the County Council boundaries of East Sussex and West Sussex and the City Council boundaries of Brighton & Hove. This land is maintained by the **South Downs Joint Committee** with legal authority resting with the relevant councils. The South Downs Joint Committee was formed in July 2005 from the Sussex Downs Conservation

---

❏ The South Downs National Park

The South Downs almost became one of the first designated national parks back in the 1950s but the proposal was rejected on the grounds that the area did not offer sufficient recreational possibilities for the public. This seems rather surprising today when you consider the number of walkers, cyclists, horse-riders and paragliders who use the hills. National Park status is not just about providing an area of fun for outdoor enthusiasts, however. It is about protecting the area from harmful development such as road building, a real problem in the South-East, and preserving the natural and cultural heritage of the area.

At present the Downs is an Area of Outstanding Natural Beauty (AONB), a designation that affords a certain degree of protection. But National Park status would allow for greater funding. In 1999 the Department for the Environment proposed that the Countryside Agency, now part of Natural England, designate the South Downs a National Park. A Designation Order was published in late 2002 and in November 2003 a public inquiry began, to hear the views of those likely to be affected by the change. A report was prepared and passed, in 2006, to the Secretary of State.

The decision was delayed owing to a legal challenge which was resolved in February 2007. The inquiry was reopened in February 2008 and closed in July that year. The Secretary of State was expected to make a decision early in 2009 but had not done so when this book went to press in February 2009. There are three options: 1) to confirm a National Park based on the original Designation Order; 2) to confirm it based on the Inspector's boundary recommendations; 3) not to confirm it, therefore not establishing a National Park. Hopefully the outcome will be one of the first two.

❑ Undergrounding power lines

In an effort to make the South Downs even more glorious than it already is – no easy task, as I am sure you'd agree – the South Downs Joint Committee have begun to remove 30km of unsightly overhead power lines and run them underground instead.

The areas chosen for this 'undergrounding' work include Butser Ancient Farm in Hampshire, the Adur Valley in West Sussex, and Bishopstone and Birling Gap in East Sussex. The sites have been chosen as they fall directly in either the Sussex Downs AONB (Area of Outstanding Natural Beauty) or the East Hampshire AONB.

While those who live in these areas may find, in the short-term, that there will be some disruption to the tranquillity of the area as contractors move in to start the digging work, there won't be any disruption to their power supply as the underground cables will be laid and connected before the overhead lines are dismantled.

Nor, it is hoped, will this be the last of such work. Indeed the Joint Committee, via their website (see box p44), have asked the public to suggest other areas which would benefit from the replacement of overhead power cables. They also list the set of criteria by which all suggestions will be judged. These include such considerations as: the area nominated must be in the countryside rather than a built-up area; that removing lines from road, rail or river crossings can be very expensive; and that both telephone lines and lines connected to the National Grid are excluded. Furthermore, only lower voltage power lines will probably be considered – higher ones on metal pylons are likely to be rejected on the grounds of cost.

Board and the East Hampshire AONB Joint Advisory Committee and it's this organisation that will be replaced with a National Park authority when the creation of the park is finally agreed. Their volunteer ranger service is well worth enquiring about if, after walking the Downs, you feel like giving something back.

The committee is also responsible for the active protection of endemic species and habitats as well as geological features along the South Downs Way. If necessary this may involve access restrictions, especially for motorised vehicles. However, promoting public access and appreciation of the Way's natural heritage is also of importance, as is educating locals and visitors about the significance of the local environment.

The **National Trail Officer** (see box below) works closely with the above organisations and councils to keep the South Downs Way in good condition although the work on the ground is often undertaken by the local highway authorities.

❑ National Trails

The South Downs Way is one of 15 National Trails (🖳 www.nationaltrails.co.uk) in England and Wales. These are Britain's flagship long-distance paths which grew out of the post-war desire to protect the country's special places, a movement which also gave birth to National Parks and AONBs. The Pennine Way was the first to be created.

National Trails in England are designated and largely funded by Natural England and are managed on the ground by a National Trail Officer. They co-ordinate the maintenance work undertaken by the local highway authority and landowners to ensure that the trail is kept to nationally agreed standards.

THE ENVIRONMENT AND NATURE

The next level of protection includes National Nature Reserves and Sites of Special Scientific Interest. There are over 200 **National Nature Reserves (NNRs)** in England. Those along the course of the South Downs Way include: Beacon Hill (see p70), just before the village of Exton; Old Winchester Hill (see p81), just after Exton; Butser Hill (see p85) several miles further along the path and Lullington Heath (p170).

There are about 4100 **Sites of Special Scientific Interest (SSSIs)** in England ranging in size from little pockets protecting wild flower meadows, important nesting sites or special geological features, to vast swathes of upland, moorland and wetland. SSSIs are a particularly important designation as they have some legal standing. They are managed in partnership with the owners and occupiers of the land who must give written notice before initiating any operations likely to damage the site and who cannot proceed without consent from Natural England. SSSIs along the South Downs Way include: Cheesefoot Head (see p75), Butser Hill (see p85), Heyshott Down (see p101), Chanctonbury Hill (see p123) and Seaford to Beachy Head (see p165).

Special Areas of Conservation (SACs) are designated by the European Union's Habitats Directive and provide an extra tier of protection to the areas that they cover. Along the South Downs Way Butser Hill NNR and SSSI is also a SAC. See Natural England's website (see box below) for further information about all of these.

The South Downs Way is included in the **South Downs Environmentally Sensitive Area** (ESA). The ESA scheme was set up by the Department for Environment, Food and Rural Affairs (DEFRA) as part of their Rural Development Programme in 1987 with an aim to protect environmentally sensitive land which didn't fall under the SSSI remit. This is done by providing financial incentives to farmers and landowners to employ agricultural methods that will conserve the landscape and wildlife. DEFRA later introduced a Countryside Stewardship Scheme but both this and the ESA scheme were replaced in March 2005 by the Environmental Stewardship Scheme (ESS).

THE ENVIRONMENT AND NATURE

❏ **Statutory bodies**
● **Department for Environment, Food and Rural Affairs** (🖳 www.defra.gov.uk) Government ministry responsible for sustainable development in the countryside.
● **Natural England** (☎ 0845 600 3078; 🖳 www.naturalengland.org.uk) Their relevant regional offices are Hampshire & the Isle of Wight (☎ 0238-028 6410) and East and West Sussex (☎ 01273-47659).
● **English Heritage** (☎ 0870-333 1181, 🖳 www.english-heritage.org.uk) Organisation whose central aim is to make sure that the historic environment of England is properly maintained. It is officially known as the Historic Buildings and Monuments Commission for England. Bramber Castle (see p126) is one of the properties it manages.
● **South Downs Joint Committee** (☎ 01243-558700, 🖳 www.southdowns.gov.uk).
● **Hampshire County Council** (☎ 0845-603 5638, 🖳 www.hants.gov.uk).
● **East Sussex County Council** (☎ 01273-481000, 🖳 www.eastsussex.gov.uk).
● **West Sussex County Council** (☎ 01243-777100, 🖳 www.westsussex.gov.uk).

There is no doubt that the AONB, NNR, SSSI, SAC and ESA/ESS designations play a vital role in safeguarding the land they cover for future generations. However, the very fact that we rely on these labels for protecting limited areas begs the question: what are we doing to the vast majority of land that remains relatively unprotected? Surely we should be aiming to conserve the natural environment outside protected areas just as much as within them.

CAMPAIGNING AND CONSERVATION ORGANISATIONS

The **National Trust** is a charity with 3.4 million members which aims to protect, through ownership, threatened coastline, countryside, historic houses, castles, gardens and archaeological remains for everybody to enjoy. In particular the NT cares for over 600 miles of British coastline, 248,000 hectares of countryside and 300 historic buildings and monuments. It manages large sections of the Downs including an area of chalk grassland on the Seven Sisters between the hamlet of Crowlink and Birling Gap (see p163), Devil's Dyke (see p133), Harting Down (see p96), and Newtimber Hill (see p133). They also own various properties on the Way, such as Monk's House (see p150) in Rodmell and the Alfriston Clergy House (see box p155), their first ever property, bought in 1896 for the sum of £10; both of these properties are open to the public.

The **Wildfowl & Wetlands Trust** (WWT) is the biggest conservation organisation for wetlands in the UK with over 4000 acres of land under their management. Their centre at Arundel (see p114) is well-known and very popular with visitors year-round.

The **Wildlife Trust** has regional branches covering the area along the South Downs Way. They undertake projects to improve conditions for wildlife and promote public awareness of it as well as acquiring land for nature reserves to protect particular species and habitats. The Sussex Wildlife Trust manages the Amberley Wild Brooks (see p112) network of ponds and marshland along with Ditchling Beacon and Malling Down, Lewes. The Hampshire and Isle of Wight Wildlife Trust manages St Catherine's Hill (see p68), Winchester.

The **Royal Society for the Protection of Birds** (RSPB) was the pioneer of voluntary conservation bodies and although it doesn't have any reserves directly on the South Downs Way, there is one near Pulborough, a couple of miles north of Storrington. The wet grassy meadows here attract ducks, geese, swans and wading birds. **Butterfly Conservation** was formed in 1968 by some naturalists who were alarmed at the decline in the number of butterflies, and moths, and who aim to reverse the situation. They now have 31 branches throughout the British Isles and operate 33 nature reserves and also sites where butterflies are likely to be found: these include Beachy Head and Malling Down.

There are also smaller conservation groups such as the **Murray Downland Trust** which manages five reserves (Heyshott Escarpment, Heyshott Down, Buriton, Under Beacon, and The Devil's Jumps) in West Sussex and East Hampshire. The Trust's main objective is to 'rescue and enhance neglected areas of unimproved chalk downland' but it also looks after some ancient monuments in the area such as the Bronze Age archaeological site (see p104).

THE ENVIRONMENT AND NATURE

❏ **Campaigning and conservation organisations – contact details**
● **National Trust** (NT; ☎ 0844-800 1895, 🖳 www.nationaltrust.org.uk).
● The umbrella organisation for the 47 wildlife trusts in the UK is **The Wildlife Trusts** (🖳 www.wildlifetrusts.org). Branches relevant to the South Downs Way are the Hampshire and Isle of Wight Wildlife Trust (🖳 www.hwt.org.uk) and the Sussex Wildlife Trust (🖳 www.sussexwt.org.uk).
● **Royal Society for the Protection of Birds** (RSPB; 🖳 www.rspb.org.uk) The largest voluntary conservation body in Europe focusing on providing a healthy environment for birds and wildlife and with over 150 reserves in the UK.
● **Butterfly Conservation** (🖳 www.butterfly-conservation.org) The two branches relevant to the South Downs Way are Hampshire and the Isle of Wight (🖳 www.hants iow-butterflies.org.uk) and Sussex (🖳 www.sussex-butterflies.org.uk) Their reserves at Yew Hill and Magdalen Hill Down are both near Winchester.
● **Wildfowl & Wetlands Trust** (WWT; ☎ 01453-891900, 🖳 www.wwt.org.uk) has a branch in **Arundel** (☎ 01903-883355, 🖳 www.wwt.org.uk/centre/116/arundel.html).
● **Murray Downland Trust** (🖳 www.murraydownlandtrust.org.uk).

THE ENVIRONMENT AND NATURE

Access to the Trust's sites is permitted except when the area should be left undisturbed for conservation reasons. The trust relies on human volunteers to help clear the land in its care but sheep are often brought in during the winter months to eat the scrub that threatens the grassland.

BEYOND CONSERVATION

The ideas embodied in nature conservation have served us well over the last century. Without the multitude of designations which protect wildlife and landscape there is no doubt that the countryside of England would be far more impoverished than it is today. However, in some respects the creation of nature reserves and other protected areas is an admission that we are not looking after the rest of our environment properly.

If we can't keep the soil, air and water free from contamination or prevent man's activities from affecting the world's climate nature reserves will have little lasting value. Similarly, if decisions made by national government, the European Union (EU) or the World Trade Organisation (WTO) continue to fragment communities and force farmers, foresters and fishermen to adopt unsustainable practices, those who are best placed to protect the land and wildlife will end up destroying it.

Those who care about the wildlife and countryside of England now need to step beyond the narrow focus of conservation. We need to find ways to reconnect with the natural world and re-learn how to live in balance with it. This not only demands action on a personal level, for which walking in the wild is surely an ideal tutor, but also a wholesale rethink of the basic assumptions underlying the political and economic policies.

Flora and fauna

The South Downs region is essentially a man-made landscape. Centuries of farming have shaped these rolling hills and left a unique habitat for a variety of common and not-so-common species. Left alone the South Downs would revert to scrub and woodland. This may not appear to be a great tragedy. However, the habitat that would be lost is a much scarcer one that provides sanctuary to a variety of endangered species which rely on the unique chalk grassland environment. The Downs are not free of trees either. The plough never reached the steep scarp slope that runs along the northern edge of the Downs. Indeed there is a healthy balance between the open grassland of the high ground and the deciduous beech woodland which can claim to be some of the oldest and most undisturbed woodland in Britain.

Any walker on the Way, however, will notice the precarious relationship between man and the Downs. This corner of England is one of the most populated parts of Europe and the demands on the land have been great. In recent times large chunks of the Downs have been eaten away to be replaced by major roads such as the A3 and M3 (see box below) and to make way for the expanding south-coast towns such as Brighton. Nevertheless, there may be some good to come out of the race to build homes and roads. More and more people are noticing the value of the South Downs as the area comes under increasing pres-

THE ENVIRONMENT AND NATURE

❏ Roads, roads, roads

Over the years the Downs have been subjected to a great deal of road building. The most notable blots on the landscape are the A3 dual carriageway through Queen Elizabeth Country Park, the A27 Brighton bypass which guides traffic across a large swathe of downland just south of Ditchling Beacon, and the highly controversial M3 link through Twyford Down.

It is the latter, however, that caught the media attention thanks largely to the unprecedented protests between 1992 and 1994 by people from all walks of life, many of whom chained themselves to the highest branches of the trees on the Down for weeks on end. Sadly for Twyford Down it was all in vain and the scheme went ahead.

The result is a desecrated chalk hill and a saving of 12 minutes on the average journey time between Southampton and London. The government tried to appease the protesters by closing the old Winchester bypass that the M3 extension replaced and returning it to its natural state. It is now almost impossible to trace the old route of the road when looking down from the top of St Catherine's Hill but in the opposite direction is the new stretch of motorway, bigger, noisier and uglier than its predecessor.

Although Twyford Down could not be saved, the two-year campaign to stop the bulldozers did appear to instigate a change in the environmental thinking of those in power and the government's road-building scheme was shelved. However, that was well over a decade ago and it appears that once again road-building schemes are being favoured over investment in public transport.

sure and this has culminated in the possible award of National Park status, with a much delayed decision expected in 2009. Whether the protection afforded by this status outweighs the increased pressure from ever-greater numbers of tourists is something of a hot debate.

Whatever happens to the Downs, one hopes that the fauna and flora of this unique environment is afforded adequate protection. Walkers are lucky enough to be travelling at a speed that allows them to appreciate the wildlife around them. Anyone who lives and works in a high-pressure environment – and particularly cities – will find a walk along the top of the Downs to be something of a therapeutic exercise. However, too many people bring the stress of work with them to the countryside, walking as if they have a train to catch. To gain more from a walk on the Downs it is worth allowing yourself the chance to wind down. Look around, not at your feet, walk slowly and take breaks. Quiet and observant walkers are far more likely to notice the plants and maybe the animals of the Downs.

FLOWERS

Many of the flowering meadows that once covered large stretches of downland farmland have been destroyed by modern farming techniques. However, in places, efforts are being made to revive these by encouraging farmers to employ more flower-friendly methods.

Meadows

The dominant grass found in fields all over the Downs is the appropriately named **sheep's fescue** (*Festuca ovina*) which was cultivated specifically for pastureland and is the grass of choice for downland sheep.

Of far greater interest are the likes of the **common poppy** (*Papaver rhoeas*) with its spectacular deep red petals. They often colonise arable fields and path edges, preferring well-disturbed soil. Entire fields turn red in the flowering season in late summer.

Earlier in the season walkers are likely to come across the likes of **cowslip** (*Primula veris*) and its head of pale yellow flowers. The flowers flop down in small bunches earning the plant the old nickname 'bunch of keys'.

Perhaps one of the most beautiful of the downland flowers is the **round headed rampion** (*Phyteuma orbiculare*). Its striking dark blue flowers have earned it the local name 'The Pride of Sussex'.

The tiny yellow flower of **tormentil** (*Potentilla tormentilla*) can be seen hugging the ground in short grassland. It gets its name from an age when it was used as a medicinal remedy for diarrhoea and haemorrhoids: the taste is so foul that it tormented whoever took it.

Another tiny flower that can also be found close to the ground is the **scarlet pimpernel** (*Anagallis avensis*), a member of the primrose family. The flowers are tiny at just 5mm in diameter but stand out from their grassy background thanks to their light red colour.

Many people assume orchids to be so rare as to be nearly impossible to find. In truth there are a number of fairly common species that may readily be seen

Foxglove
Digitalis purpurea

Early Purple Orchid
Orchis mascula

Bee Orchid
Orchis apifera

Herb-Robert
Geranium robertianum

Bell Heather
Erica cinerea

Heather (Ling)
Calluna vulgaris

Red Campion
Silene dioica

Rosebay Willowherb
Epilobium angustifolium

Bluebell
Endymion non-scriptus

Gorse
Ulex europaeus

Common Ragwort
Senecio jacobaea

Honeysuckle
Lonicera periclymemum

Tormentil
Potentilla erecta

Birdsfoot-trefoil
Lotus corniculatus

Scarlet Pimpernel
Anagallis arvensis

Yarrow
Achillea millefolium

Hogweed
Heracleum sphondylium

Ramsons (Wild Garlic)
Allium ursinum

Common Fumitory
Fumaria officinalis

Old Man's Beard
Clematis vitalba

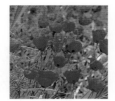

Common Poppy
Papaver rhoeas

Silverweed
Potentilla anserina

Self-heal
Prunella vulgaris

Violet
Viola riviniana

Meadow Buttercup
Ranunculis acris

Primrose
Primula vulgaris

Cowslip
Primula veris

Dog Rose
Rosa canina

Common Hawthorn
Crataegus monogyna

Ox-eye Daisy
Leucanthemum vulgare

Peacock
Inachis io

Small Tortoiseshell
Aglais urticae

Common Blue
Polyommatus icarus

Painted Lady
Cynthia cadui

Chalkhill Blue
Polyommatus/Lysandra coridon

Brimstone
Gonepteryx rhamni

Small Garden/Cabbage White
Pieris/Artogeia rapae

Red Admiral
Vanessa atalanta

Meadow brown
Maniola jurtina

Large Garden/Cabbage White
Pieris brassicae

White Admiral
Limenitis camilla

flowering on the Downs, usually around mid-summer. These include the **early purple orchid** (*Orchis mascula*) which can be seen in rough grassland. It stands about 10-15cm tall and has an elongated head of pinky-purple flowers.

There are of course some species that do fit the rare orchid label including the **fly orchid** (*Ophrys insectifera*) with flowers resembling small insects. These cleverly designed flowers attract wasps which pick up the pollen and take it on to the next insect-shaped flower they see. Another orchid with the same tactic is the **bee orchid** (*Ophrys apifera*) whose flowers are shaped like, well, bees.

Apart from the orchids, one of the most endangered and also one of the most striking flowering plants that may be seen, particularly on the Downs above Eastbourne, is **pheasant's-eye** (*Adonis annua*) with its blood red petals and large seed head.

In overgrown areas thorny **gorse** (*Ulex europeous*) bushes brighten up the summer with their small yellow flowers that burst open from February until June.

Woodland and hedgerows

There are several flowering plants associated with open woods and woodland edges. In May the pink flowers of the slightly inaccurately named **red campion** (*Silene dioica*) come into view along woodland edges and at the foot of hedgerows while deeper into the woods the floor becomes covered with **bluebells** (*Hyacinthoides non-scripta*) in the early spring. Other common woodland flowering plants include the **wood anemone** (*Anemone nemorosa*) with its round white flowers. Wood anemones cover forest floors in a similar way to bluebells. A more isolated flower, although sometimes seen growing in small groups, is the **primrose** (*Primula vulgaris*) with cheerful yellow flowers.

Bramble (*Rubus fruticosus*) is a common woodland and hedgerow species with small sharp thorns. It spreads rapidly, engulfing everything in its path. In its favour, blackberries appear on the branches in the autumn to provide sustenance for hungry birds and greedy walkers.

In hedgerows and along woodland edges you'll see the distinctive feathery climber, **old man's beard** (*Clematis vitalba*), also known as traveller's joy. The feathery part of the plant is actually the fruit.

The **foxglove** (*Digitalis purpurea*) is a very tall and graceful plant with white or purple trumpet-like flowers. It is commonly spotted along hedgerows, roadside verges and in shady woodland. Other fairly common woodland species that are just as comfortable on hedgebanks include the **forget-me-not** (*Myosotis arvensis*) which has very small blue flowers and **cow parsley** (*Anthriscus sylvestris*), a tall plant with a head of white flowers.

Perhaps the most unusual and to some eyes the ugliest of plants, found in dark corners of beech woodland, is the **bird's nest orchid** (*Neottia nidus-avis*), so-called because of its nest-like root system that intertwines across the ground.

TREES

Over the last few hundred years the once-extensive forest cover in southern England has been fragmented into a patchwork of copses and coppiced

THE ENVIRONMENT AND NATURE

woodland. Trees were felled for fuel and for shipbuilding and, in the case of the South Downs, to clear land for agricultural needs. In more recent times many of the hedgerows that helped create the familiar patchwork landscape have been grubbed up to create much larger fields.

Nevertheless, there are parts of the Downs that have survived the threat from axe and chainsaw. The north-facing scarp slope was, and still is, too steep for clearing and too inaccessible for ploughing. Consequently, this is where most of the trees are found. Although there are still areas of semi-natural or ancient mixed woodland, much of the remaining woodland has been coppiced, an old method of promoting growth of more numerous and narrower trunks by cutting a tree at its base. Coppicing was common in hazel stands and the resulting product used in constructing fences and making furniture.

Although coppicing died out around 100 years ago it is still practised in some parts today by enthusiasts of old woodland crafts and also by conservationists who recognise that coppiced woodland can be beneficial to certain species.

Most of the woodland the walker will encounter on the Downs is mixed deciduous, made up largely of beech and ash but there are many other species to look out for.

Tree species

The **beech** (*Fagus sylvatica*) with its thick, silvery trunk is one of the most attractive native trees. It can grow to a height of 40 metres with the high canopies blocking out much of the light. As a result the floors of beech woodlands tend to be fairly bare of vegetation. They favour well-drained soil, hence their liking for the steep scarp slope. In autumn the colours of the turning leaves can be quite spectacular.

One species that does survive the shady floor of beech woodland is the distinctive **common holly** (*Ilex aquifolium*) with its dark waxy leaves which have sharp points. Holly varies in size, usually growing as a sprawling bush on the woodland floor or in hedgerows but also as a tree when established in more isolated locations.

Famous for its life expectancy, lasting for well over a thousand years in some cases, the **common yew** (*Taxus baccata*) is abundant in churchyards but there are also natural stands on the scarp slope and also among beech woodland. The dark glossy needles are quite distinctive as is the flaky red bark of the often gnarled and twisted old trunks and branches. Do not be tempted to eat the bright red berries; they're poisonous. Another tree with red berries is the **hawthorn** (*Crataegus monogyna*). It has small leaves and is usually found in hedgerows but can also grow as a small tree. In early autumn the berries provide food for woodland birds and are particularly popular with blackbirds.

MAMMALS

The well-drained soil of chalk downland is ideal habitat for the **badger** (*Meles meles*), a sociable animal with a distinctive black-and-white-striped muzzle.

THE ENVIRONMENT AND NATURE

Badgers live in family groups in large underground 'setts'. They are rarely spotted since they tend to emerge after dark to hunt for worms in the fields. Sadly, they are more commonly seen dead on the road: after hedgehogs they are the most inept at crossing roads.

The **fox** (*Vulpes vulpes*) is another common mammal on the Downs. Although they prefer to come out at night they are not exclusively nocturnal; particularly in summer they can be spotted in broad daylight in some of the quieter corners of the hills though the best time to spot a fox is at dusk when you might see one trotting along a field or woodland edge.

The **rabbit** (*Oryctolagus cuniculus*) is seemingly everywhere on the Downs. The well-drained, steep grassland is ideal for their warrens.

The **grey squirrel** (*Sciurus carolinensis*) was introduced from North America at the beginning of the 20th century. Its outstanding success in colonising Britain is very much to the detriment of other native species including the red squirrel. Greys are bigger and stockier than reds and to many people the reds, with their tufted ears, bushy tails and small beady eyes, are the far more attractive of the two. Sadly there are no red squirrels anywhere on the Downs.

The **roe deer** (*Capreolus capreolus*) is a small, native species of deer that tends to hide in woodland. They can sometimes be seen, alone or in pairs, on field edges or clearings in the forest but you are more likely to hear the sharp dog-like bark made when they smell you coming.

At dusk **bats** can be seen hunting for moths and flying insects along hedgerows, over rivers and around street lamps. Bats have had a bad press thanks to Dracula and countless other horror stories but anyone who has seen one up close knows them to be harmless and delightful little creatures. As for their blood-sucking fame, the matchbox-sized species of Britain would do well with their tiny teeth to break your skin let alone suck your blood. Their reputation is improving all the time thanks to the work of the many bat conservation groups around the country. All fourteen species in Britain are protected by law. The commonest species is the **pipistrelle** (*Pipistrellus pipistrellus*) but you may also be lucky enough to see **Daubenton's** (*Myotis daubentonii*) hunting for mosquitoes over rivers and ponds.

If the Downs were made for any one species it is probably the **brown hare** which, if you are observant, can be seen racing across the fields on the hilltops. Hares are bigger than rabbits, with longer hind legs and ears, and are arguably far more graceful than their more prolific little cousins. Some other small but fairly common species to keep an eye out for include the carnivorous **stoat** (*Mustela erminea*), its smaller cousin the **weasel** (*Mustela nivalis*), the **hedgehog** (*Erinaceus europaeus*) and a number of species of **voles**, **mice** and **shrews**.

REPTILES

The **adder** (*Vipera berus*) is the only poisonous snake in Britain. It is easily recognised by the distinctive zig-zag markings down its back and a diamond shape on the back of its head. On summer days adders bask in sunny spots such as on a warm rock or in the middle of a path so watch your step. Adders tend to move out of the way quickly but should you be unlucky enough to inadvertently step on one and get bitten sit still and send someone else for help. Their venom is designed to kill small mammals, not humans. A bite is unlikely to be fatal to an adult but *is* serious enough to warrant immediate medical attention, especially in the case of children. Nevertheless, the likelihood of being bitten is minuscule. Walkers are far more likely to frighten the adder away once it senses your footsteps.

The **grass snake** (*Natrix natrix*), an adept swimmer, is a much longer, slimmer snake with a yellow collar around the neck. It's non-venomous but does emit a foul stench should you attempt to pick one up. It's much better for you and the snake to leave it in peace.

The **common lizard** (*Lacerta vivipara*) is a harmless creature which can often be seen basking in the sun on rocks and stone walls. However, you are far more likely to hear them scuttling away through the undergrowth as you approach.

A curious beast, looking like a slippery eel or small snake, is the **slow worm** (*Anguis fragilis*) which despite the name is neither a worm nor indeed an eel or snake but a legless lizard. Usually a glossy grey or copper colour, they can be seen on woodland floors and in grassland. They are completely harmless and usually slip away into the leaf litter when they hear footsteps.

BIRDS

The chalk grassland of the Downs is ideal for a variety of bird species but the grassy hillsides are not the only habitat on the Downs. There are many woodland species in the beech forests on the steep scarp slope, freshwater species on the rivers and sea birds by Cuckmere Haven and the Seven Sisters cliffs. The following list gives just a few of the birds that may be seen while walking on the Downs.

Scrubland and chalk grassland

One of the most attractive birds the Downs walker might spot, usually seen feeding on open arable farmland, is the **lapwing** (*Vanellus vanellus*), also known as the peewit. It has long legs, a short bill and a distinctive long head crest. Sadly, this attractive bird is declining in numbers. The name comes from its lilting flight, frequently changing direction with its large rounded wings. It is also identified by a white belly, black and white head, black throat patch and distinctive dark green wings.

LAPWING/PEEWIT
L: 320MM/12.5"

Towards dusk **barn owls** (*Tyto alba*) hunt for voles along field and woodland edges. To see a barn owl, with its ghostly white plumage, is a

BARN OWL
L: 355MM/14"

real treat but their dwindling numbers make such a sighting increasingly rare.

The colourful little **stonechat** (*Saxicola rubicola*) with its deep orange breast and black head is among the more commonly sighted of Downland birds. They are easily identified by their habit of flitting from the top of one bush to another, only pausing to call out across the fields. The stonechat's call sounds much like two stones being struck together, hence the name stonechat.

STONECHAT
L: 135MM/5.25"

The **yellowhammer** (*Emberiza citrinella*), also known as the yellow bunting, can sometimes be seen perched on the top of gorse bushes. Most field guides to birds along with most old romantic country folk claim that the distinctive song of the yellowhammer sounds like 'a little bit of bread and no cheese'. At a push they are right but the yellowhammer is certainly no talking parrot.

YELLOWHAMMER
L: 160MM/6.25"

The call of the **skylark** (*Alauda arvensis*) can probably be considered the sound of the Downs. This small, buff-coloured, ground-nesting lark is usually heard but not often seen. The distinctive flight pattern, rising steadily upwards on rapid wingbeats whilst twittering relentlessly, is what makes the skylark such a distinctive little bird. However, it is virtually impossible to see it against the blue sky but if you look carefully you might just spot it way up high.

Woodland

A common raptor that is often heard before it's seen is the **buzzard** (*Buteo buteo*), a large broad-winged bird of prey which looks much like a small eagle. It is dark brown in appearance but slightly paler on the underside of the wings. It has a distinctive mewing call and can be spotted soaring ever higher on the air thermals or sometimes perched on the top of fenceposts.

SKYLARK
L: 185MM/7.25"

Buzzards are not so common towards the eastern end of the Downs where the woodland cover is not so great. They are far easier to spot above the dense woodland on the West Sussex Downs and around the Meon Valley in Hampshire.

THE ENVIRONMENT AND NATURE

The **kestrel** (*Falco tinnunculus*), a small falcon, is much smaller than the buzzard and is far more commonly seen. It hovers expertly in a fixed spot above grassland and roadside verges, even in the strongest of winds, hunting for mice and voles. Similar in size and appearance but rarely seen is the **hobby** (*Falco subbuteo*) which appears in the summer months, often on the margins of woodlands.

The **green woodpecker** (*Picus viridis*) is not all green, sporting a bright red and black head. They are sometimes spotted clinging to a vertical tree trunk or feeding on the ground in open fields. The most common view, however, is as the bird flies away when disturbed. The undulating flight pattern is characterised by rapid wing beats as the bird rises followed by a pause when the bird slowly drops. This is accompanied by a loud laughing call that has earned the bird its old English name of yaffle.

GREEN
WOODPECKER
L: 330MM/13"

The **woodcock** (*Scolopax rusticola*), with its long straight beak and plump body, is common in damp woodland where it can lie hidden thanks to its leafy brown plumage. It is most easily sighted in the spring at dusk and dawn. This is when the males perform their courtship flight, known as 'roding', which involves two distinct calls, one a low grunting noise, the other a sharp 'k-wik k-wik' call.

WOODCOCK
L: 330MM/13"

BUTTERFLIES [see colour plate opp p49]

The Downs are famous for their butterflies. Many of the National Nature Reserves in the area have been set up specifically because of the variety and number of butterflies. One of the most prevalent is the **meadow brown** (*Maniola jurtina*), a very common species, dusty brown in colour with a rusty orange streak and dark, false eyes. They can be seen in meadows all across the Downs. The small **gatekeeper** (*Pyronia tithonus*) likes similar habitat and is also widespread throughout the Downs. They are identified by their deep orange and chocolate-brown markings.

The **peacock** (*Inachis io*) is surely Britain's most beautiful butterfly; it's quite common in this area. The markings on the wings are said to mimic the eyes of an animal to frighten off predators. Also common is the impressive **red admiral** (*Vanessa atalanta*). Owing to climate change it is now starting to overwinter in Britain and appears to be thriving. The **brimstone** (*Gonepteryx rhamni*) is also widespread; the **white admiral** (*Limenitis camilla*), however, is declining in numbers but may still be seen in some woodland sites. Although it has also recently been in decline in other parts of the country, the **small**

❏ Flint

Flint is a mineral found in bands within chalk and has played a big part in the history of the Downs. When man first found the ability to make tools the folk who lived on the Downs used flakes of flint to make arrowheads and knives. It was also found to be a very useful stone for starting fires. Today flint can be seen in local village architecture, being a very versatile building brick. The traditional Sussex Downs house and barn would not be the same if it were not for flint.

---

tortoishell (*Aglais urticae*) is still widespread here and also in towns and villages. Other very common butterflies include the **small white** (*Pieris/Artogeia rapae*) and the **large white** (*Pieris brassicae*). Both can travel large distances, some migrating from continental Europe each year.

Along many of the country lanes and tracks the **speckled wood** (*Pararge aegeria*) can be seen basking on hedgerows. It is a small dark butterfly with a few white spots and six small false eyes at the rear.

There are a number of butterflies that are synonymous with chalk downland, notably the butterflies known as blues. The **holly blue** (*Celastrina argiolus*) and **Chalkhill blue** (*Polyommatus/Lysandra coridon*) are both similar in appearance, being very small and pale blue in colour, although the Chalkhill blue has a dark strip on the edge of each wing. The **common blue** (*Polyommatus icarus*) is even smaller and as the name suggests is the most common of the blues. The underside of its wings is a dusty brown colour with small orange and white spots.

Another rare downland butterfly is the **Duke of Burgundy fritillary** (*Hamearis lucina*) which you may be lucky enough to see on Beacon Hill. It has pale orange spots on small dark wings. Another rarity that relies on chalk grassland is the **silver spotted skipper** (*Hesperia comma*), a diminutive yellow butterfly with small white flashes on the undersides of the wings.

Finally, the **brown argus** (*Aricia agestis*), a small dark butterfly with distinctive orange spots along the edges of each wing, is another that is restricted to chalk grassland; it can sometimes be seen flying close to the ground.

THE ENVIRONMENT AND NATURE

❏ Dew ponds

The chalk soil of the Downs is highly permeable so there is rarely any standing or free-flowing water available for livestock. To combat the problem farmers have, since prehistoric times, constructed dew ponds. These small, circular ponds are designed to collect and retain water for the sheep and cattle that graze the dry hilltops. Despite their name, dew accounts for very little of the moisture that collects in these man-made bowls; most of it is rainwater. The water is prevented from filtering through the chalk thanks to a base layer of straw and clay, although modern-day dew ponds usually have a layer of concrete instead.

Many dew ponds are hundreds of years old and in a state of disrepair, being overgrown and barely recognisable as ponds. However, in recent years many have been restored, either because of their historic interest or simply to be used again for their original purpose. Good examples of dew ponds can be seen near Chanctonbury Ring and also between Southease and Alfriston.

Minimum impact walking

Walk as if you are kissing the Earth with your feet **Thich Nhat Hanh** *Peace is every step*

The popularity of the 'Great Outdoors' as an escape route from the chaos of modern living has experienced something of a boom over the last decade or so. It is therefore important to be aware of the pressures that each of us as visitors to the countryside exert upon the land. The South Downs are particularly vulnerable, situated as they are in the most populous corner of the British Isles. Thousands of people explore the network of trails that criss-cross these historic chalk hills.

Minimum impact walking is all about a common-sense approach to exploring the countryside, being mindful and respectful of the wildlife and those who live and work on the land. Those who appreciate the countryside will already be aware of the importance of safeguarding it. Simple measures such as not dropping litter, keeping dogs on leads to avoid scaring sheep and leaving gates as you find them will already be second nature to anyone who regularly visits the countryside. However, there are a number of other measures that are not quite so well known and are worth repeating here.

ECONOMIC IMPACT

Rural businesses and communities in Britain have been hit hard in recent years by a seemingly endless series of crises. In addition, they have to compete with the omnipresence of chain supermarkets that are now so common in towns across Britain. Faced with such competition local businesses struggle to survive. Visitors to the countryside can help these local businesses by 'buying locally'. It benefits the local economy as well as the consumer.

Buy local
Look and ask for local produce to buy and eat. Not only does this cut down on the amount of pollution and congestion that the transportation of food creates, so-called 'food miles', but also ensures that you are supporting local farmers and producers – the very people who have moulded the countryside you have come to see and who are in the best position to protect it. If you can find local food which is also organic so much the better.

Support local businesses
It's a fact of life that money spent at local level – perhaps in a market, or at the greengrocer, or in an independent pub – has a far greater impact for good on

that community than the equivalent spent in a branch of a national chain store or restaurant. While no-one would advocate that walkers should boycott the larger supermarkets, which after all do provide local employment, it's worth remembering that businesses in rural communities rely heavily on visitors for their very existence. If we want to keep these shops and post offices, we need to use them. The more money that circulates locally and is spent on local labour and materials, the greater the impact on the local economy and the more power the community has to effect the changes it wants to see. See also box p140.

Encourage local cultural traditions and skills

No two parts of the countryside look the same. Buildings, food, skills and language evolve out of the landscape and are moulded over hundreds of years to suit the locality. Discovering these cultural differences is part of the pleasure of walking in new places. Visitors' enthusiasm for local traditions and skills brings awareness and pride, nurturing a sense of place; an increasingly important role in a world where economic globalisation continues to undermine the very things that provide security and a feeling of belonging.

ENVIRONMENTAL IMPACT

By choosing a walking holiday you are already minimising your impact on the environment. Your interaction with the countryside and its inhabitants, whether they be plant, animal or human, can bring benefits to all. The following are some ideas on how you can go a few steps further in helping to minimise your impact on the natural environment while walking the South Downs Way.

Use public transport whenever possible

Both Sussex and Hampshire are blessed with an excellent public transport system (see pp38-40). There are various bus routes which drop off and pick up passengers at convenient start and finish points for day walks along the Downs and there are many buses linking the Way with nearby towns and villages. There are also plenty of bus and train links to get the walker to the Downs in the first place, making a car quite unnecessary.

Never leave litter

Leaving litter shows a total disrespect for the natural world and others coming after you. As well as being unsightly, litter kills wildlife, pollutes the environment and can be dangerous to farm animals. Please take your rubbish with you so you can dispose of it in a bin in the next village. It would be very helpful if you could pick up litter left by other people, too.

● **Is it OK if it's biodegradable?** No. Apple cores, banana skins, orange peel and the like are an eyesore, encourage flies, ants and wasps and ruin a picnic spot for others. They also promote a higher population of scavengers such as carrion crows and magpies, an explosion of which can have a detrimental effect on rarer bird species.

MINIMUM IMPACT & OUTDOOR SAFETY

Those who use the excuse that orange peel is natural and biodegradable are simply fishing for an excuse to clear their conscience. Biodegradable? Yes, but surprisingly slowly (see below). Natural? The South Downs have never been known for banana plantations and orange groves.

● **The lasting impact of litter** A piece of orange peel left on the ground takes six months to decompose; silver foil 18 months; a plastic bag 10 years; clothes 15 years; and an aluminium can 85 years.

Erosion

● **Stay on the main trail** The effect of your footsteps may seem minuscule but when they are multiplied by several thousand walkers each year they become rather more significant. Avoid taking shortcuts, widening the trail or taking more than one path; your boots will be followed by many others. This is particularly pertinent on the South Downs where there is such a huge volume of visitors.

● **Consider walking out of season** Unfortunately, most people prefer to walk in the spring and summer which is exactly the time of year when the vegetation is trying to grow. Walking on the South Downs in the autumn and winter can be just as enjoyable as in the high season and eases the burden on the land during the busy summer months. The quieter season also gives the walker a greater chance of a peaceful walk away from the crowds and there are fewer people competing for accommodation.

Respect all wildlife, plants and trees

If you come across wildlife keep your distance and don't watch for too long. Your presence can cause considerable stress, particularly if the adults are with young or in winter when the weather is harsh and food is scarce.

Young animals are rarely abandoned. If you come across young birds keep away so that their mother can return. Never pick flowers, leave them for others to enjoy too and try to avoid breaking branches off or damaging trees in any way.

The code of the outdoor loo

As more and more people discover the joys of the outdoors, issues like toilet business rapidly gain importance. How many of us have shaken our heads at the sight of toilet paper strewn beside the path or, even worse, someone's dump left in full view? In some parts of the world where visitor pressure is higher than in Britain walkers and climbers are required to pack out their excrement. This could soon be necessary here. Human excrement is not only offensive to our senses but, more importantly, can infect water sources.

● **Where to go** Wherever possible **use a toilet**. Public toilets are marked on the trail maps in this guide and you will also find facilities in pubs, cafés and campsites along the Way.

If you do have to go outdoors choose a site at least **30 metres away from running water** and 200 metres from any high-use areas such as hostels and beaches, or from any sites of historic or archaeological interest. Carry a small trowel and dig a small hole about 15cm (6") deep in which to bury your excrement. It decomposes quicker when in contact with the top layer of soil or leaf mould. Use a stick to stir loose soil into your deposit as well, as this speeds up decomposition even more. Do not squash it under rocks as this slows down the composting process. If you have to use rocks to cover it make sure they are not in contact with your faeces.

● **Toilet paper and tampons** Toilet paper takes a long time to decompose whether buried or not. It is easily dug up by animals and may then blow into water sources or onto the path. The best method for dealing with it is to **pack it out**. Put the used paper inside a paper bag which you then place inside a biodegradable bag. Then simply empty the contents of the paper bag at the next toilet you come across and throw the bag away. You should also pack out **tampons** and **sanitary towels** in a similar way; they take years to decompose and will be dug up and scattered about by animals.

Wild camping

There is very little opportunity for wild camping along the length of the Downs. Most of the land is private farmland and much of this is arable cropland. If the urge to camp away from an organised site is too much to resist always ask the landowner first. If the opportunity for wild camping is there take it. Camping in such an independent way is an altogether more fulfilling experience than camping on a designated site.

Living in the outdoors without any facilities allows the walker to briefly live in a simple and sustainable way in which everyday activities from cooking and eating to personal hygiene suddenly take on greater importance. Remember that by camping off the beaten track one takes on added responsibilities. By taking on board the following suggestions for minimising your impact the whole experience of wild camping will be a far more satisfying one.

● **Be discreet** Camp alone or in small groups and spend only one night in each place. Pitch your tent late in the day and move off as early in the morning as you can.

● **Never light a fire** The deep burn caused by camp fires, no matter how small, seriously damages the turf and can take years to recover. Cook on a camp stove instead.

● **Don't use soap or detergent** There is no need to use soap; even biodegradable soaps and detergents pollute streams. You won't be away from a shower for more than a couple of days. Wash up without detergent; use a plastic or metal scourer, or failing that some bracken or grass.

● **Leave no trace** Enjoy the skill of moving on without leaving any sign of having been there. Make a final check of your campsite before heading off; pick up any litter that you or anyone else has left, so leaving the place in a better state than you found it.

MINIMUM IMPACT & OUTDOOR SAFETY

ACCESS

The south-east corner of England is the most populated area of the British Isles and is criss-crossed by some of the busiest roads in the country. Thankfully, there are also countless public footpaths and rights of way for the large local population and visitors alike. But what happens if you want to explore some of the local woodland or tramp across a meadow? Most of the land on the South Downs is agricultural land and, unless you are on a right of way, it's off limits. However, the 'Right to Roam' legislation (see below) has opened up some previously restricted land to walkers.

Rights of way

As a designated National Trail (see box p43) the South Downs Way is a public right of way – this is either a footpath, a bridleway or a byway; the South Downs Way is made up of all three.

Rights of way are theoretically established because the owner has dedicated them to public use. However, very few rights of way are formally dedicated in this way. If the public has been using a path without interference for 20 years or more the law assumes the owner has intended to dedicate it as a right of way. If a path has been unused for 20 years it does not cease to exist; the guiding principle is 'once a highway, always a highway'.

On a public right of way you have the right to 'pass and repass along the way' which includes stopping to rest or admire the view or to consume refreshments. You can also take with you a 'natural accompaniment' which includes a dog but obviously could also be a horse on bridleways and byways. All 'natural accompaniments' must be kept under close control (see p17).

Farmers and land managers must ensure that paths are not blocked by crops or other vegetation, or otherwise obstructed, and the route is identifiable and the surface is restored soon after cultivation. If crops are growing over the path you have every right to walk or ride through them, following the line of the right of way as closely as possible. If you find a path blocked or impassable you should report it to the appropriate highway authority. Highway authorities are responsible for maintaining public rights of way. Along the South Downs Way the highway authorities are Hampshire County Council, East Sussex County Council and West Sussex County Council (see box p44). The councils are also the surveying authority with responsibility for maintaining the official definitive map of public rights of way.

Right to roam

For many years groups such as the **Ramblers Association** (see box p34) and the **British Mountaineering Council** (🖳 www.thebmc.co.uk) campaigned for new and wider access legislation. This finally bore fruit in the form of the Countryside & Rights of Way Act of November 2000, colloquially known as the CRoW Act or 'Right to Roam'. It came into full effect on 31 October 2005 and gave access for 'recreation on foot' to mountain, moor, heath, down and registered common land in England and Wales. In essence it allows walkers the freedom to roam responsibly away from footpaths, without being accused of trespass, on about four million acres of open, uncultivated land. The areas of access land open to walkers are shown on new edition OS Explorer maps.

'Right to Roam' does not mean free access to wander over farmland, woodland or private gardens and much of the true chalk grassland of the South Downs has long since been ploughed up. Along with this, most of that which remains is already annexed as national and local nature reserves where access is relatively unrestricted anyway, so the results of the CRoW Act on the South Downs Way might not be quite as liberating as expected.

For those who wish to get off the beaten track and away from the crowds there are plenty of lesser-known rights of way. Follow any of these and you are likely to spend the whole day alone, which is not an easy thing to do in this part of England. However, if you want to leave the path entirely and beat your own trail through the woods and fields always check with local landowners.

Those who do exercise their 'right to roam' should remember that this added freedom comes with the responsibility to respect the immediate environment. This is particularly pertinent on the South Downs where most of the land is worked by farmers and is the home to a variety of wildlife. Always keep this in mind and try to avoid disturbing domestic and wild animals.

The Countryside Code

The countryside is a fragile place which every visitor should respect. The countryside code seems like common sense but sadly some people still seem to have no understanding of how to treat the land they walk on. Everyone visiting the countryside has a responsibility to minimise the impact of their visit so that other people can enjoy the same peaceful landscapes. It does not take much effort. It really is common sense. Below is an expanded version of the revised Countryside Code, launched in July 2004 under the new logo 'Respect, Protect and Enjoy':

> ❏ **The Countryside Code**
> ● Be safe – plan ahead and follow any signs
> ● Leave gates and property as you find them
> ● Protect plants and animals, and take your litter home
> ● Keep dogs under close control
> ● Consider other people

● **Be safe** Walking on the South Downs Way is pretty much hazard free but you're responsible for your own safety so follow the simple guidelines outlined on p63.

● **Leave all gates as you found them** Normally a farmer leaves gates closed to keep livestock in but may sometimes leave them open to allow livestock access to food or water. Leave them as you find them and if there is a sign, follow the instructions.

● **Leave livestock, crops and machinery alone** Help farmers by not interfering with their means of livelihood.

● **Take your litter home** 'Pack it in, pack it out'. Litter is not only ugly but can be harmful to wildlife. Small mammals often become trapped in discarded cans

❏ **Lambing**

Most of the South Downs Way passes through private farmland, some of which is pasture for sheep. Lambing takes place from mid-March to mid-May when dogs should not be taken along the path. Even a dog secured on a lead is liable to disturb a pregnant ewe. If you should see a lamb or ewe that appears to be in distress contact the nearest farmer.

and bottles. Many walkers think that orange peel and banana skins do not count as litter. Even biodegradable foodstuffs attract common scavenging species such as crows and gulls to the detriment of less dominant species.

● **Keep your dog under control** Across farmland dogs should be kept on a lead. During lambing time they should not be taken with you at all (see box above).

● **Enjoy the countryside and respect its life and work** Access to the countryside depends on being sensitive to the needs and wishes of those who live and work there. Being courteous and friendly to those you meet will ensure a healthy future for all based on partnership and cooperation.

● **Guard against all risk of fire** Accidental fire is a great fear of farmers and foresters. Never make a campfire and take matches and cigarette butts out with you to dispose of safely.

● **Keep to paths across farmland** Stick to the official path across arable or pasture land. Minimise erosion by not cutting corners or widening the path.

● **Use gates and stiles to cross fences, hedges and walls** The South Downs Way is well supplied with stiles where it crosses field boundaries. On some of the side trips you may find the path less accommodating. If you have to climb over a gate because you can't open it always do so at the hinged end.

● **Help keep all water clean** Leaving litter and going to the toilet near a water source can pollute people's water supplies. See p57 and p58 for more advice.

● **Take special care on country roads** Drivers often go dangerously fast on narrow winding lanes. To be safe, walk facing the oncoming traffic and carry a torch or wear highly visible clothing when it's getting dark.

● **Protect wildlife, plants and trees** Care for and respect all wildlife you come across along the South Downs Way. Don't pick plants, break trees or scare wild animals. If you come across young birds that appear to have been abandoned leave them alone.

● **Make no unnecessary noise** Enjoy the peace and solitude of the outdoors by staying in small groups and acting unobtrusively.

MINIMUM IMPACT & OUTDOOR SAFETY

Outdoor safety and health

AVOIDANCE OF HAZARDS

Walking does not come much more hazard-free than on the South Downs; however, these low southern hills should be given as much respect as their loftier counterparts. Good preparation is just as important here as it is on the northern mountains.

The following common-sense advice should ensure that those out for a day walk as well as those embarking on the whole route enjoy a safe walk. Always make sure you have **suitable clothes** to keep you warm and dry, whatever the conditions, as well as a spare change of inner clothes. Every rucksack should have inside it a compass, torch and simple first-aid kit (see p32). A whistle is unlikely to be necessary due to the close proximity of people and villages but it does not hurt to take one anyway. The **emergency signal** is six blasts on the whistle or six flashes with a torch.

Take more **food** than you expect to eat. High-energy snacks such as chocolate, fruit, biscuits and nuts are useful for those last few gruelling miles each day. With the Downs being made of permeable chalk there is a distinct lack of running water so make sure you have at least a one-litre **water bottle** or **pouch** that can be refilled when the opportunity arises.

You need to drink plenty of water when walking; 3-4 litres per day depending on the weather. There are a few drinking water taps placed conveniently along the path. These are marked on the maps in Part 4. If you start to feel tired, lethargic or get a headache it may be that you are not drinking enough. Thirst is not a good indicator of when to drink; stop and have a drink every hour or two. A good indicator of whether you are drinking enough is the colour of your urine – the lighter the better. If you are not needing to urinate much and your urine is dark yellow you may need to increase your fluid intake.

It is a good idea to be aware of where you are throughout the day. **Check your location** on the map regularly. Getting lost on the Downs is unlikely to be a major cause for concern but it can turn a pleasant day's walk into a stressful trudge back in the dark, praying that the pub chef has not gone home. If you do get lost it is unlikely to be long before someone passes by who does know their Bottoms from their Downs.

If you are walking alone you must appreciate and be prepared for the increased risk. It is always a good idea to leave word with somebody about where you are going; you can always ring ahead to book accommodation and let them know you are walking alone and what time you expect to arrive. Don't forget to contact whoever you have left word with to let them know you've arrived safely. Carrying a mobile phone can be useful though you cannot rely on getting good reception.

To ensure you have a safe trip it is well worth following this advice:

● Keep to the path – avoid steep sections of the escarpment and old quarries
● Be aware of the increased possibility of slipping over in wet or icy weather
● Wear strong sturdy boots with good ankle supports and a good grip. In very dry stable weather trainers or sandals are fine
● Be extra vigilant with children
● In an emergency dial ☎ 999.

FOOTCARE

Caring for your feet is vital; you're not going to get far if they are out of action. Wash and dry them properly at the end of the day, change your socks every few days and if it is warm enough take your boots and socks off when you stop for lunch to allow your feet to dry out in the sun.

It is important to 'break in' new boots before embarking on a long walk. Make sure the boots are comfortable and try to avoid getting them wet on the inside. If you feel any 'hot spots' stop immediately and apply a few strips of zinc oxide tape and leave them on until the area is pain free or the tape starts to come off. If you have left it too late and a blister has developed you should surround it with 'moleskin' or any other blister treatment to protect it from abrasion. Popping it can lead to infection. If the skin is broken keep the area clean with antiseptic and cover with a non-adhesive dressing material held in place with tape.

SUNBURN

It can happen, even in England and even on overcast days. The only surefire way to avoid it is to stay wrapped up but that's not really an option. What you must do, therefore, is to smother yourself in sunscreen (with a minimum factor of 15) and apply it regularly throughout the day. Don't forget your lips, nose, the back of your neck and even under the chin to protect you against rays reflected from the ground.

HYPOTHERMIA

Also known as exposure, this occurs when the body can't generate enough heat to maintain its normal temperature, usually as a result of being wet, cold, unprotected from the wind, tired and hungry. The risk of hypothermia while walking on the Downs is extremely small. However, it is worth being aware of the dangers. Hypothermia is easily avoided by wearing suitable clothing, carrying and

(**Opposite**): Winchester Cathedral (see p68), built over 900 years ago, marks the start (or the end) of the South Downs Way. This magnificent building is one of the best examples of the Gothic Perpendicular style.

eating enough food and drink, being aware of the weather conditions and checking the morale of your companions.

Early signs to watch for are feeling cold and tired with involuntary shivering. Find some shelter as soon as possible and warm the victim up with a hot drink and some chocolate or other high-energy food. If possible give them another warm layer of clothing and allow them to rest until feeling better.

If allowed to worsen, strange behaviour, slurring of speech and poor co-ordination will become apparent and the victim can quickly progress into unconsciousness, followed by coma and death. In the unlikely event of a severe case of hypothermia, quickly get the victim out of wind and rain, improvising a shelter if necessary.

Rapid restoration of bodily warmth is essential and best achieved by bareskin contact: someone should get into the same sleeping bag as the patient, both having stripped to their underwear with any spare clothing under or over them to build up heat. Send urgently for help.

HYPERTHERMIA

Hyperthermia occurs when the body generates too much heat, eg heat exhaustion and heatstroke. Not an ailment that you would normally associate with the south of England, heatstroke is a serious problem nonetheless. Symptoms of **heat exhaustion** include thirst, fatigue, giddiness, a rapid pulse, raised body temperature, low urine output and, if not treated, delirium and finally a coma. The best cure is to drink plenty of water.

Heatstroke is another matter altogether, and even more serious. A high body temperature and an absence of sweating are early indications, followed by symptoms similar to hypothermia (see opposite) such as a lack of co-ordination and convulsions. Coma and death will follow if treatment is not given instantly. Sponge the victim down, wrap them in wet towels, fan them, and get help immediately.

WEATHER FORECASTS

The South Downs is one of the driest parts of what is a notoriously wet island. However, the weather can still change from blazing sunshine to a stormy wet gale in the space of a day. The wind, in particular, can be surprisingly severe along the top of the Downs. Couple this with rain and a nice walk can turn into a damp battle against the elements.

Try to get the local weather forecast from the newspaper, TV or radio or one of the weather telephone forecasts before you set off and alter your plans for the day accordingly. These are frequently updated and generally reliable. Calls to **Weather call** (☎ 09068-500402) are charged at the expensive premium rate.

(Opposite) Top: Each day on the South Downs Way you'll be treated to wide views of open landscape such as this vista from Old Winchester Hill. **Bottom left**: A statue of King Alfred the Great (849-99) stands in his capital, Winchester, on the Broadway. **Bottom right**: Also in Winchester is a medieval table said to be King Arthur's Round Table (see p69).

MINIMUM IMPACT & OUTDOOR SAFETY

For detailed weather outlooks online, including local five-day forecasts, log on to ▭ www.bbc.co.uk/weather or ▭ www.metoffice.gov.uk/weather/uk/index.html.

DEALING WITH AN ACCIDENT

● Use basic first aid to treat the injury to the best of your ability.

● Try to attract the attention of anybody else who may be in the area. The emergency signal is six blasts on a whistle, or six flashes with a torch.

● If possible leave someone with the casualty while others go to get help. If there are only two people, you have a dilemma. If you decide to get help leave all spare clothing and food with the casualty.

● Telephone ☎ 999 and ask for the emergency services. They will assist in both offshore and onshore incidents. Be sure you know exactly where you are before you call. Report the exact position of the casualty and their condition.

PART 4: ROUTE GUIDE & MAPS

Using this guide

This route guide has been divided according to logical start and stop points. However, these are not intended to be strict daily stages since people walk at different speeds and have different interests. The maps can be used to plan how far to walk each day. The **route summaries** below describe the trail between significant places and are written as if walking the path from west to east. To enable you to plan your own itinerary **practical information** is presented clearly on the trail maps. This includes walking times for both directions, all places to stay, camp and eat, as well as shops where you can buy supplies. Further service **details** are given in the text under the entry for each place.

For an overview of this information see Itineraries, pp26-7.

TRAIL MAPS

Scale and walking times   [see map key, p177]
The trail maps are to a scale of 1:20,000 (1cm = 200m; 3¹/₈ inches = one mile). Walking times are given along the side of each map and the arrow shows the direction to which the time refers. Black triangles indicate the points between which the times have been taken. **See note below on walking times.**

The time-bars are a tool and are not there to judge your walking ability. There are so many variables that affect walking speed, from the weather conditions to how many beers you drank the previous evening. After the first hour or two of walking you will see how your speed relates to the timings on the maps.

Up or down?
The trail is shown as a dotted line. An arrow across the trail indicates the slope; two arrows show that it is steep. Note that the arrow points towards the higher part of the trail. If, for example, you are walking from A (at 80m) to B (at 200m) and the trail between the two is short and steep it would be shown thus:

A— — — >> — — – B. Reversed arrow heads indicate downward gradient.

Accommodation
Apart from in large towns where some selection of places has been necessary, almost everywhere to stay that is within easy reach of the trail is marked.

❏ **Important note – walking times**
Unless otherwise specified, **all times in this book refer only to the time spent walking.** You will need to add 20-30% to allow for rests, photography, checking the map, drinking water etc. When planning the day's hike count on 5-7 hours' actual walking.

ROUTE GUIDE AND MAPS

Details of each place are given in the accompanying text. Unless otherwise specified **B&B prices** are summer high-season prices per room assuming two people sharing. The number and type of rooms are given after each entry: S = single room, T = twin room, D = double room, F = family room (sleeps at least three people).

Other features
Other features are marked on the map only when they are pertinent to navigation. Not all features are marked all the time.

The route guide

WINCHESTER   MAP 1, p71
Winchester is a city steeped in history. The area was settled as long ago as 450BC when the nearby **St Catherine's Hill** was home to a Celtic tribe.

After the Roman occupation came the Dark Ages of 400-600AD during which time it is believed that **King Arthur** (see opposite) reigned from here. Many romantics today believe the city to be the site of legendary Camelot.

Things brightened up after the Dark Ages when in 871 **King Alfred the Great** (849-899) made the city the capital of Saxon England. He has probably had the greatest influence on the city so it is not surprising that a **bronze statue** of him, constructed in 1901, stands in the Broadway.

St Swithun (see box below) is also inextricably linked with Winchester.

In 1066 **William the Conqueror** arrived in Hastings and made his way to

Winchester where he duly took charge and ordered the building of the castle. Soon after, in 1079, work began on the cathedral.

Other famous people who have links with the city include **Winston Churchill** and **Eisenhower** who reviewed their troops at Peninsula Barracks the day before D-Day. More tenuous associations with the city include **John Keats** who was inspired to pen *Ode to Autumn* while wandering around the water meadows here in 1819.

The city has had a long and at times turbulent history but it is well worth spending an afternoon or the whole day exploring the compact city's many sights.

What to see and do
Winchester Cathedral (☎ 01962-857200, 🖥 www.winchester-cathedral.org.uk; Mon-Sat 8.30am-6pm, Sun 8.30am-5.30pm, free but suggested donation of £4-5) stands elegantly in parkland in the city centre. The

---

❏ The Legend of St Swithun
St Swithun, once bishop of Winchester, died in 862AD. Before his death he asked to be buried outside the Old Minster and was duly interred in accordance with his wishes. St Swithun, however, had not counted upon the wishes of Bishop Aethelwold who on 15 July 971 decided to extend the Minster. The expansion plans required the temporary opening of St Swithun's grave before he was carefully re-interred within the new Minster's walls. On the day of the re-interment it began to rain and did not stop for forty days. To this day the legend says that if it rains on St Swithun's Day it will rain for forty days. Some would say this is not unusual for England in July.

❏ Jane Austen

Jane Austen, born near Basingstoke in Hampshire in 1775, is one of the most important English novelists, having penned such classics as *Pride and Prejudice*, *Persuasion* and *Northanger Abbey*. In 1816 she began writing *Sanditon* but in the same year she contracted Addison's disease and the novel was never completed. As her condition worsened she moved to a house in Winchester where she spent the last few weeks of her life, dying at the age of 41 on 18 July 1817.

spectacular nave is said to be the longest Gothic cathedral nave in the world. The best time to visit the cathedral is from 5.30pm daily (except Wed and Sun) or during the Sunday morning service when the choir can be heard.

The cathedral has witnessed many a historic event: **Henry III** was baptised here in 1207 and it was also the scene of the marriage of **Mary Tudor** to **Philip of Spain** in 1554. In more recent history it became the final resting place in 1817 of **Jane Austen** (see box above). Her grave and memorial can be seen in the north aisle of the cathedral.

Tours include Cathedral Tours (Mon-Sat hourly between 10am and 3pm), Tower Tours (Jun-Sep Mon-Sat 2.15pm plus Sat 11.30am, Oct-May Sat 11.30am & 2.15pm, Wed 2.15pm; £5) and Crypt Tours (Mon-Sat 10.30am, 12.30pm & 2.30pm).

Even though the cathedral is the centrepiece of the city there are other equally fascinating places such as the remains of **Wolvesey Castle** (Apr-Sep daily 10am-5pm; free), the palace (residence) for the bishops of Winchester till about the 1680s.

On College St, not far from Wolvesey Castle, is the house where **Jane Austen** died. (It's the yellow building next to the college although be aware that this is a private residence so don't peer through the windows).

Also near the cathedral is the **City of Winchester Museum** (☎ 01962-863064, 🖳 www.winchester.gov.uk/museums; Apr-Oct Mon-Sat 10am-5pm, Sun noon-5pm, Nov-Mar Tue-Sat 10am-4pm, Sun noon-4pm, admission free). The museum traces the history of the city from the Romans to the Victorians and most things in between.

Some of the exhibits in Winchester's museums can be viewed online at 🖳 www .winchestermuseumcollections.org.uk.

Next to **Westgate**, one of two city gates, is **Great Hall** (☎ 01962-846476, 🖳 www.hants.gov.uk/greathall/index.html, Castle Ave; daily 10am-5pm, free but donations of 50p-£1 are welcome; tours are available on request), the only surviving part of Winchester Castle. Here you can see the table of King Arthur and his Knights of the Round Table. The table has hung in the Great Hall for at least 600 years. The Great Hall is also famous for the trying of **Sir Walter Raleigh** for treason in 1603.

In the heart of the city is **City Mill** (☎ 01962-870057, 🖳 www.nationaltrust.org .uk/winchestercitymill; Feb half term and Mar-Christmas, daily in school holiday periods summer 11am-5pm, winter to 4.30pm, at other times Wed-Sun 11am-5pm; admission £3.50/£3.95 with gift aid; NT and Wildlife Trust members free), a working water mill sitting astride the River Itchen. Although it has been around for centuries it was restored to full working order in 1744. On most Saturdays and Sundays (2-4pm) visitors can watch demonstrations of flour milling. Call to check the details if you are interested in seeing this.

It is possible to visit **Winchester College** (☎ 01962-621209, 🖳 www.win chestercollege.co.uk; one-hour tours, Mon, Wed, Fri & Sat 10.45am, noon, 2.15pm & 3.30pm, Tue & Thur 10.45am & noon, Sun 2.15pm & 3.30pm, year-round except Christmas and New Year; admission £4) which was founded in 1382 by William of Wykeham, then Bishop of Winchester, and is said to be the oldest continuously running school in the country. Originally it was home to 70 pupils but it now has more than 700. Amongst the buildings included in the tour are the 14th-century chapel, the College Hall, the 17th-century schoolroom and the medieval cloister.

Services

The **tourist information centre** (TIC; ☎ 01962-840500, 🖳 www.visitwinchester.co .uk; May-Sep Mon-Sat 9.30am-5.30pm, bank holiday Mondays 10am-4pm, Sun 11am-4pm, Oct-Apr Mon-Sat 10am-5pm) is on the ground floor of the Guildhall on Broadway. They have an accommodation-booking service though they charge a rather steep £4 (or £5 if booking over the phone) fee and they also take a 10% deposit for the first night's accommodation at the time of booking, though this is deducted from the cost of the accommodation. All in all you're better off phoning around yourself.

Those arriving or leaving by coach will find the main **bus station** opposite the TIC. The **train station** is about five minutes' walk from the city centre on Station Rd (see pp38-40, for details of public transport to and from Winchester).

On the pedestrianised High St there are countless **banks** and **cash machines** while the main **post office** (Mon-Sat 9am-5.30pm) is now housed in the local branch of WH Smith at the top of the High St.

There are several **supermarkets**; the biggest, Sainsbury's, adjoins **Brooks Shopping Centre** on Middle Brook St.

Last-minute hiking equipment (including blister kits) can be found in any of the **outdoor shops**, including Millets and Blacks, which are situated on the High St. **Lloyds Pharmacy** (Mon, Wed-Fri 8.45am-5.30pm, Tues & Sat 9am-5.30pm) is near the TIC at 155 High St.

Free **internet access** can be found inside the Discovery Centre (Mon-Fri 9am-7pm, Sat 9am-5pm, Sun 10am-4pm) on Jewry St.

Where to stay

Being a popular tourist destination, Winchester is blessed with plenty of affordable and not-so-affordable guest-houses and hotels. However, the demand on accommodation throughout the year is such that booking well in advance is strongly recommended to avoid a night on the park bench by the cathedral.

Close to the city centre and offering the chance to stay in a traditional old inn is *The Westgate Hotel* (☎ 01962-820222; 6D en suite, 1D/1T shared bathroom) at 2 Romsey Rd. B&B here is from £70 to £85; there is no single occupancy rate.

Slightly further out is *5 Clifton Terrace* (☎ 01962-890053; 1D, T or F/1D, both with private bathroom) with B&B for £69-75, or £55-59 if you're on your own.

Another good bet is *53a Parchment Street* (☎ 01962-849962; 1D en suite), a terraced townhouse on a quiet street yet close to the hubbub of the centre. B&B costs from £65, or £55 for single occupancy.

Also very convenient for the city centre is *63 Upper Brook St* (☎ 01962-620367; 1S/1T, private bathroom) where B&B is £70 and the single £35. It's quite a small place but the location and prices are hard to beat. If you stay here be aware that they have no facilities for self-catering and also do not permit people to bring takeaway meals into their room.

Those wishing to start (or end) their walk on the South Downs with a touch of luxury should aim for the *Winchester Royal* (☎ 01962-840840, 🖳 www.thewin chesterroyalhotel.co.uk; 10S/33D/28T/3 suites, all en suite) on St Peter St. This 16th-century townhouse was once a bishop's residence then a convent but now offers luxurious hotel accommodation with four-poster beds in some of the rooms and a walled garden. Prices start at £120 for two sharing and for the single rooms; they also have special offers so check their website for details.

Further from the bustling centre are several affordable guesthouses in a Victorian part of town: *5 Compton Road* (☎ 01962-869199, 🖳 www.winchesterbed andbreakfast.net; 2D or T, both rooms share a bathroom) with B&B from £55, £40 single occupancy. They serve a healthy breakfast here (cereals, fruit etc; a cooked one is £4 more), will prepare packed lunches and

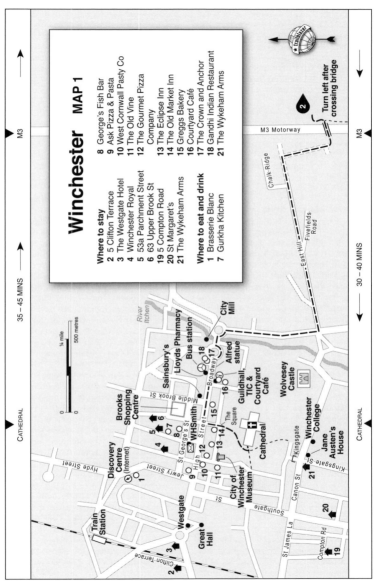

Winchester MAP 1

Where to stay
2   5 Clifton Terrace
3   The Westgate Hotel
4   Winchester Royal
5   53a Parchment Street
6   63 Upper Brook St
19 5 Compton Road
20 St Margaret's
21 The Wykeham Arms

Where to eat and drink
1   Brasserie Blanc
7   Gurkha Kitchen
8   George's Fish Bar
9   Ask Pizza & Pasta
10 West Cornwall Pasty Co
11 The Old Vine
12 The Gourmet Pizza Company
13 The Eclipse Inn
14 The Old Market Inn
15 Greggs Bakery
16 Courtyard Café
17 The Crown and Anchor
18 Gandhi Indian Restaurant
21 The Wykeham Arms

have drying facilities. Subject to a small charge, and a two-night booking, they will pick walkers up from Exton and take them back the next day. Nearby is *St Margaret's* (☎ 01962-861450, 🖳 www.win chesterbandb.com; 2S/1D/1T; shared bathroom), 3 St Michael's Rd, offering B&B from £58-60 two sharing, the singles costing £38 per night.

Close by at 75 Kingsgate St is *The Wykeham Arms* (☎ 01962-853834, 🖳 www .fullershotels.com; 2S/9D/2T, all en suite), a cosy inn with quality rooms priced from £115 (£99 single occupancy): the singles cost £65. It's named after William of Wykeham who founded Winchester College (see p69).

Where to eat and drink

There are plenty of places to eat in Winchester from little street cafés to traditional old timber-framed pubs. *Courtyard Café* (☎ 01962-855385; Mon-Sat 9.30am-5pm, Sun 10am-4pm) is, like the TIC, hidden inside the **Guildhall**.

Near the TIC is *The Crown and Anchor* (☎ 01962-620849; food Mon-Sat noon-6pm, Sun noon-4pm), which has no-nonsense dishes such as burgers from £7.25.

For quick eats, *Greggs Bakery* (☎ 01962-813580; Mon-Sat 8am-6pm, Sun 9.30am-4.30pm), on the High St, is a good place to go for ideas for packed lunches as is the wonderful **Winchester street market** (☎ 01962-848325) held Wednesday to Saturday (8am-5pm) on Middle Brook St, though the exact location is dependent on the weather. The farmer's market (see box p15) is also held here on the first and third Sundays of the month.

There's also *West Cornwall Pasty Company* (Mon-Sat 8.10am-6pm, Sun 9.15am-5pm), with pasties starting at just £2. More simple yet filling fare can be found at *George's Fish Bar* (Mon 10.30am-9pm, Tue-Fri 10.30am-late, Sat 10am-late) on St George's St.

One of the most attractive and historic pubs in the city is at 25 The Square: *The Eclipse Inn* (☎ 01962-865676; food Mon-Fri noon-2.30pm, Sat & Sun noon-3.30pm)

is a tiny whitewashed, timber-framed house which once served as a 16th-century rectory and is rumoured to be haunted. They are now just as famous for their Sunday roasts (£7.50) which boast – if you can believe it – up to 17 different vegetables on the plate! Further along The Square is *The Old Market Inn* (☎ 01962-627341; food Mon-Sat noon-9pm, Sun noon-6pm); a healthy portion of fish & chips is £6.75 or a peppered steak £11.95. *The Wykeham Arms* (see Where to stay: Mon-Sat noon-2.30pm, Sun noon-1.45pm; daily 6.30-8.45pm) serves standard pub fare using local produce; on Sunday lunchtimes it serves a two-course (£15.50) and a three-course (£19.50) set menu.

In the other direction, on Minster St, *The Old Vine* (☎ 01962-854616; food Mon-Fri noon-2.30pm & 6.30-9.30pm, Sat noon-3pm & 6.30-9.30pm, Sun noon-3pm & 6.30-9pm), another old pub but one that was completely refurbished a few years ago, offers salmon fillet for £12.95.

For something Italian you could try *Ask Pizza & Pasta* (☎ 01962-849464; Sun-Thur noon-11pm, Fri & Sat noon-11.30pm) on the High St; they have a large range of pizzas and pasta dishes from £5.95. Pastries and coffee are served daily from 9am-noon.

If this place is full the *Gourmet Pizza Company* (☎ 01962-842553; Mon-Sat 11am-11pm, Sun 11am-10.30pm) serves much the same fare with pizzas from £5.95 and fresh pasta from £8.15 though child portions (£3.50) are also available to adults.

Spicier food can be found at the *Gandhi Indian Restaurant* (☎ 01962-863940; daily noon-2.30pm & 6pm-midnight) near the roundabout at the bottom of Broadway; typical tandoori dishes start at £6.45. For more subcontinental fare though with a Himalayan twist there's also *Gurkha Kitchen* (☎ 01962-844409; daily noon-2.30pm & 6-11pm), a Nepalese restaurant and takeaway just off the main drag on Parchment St.

Finally, for some top-notch food check out *Brasserie Blanc* (☎ 01962-810870, 🖳 www.brasserieblanc.com/locations/winchester.html; Mon-Fri noon-2.45pm &

5.30-10pm, Sat noon-10.30pm, Sun noon-9pm). The menu changes seasonally and they use local produce; main courses cost around £14. If you started in Eastbourne and are consequently looking for somewhere to celebrate the end of your trek this is a fine choice; though do make sure you tidy yourself up first.

Moving on

There are regular **trains** to London Waterloo, Southampton and Portsmouth as well as to Reading and along the coast to Brighton. Cross Country run services between Bournemouth and Manchester via Winchester.

From the **bus station** there is a regular National Express **coach** service to Heathrow Airport and London; Megabus's London to Bournemouth and Leeds to Portsmouth (via Birmingham) services also stop in Winchester (see box p37). For Southampton you should take bluestar's No 1 bus or Stagecoach's No 46 while for Petersfield and the villages in between take Stagecoach's No 67; see the public transport map and table, pp38-40.

WINCHESTER TO OLD WINCHESTER HILL   MAPS 1-7

(Note: The route from Winchester used to go to Exton but from summer 2009 will bypass the village: see p82 and Maps 7a and 7b pp80-1.)

These **12 miles/19.5km** begin at the cathedral in the centre of Winchester. The route takes you from the cathedral grounds, along the main shopping street and over the River Itchen. It does not take long for the South Downs Way to leave the city and enter the rolling East Hampshire countryside but first you must cross the M3.

On crossing the bridge spanning the noisy motorway spare a thought for the remains of **Twyford Down**. This once beautiful hill a few miles to the south was, despite vociferous and well-publicised demonstrations, ruthlessly sliced in two as part of a highly controversial road improvement scheme (see box p47).

Once away from the noise of the road the path crosses a field before arriving at **Chilcomb** (see below). The church aside, there's little in the way of shops or services to keep you in Chilcomb so once you have admired the thatched cottages head on up the lane for the gradual but steady ascent to **Cheesefoot Head** (Map 3) where there are great views to the north over the Itchen Valley.

CHILCOMB   MAP 2, p74

Chilcomb is the first of several beautiful Hampshire villages passed through on the way to Sussex. In fact Chilcomb is one of the older settlements, with a **church** (off the path to the south) that pre-dates Winchester Cathedral.

For accommodation, campers will find pitches from around £12 for a two-man tent at *Morn Hill Camping and Caravan Site* (☎ 01962-869877; mid Mar to end Sep). To get there turn left where the path hits the junction of lanes just before Chilcomb.

Follow the lane up to the busy A31 then follow this road as far as the big roundabout a mile further east.

There's also a B&B, *Complyns* (☎ 01962-861600, ☐ www.complyns.co.uk; 1D/1T, shared bathroom), a seventeenth-century former farmhouse with rooms for £58 or £30-35 single occupancy. They have a boiler house where you can dry clothes and packed lunches are available on request.

ROUTE GUIDE AND MAPS

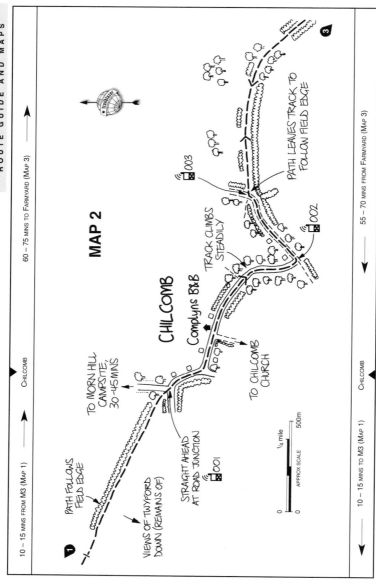

10 – 15 MINS FROM M3 (MAP 1)   CHILCOMB   60 – 75 MINS TO FARMYARD (MAP 3)

MAP 2

CHILCOMB

Complyns B&B

PATH FOLLOWS FIELD EDGE

VIEWS OF TWYFORD DOWN (REMAINS OF)

STRAIGHT AHEAD AT ROAD JUNCTION

001

TO MORN HILL CAMPSITE, 30-45 MINS

TO CHILCOMB CHURCH

TRACK CLIMBS STEADILY

002

003

PATH LEAVES TRACK TO FOLLOW FIELD EDGE

APPROX SCALE
¼ mile
500m

10 – 15 MINS TO M3 (MAP 1)   CHILCOMB   55 – 70 MINS FROM FARMYARD (MAP 3)

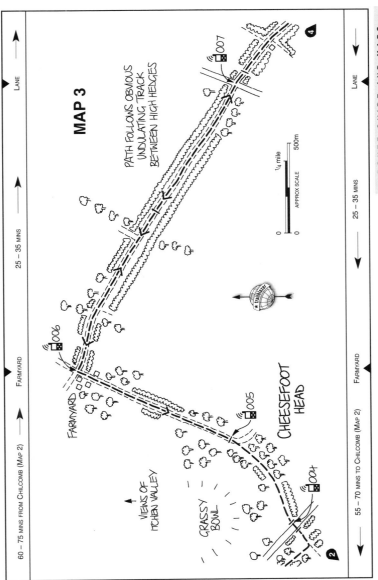

MAP 3

PATH FOLLOWS OBVIOUS
UNDULATING TRACK
BETWEEN HIGH HEDGES

007

4

LANE

25 – 35 MINS

FARMYARD

006

FARMYARD

005

CHEESEFOOT
HEAD

004

2

VIEWS OF
ITCHEN VALLEY

GRASSY
BOWL

60 – 75 MINS FROM CHILCOMB (MAP 2)

55 – 70 MINS TO CHILCOMB (MAP 2)

APPROX SCALE

¼ mile   500m

0

0

LANE

25 – 35 MINS

FARMYARD

CHERITON   MAP 4a

On hot sunny days the locals can be seen paddling in the clear waters of the tiny River Itchen, which bubbles out of the chalk about a mile south of Cheriton and runs straight through the village passing beautiful thatched houses and the village green. The village is some 40 to 50 minutes from the official route of the South Downs Way so unfortunately, unless you are planning on staying the night here, you are likely to miss Cheriton's quaint charms.

Those who do make the visit should bear in mind that it was not always such a peaceful and charming spot. In 1644, during the English Civil War, the Battle of Cheriton took place just to the east of the village, off Lamborough Lane. The clash between the Parliamentarians and the Royalists resulted in the deaths of 2000 men with the Parliamentarians coming out on top. To this day it is claimed that 'Lamborough Lane ran with the blood of the slain'.

In the centre of the village is a very useful combined **post office**, **shop**, **newsagent** and **off-licence** (☎ 01962-771251; Mon-Sat 7am-6pm, Sun 7am-1pm) that is open long hours but note that the post office part opens on Monday and Thursday only (9am-1pm).

Accommodation-wise, the 14th-century, thatched *Old Kennetts Cottage* (☎ 01962-771863, 💻 dglssmith@aol.com; 1S/1D private shower room) has a self-contained part of the house for guests costing £65 for the double and the single costs £45.

The charming *Flowerpots Inn* (☎ 01962-771318; 1D/3T all en suite; food daily noon-2pm & 7-9pm, except Sun &

Bank hol eves, though these hours can vary depending on demand) on the outskirts of the village has a range of excellent beers; the Flowerpots Bitter is definitely worth a taste though the pub is closed 2.30-6pm (3-7pm on Sundays). As well as the beer they have a decent bar menu and B&B from £70, or £45 for single occupancy.

Stagecoach **bus** No 67 passes through Cheriton on its way between Winchester and Petersfield and stops in the centre of the village, next to the church; see the public transport map and table, pp38-40.

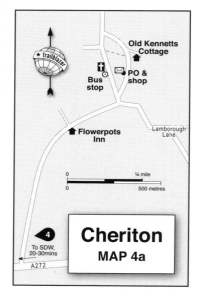

The route continues along leafy country lanes and tracks through a typically English landscape of patchwork fields, hedgerows and pockets of woodland. Along this section is *The Milbury's* (Map 5, p78; ☎ 01962-771248; food daily noon-2pm, Mon-Fri 6.30-9pm, Sat 6-9pm) which makes an ideal lunch stop; the liver sautéed with bacon and onions (£8.95) is delicious. Even if you do not plan on eating here it is still worth dropping in for a drink, though the pub is closed 3-6pm. While you're here you should take a few minutes to admire the 250-year-old **indoor treadmill** and 300ft-deep (92m) well which is lit all the way to the bottom. *(cont'd on p82)*

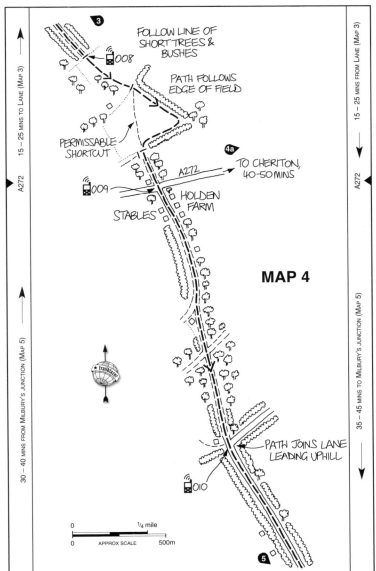

FOLLOW LINE OF
SHORT TREES &
BUSHES

008

PATH FOLLOWS
EDGE OF FIELD

PERMISSABLE
SHORTCUT

4a

A272

TO CHERITON,
40-50 MINS

009

HOLDEN
FARM

STABLES

MAP 4

PATH JOINS LANE
LEADING UPHILL

010

15 – 25 MINS TO LANE (MAP 3)   A272   15 – 25 MINS FROM LANE (MAP 3)

30 – 40 MINS FROM MILBURY'S JUNCTION (MAP 5)   35 – 45 MINS TO MILBURY'S JUNCTION (MAP 5)

trailblazer

0   ¼ mile

0   500m
APPROX SCALE

3

5

ROUTE GUIDE AND MAPS

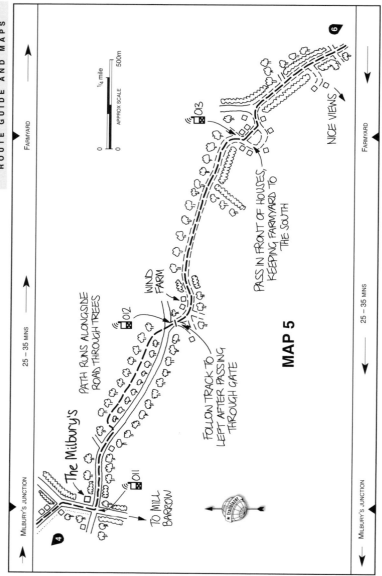

FARMYARD

25 – 35 MINS

MILBURY'S JUNCTION

¼ mile

500m

0

0

APPROX SCALE

The Milbury's

PATH RUNS ALONGSIDE ROAD THROUGH TREES

WIND FARM

012

011

TO MILL BARROW

FOLLOW TRACK TO LEFT AFTER PASSING THROUGH GATE

MAP 5

PASS IN FRONT OF HOUSES, KEEPING FARMYARD TO THE SOUTH

03

NICE VIEWS

FARMYARD

25 – 35 MINS

MILBURY'S JUNCTION

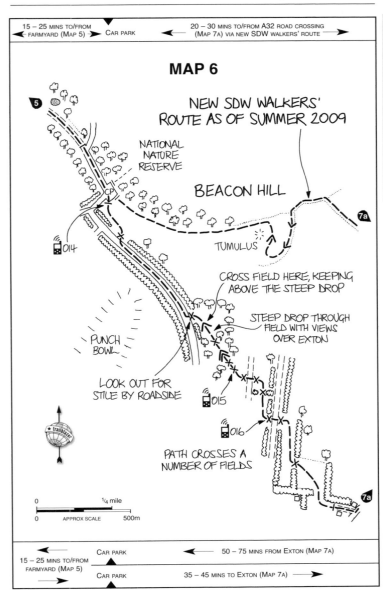

MAP 6

NEW SDW WALKERS' ROUTE AS OF SUMMER 2009

NATIONAL NATURE RESERVE

BEACON HILL

7a

TUMULUS

☐014

CROSS FIELD HERE, KEEPING ABOVE THE STEEP DROP

STEEP DROP THROUGH FIELD WITH VIEWS OVER EXTON

PUNCH BOWL

LOOK OUT FOR STILE BY ROADSIDE

☐015

☐016

PATH CROSSES A NUMBER OF FIELDS

7a

trailblazer

0   ¼ mile

0   APPROX SCALE   500m

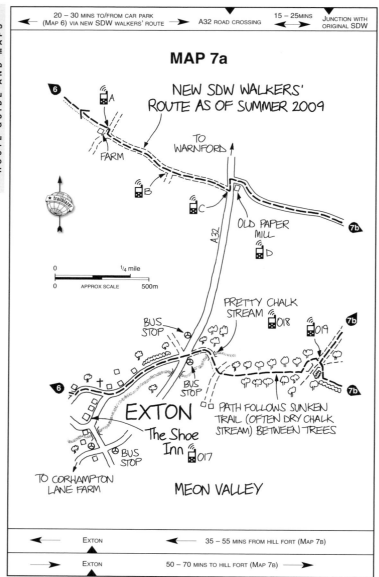

← 20 – 30 MINS TO/FROM CAR PARK (MAP 6) VIA NEW SDW WALKERS' ROUTE → | A32 ROAD CROSSING | 15 – 25MINS ←→ | JUNCTION WITH ORIGINAL SDW

MAP 7a

NEW SDW WALKERS' ROUTE AS OF SUMMER 2009

6

A

FARM

TO WARNFORD

B

C

OLD PAPER MILL

D

A32

7b

★ trailblazer

0   ¼ mile
0   APPROX SCALE   500m

PRETTY CHALK STREAM

018

019

7b

BUS STOP

BUS STOP

6

EXTON

The Shoe Inn   017

PATH FOLLOWS SUNKEN TRAIL (OFTEN DRY CHALK STREAM) BETWEEN TREES

7b

BUS STOP

TO CORHAMPTON LANE FARM

MEON VALLEY

← EXTON | ← 35 – 55 MINS FROM HILL FORT (MAP 7B)

→ EXTON | 50 – 70 MINS TO HILL FORT (MAP 7B) →

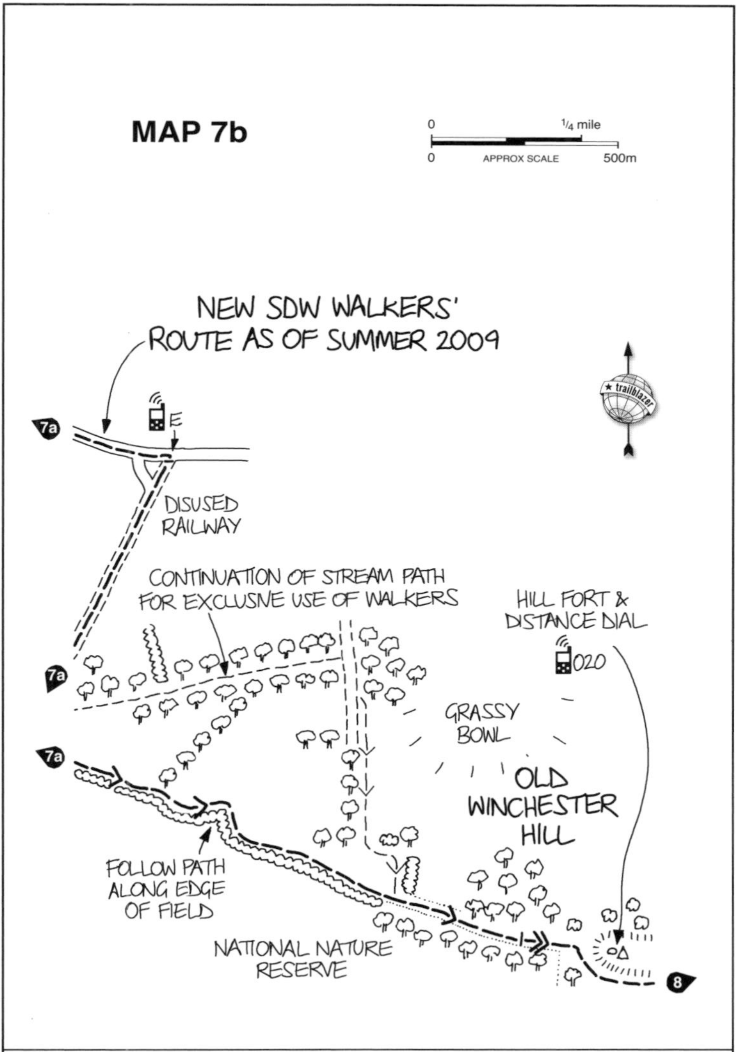

MAP 7b

0   ¼ mile

0   APPROX SCALE   500m

NEW SDW WALKERS'
ROUTE AS OF SUMMER 2009

7a

E

DISUSED
RAILWAY

CONTINUATION OF STREAM PATH
FOR EXCLUSIVE USE OF WALKERS

HILL FORT &
DISTANCE DIAL

020

7a

GRASSY
BOWL

7a

OLD
WINCHESTER
HILL

FOLLOW PATH
ALONG EDGE
OF FIELD

NATIONAL NATURE
RESERVE

8

35 – 55 MINS TO EXTON (MAP 7A)   HILL FORT ◄

50 – 70 MINS FROM EXTON (MAP 7A) ►   HILL FORT →

(cont'd from p76) The pub's name refers to the Mill Barrow, a Bronze Age burial ground just a short distance to the south-east.

The highlight of the day appears rather unexpectedly at the top of **Beacon Hill** (Map 6, p79), a National Nature Reserve and the first real taste of steep downland scenery. The view over the Meon Valley to Old Winchester Hill is a fine reward for the day's effort. Beacon Hill is one of a number of hills in southern England where beacons or bonfires were lit to warn of invasions, most notably in the 16th century because of the Spanish Armada.

The course of the South Downs Way across the Meon Valley is changing. After a lengthy battle between Hampshire County Council (HCC) and the landowners concerned, the new path has now been given the go-ahead. This new route no longer calls in at Exton, but instead heads across Beacon Hill and continues north of the village. By way of compensation for losing a visit to pretty Exton, the new path offers stunning views east and south from the summit of the hill.

That said, although the new route has been agreed, at the time of writing (December 2008) the actual path had yet to be finished and there are still fences to be removed and signposts to be placed. It is unsure when the new route will finally be established and opened to the public. As such, in this book (see Maps 7a and 7b, pp80-1) we have marked both trails; and the best advice we can give you is to follow the signposts closely when you come to this section, to ensure you are on the correct trail.

EXTON   MAP 7a, p80

The Meon valley is known for its natural beauty and also for the Meon villages, all of which claim to be the prettiest in the area. Exton is the smallest of them, if you discount the adjoining hamlets of Meonstoke and Corhampton, and dates back to at least 940AD when it was first mentioned in official documents. It also merited an entry in the Domesday Book of 1086 in which it is described as a hamlet of one church and two mills. This guidebook today describes it as a charming hamlet of attractive old cottages and one rather good public house. And though the new route (see above) takes you away from the village, those in need of a pint or a spot of lunch could do worse than to call in at the pub (see Where to stay and eat), and there is also somewhere to stay nearby.

The **bus stop** is situated on the main road just outside the village. Brijan Tours' bus No 17 heads to East Meon and onto Petersfield from here; see the public transport map and table, pp38-40.

Where to stay and eat

A little way from the village, about a mile down Corhampton Lane (off Map 7a), is *Corhampton Lane Farm* (☎ 01489-877506; 1S/1T, shared shower room) with simple **camping** pitches for £5 per camper and B&B for £60, or £35 for the single room. Campers can use the toilet and wash basin in the barn. The owner can put up a camp bed in either of the rooms if an extra bed is needed. All rates include a 'free taxi service' by the owner from/to Exton provided he knows your expected time of arrival by noon on the day concerned.

There is only one choice in terms of food but it is a good one: *The Shoe Inn* (☎ 01489-877526; food Sun noon-2pm & 6-8.30pm, Mon noon-2pm, Tue-Thur noon-2pm & 6-9pm, Fri & Sat noon-2pm & 6-9.30pm) is a friendly village pub with real ales and real food though it's closed every afternoon (3-6pm). The pub's name derives from the building next door which used to be the village cobbler's.

OLD WINCHESTER HILL TO BURITON   MAPS 7b-12

This fine stretch of the Way covering **12¹/₂ miles/20km** takes the walker over **Old Winchester Hill** (Map 7b, p81), a typical downland hill of chalk grassland and steep ancient woodland and a National Nature Reserve. The top of the hill boasts one of the finest Iron Age hill-fort sites in the south. The old earthworks clearly mark the outline of the fort and a display board has an artist's impression of how it once would have looked when the earthy banks were lined with the wooden stakes that formed the walls of the fort.

It is clear why it was positioned here since the views in all directions are spectacular, stretching as far as the Isle of Wight on a clear day. One would assume, however, that the soldiers of the time appreciated the views for the strategic advantage it gave them and not just because they were so magnificent. After descending off Old Winchester Hill there is the option of a short and highly recommended detour into East Meon.

However, right on the SDW, just before the turn-off to East Meon, is *Meon Springs* (Map 8; ☎ 01730-823134, 🖥 www.meonsprings.com), a fly-fishing base where you can pick up refreshments (they have a licensed bar) and bike spares, fill up your water bottles and **camp** (£5 per person) if you have a tent. The site has a toilet and washing facilities.

EAST MEON   MAP 8a
East Meon is only a half-hour detour from the official path and is well worth the effort for a lunch stop or overnight stay. There are records of a settlement at East Meon stretching as far back as 400AD and the whole area was once a royal estate belonging to King Alfred. Anyone visiting the village should take a look at the 900-year-old **church** at the foot of the hill where one can also admire the 14th-century **courthouse** which was once part of a monastery.

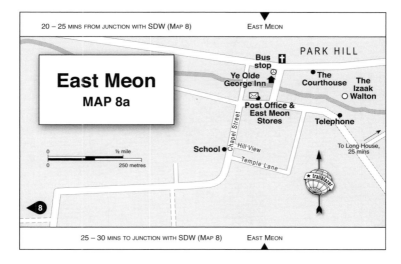

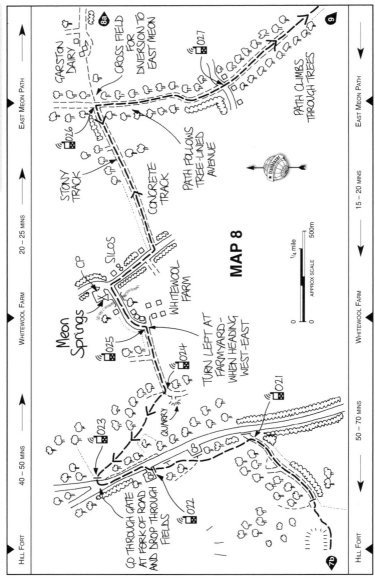

ROUTE GUIDE AND MAPS

MAP 8

APPROX SCALE

0   ¼ mile
0   500m

Hill Fort 40 – 50 MINS Whitewool Farm 20 – 25 MINS East Meon Path

Hill Fort 50 – 70 MINS Whitewool Farm 15 – 20 MINS East Meon Path

GARSTON DAIRY

CROSS FIELD FOR DIVERSION TO EAST MEON

027

STONY TRACK

026

CONCRETE TRACK

PATH FOLLOWS TREE-LINED AVENUE

PATH CLIMBS THROUGH TREES

9

8a

CP

SILOS

Meon Springs

025

WHITEWOOL FARM

024

TURN LEFT AT FARMYARD – WHEN HEADING WEST-EAST

023

QUARRY

021

GO THROUGH GATE AT FORK OF ROAD AND DROP THROUGH FIELDS

022

7b

The **post office** (Mon-Fri 9am-5.30pm, Sat 9am-noon) and **East Meon Stores** (Mon-Fri 7am-6pm, Sat 7am-5pm, Sun 8am-4pm) are on the High St. The Stores are surprisingly well stocked and also sell a good range of postcards of the surrounding area.

Stagecoach **bus** No 67 wends its way through the village on its way between Winchester and Petersfield. Brijan Tours' bus No 17 also passes through and serves both Bishops Waltham and Petersfield; see the public transport map and table, pp38-40.

Where to stay and eat

There are several accommodation options in and around East Meon. In the centre of the village, *Ye Olde George Inn* (☎ 01730-823481; 3D/2T, all en suite, food Mon-Sat noon-2.30pm & 6.30-9.30pm, Sun noon-3pm) has B&B from £40, or £50 for single

occupancy. It also has an à la carte restaurant though you'd be advised to book ahead at weekends.

Long House (☎ 01730-823239; 2D/1T) lies just round the corner from the end of Frogmore Lane, about a mile away from the village on the road to Ramsdean. B&B in this friendly establishment with the world's most powerful shower is from £30 to £35 per person (there is no single supplement). One double is en suite and the other rooms share facilities. They also have some space for **campers** (£5 per person). Booking is essential for both camping and B&B; packed lunches are available by prior arrangement.

The Izaak Walton (☎ 01730-823252; food Tue-Sat noon-2pm & 7-9pm, Sun roast noon-4pm), a pub named after a famous local angler, serves high-quality local cuisine in its restaurant section.

After the turn off there is a tough pull up the slope towards **HMS Mercury** (Map 9, p86). Right on the South Downs Way on the edge of the HMS Mercury complex, a Naval Signal School, situated about two miles past the village, is *Wetherdown Hostel* (☎ 01730-823549, 🖳 www.sustainability-centre.org; 35 beds), which is part of the Sustainability Centre where everything is environmentally friendly and they use renewable energy. They offer B&B for £22.50 per person in bunk rooms (£25 single occupancy; groups of eight or more £19.50 per person) and **camping** (£5 per night plus £3.50 per person). They also have two tipis (tepees) and charges are £10 per person plus £5 for a tipi with carpets and chairs. A yurt is also available for hire. From 2009 the campsite will have showers, running water, a toilet and barbecue. Campers may appreciate the fact that they allow camp fires (£5 for firewood). Dogs are welcome and packed lunches (£3.50) are available if requested in advance.

It is at the HMS Mercury complex that the true line of the Downs begins, stretching east as a high-level ridge, interrupted only by a few river valleys, all the way to Beachy Head near Eastbourne.

The Way continues along the broad ridge with fine views over the Meon valley to the north culminating in the highest point of the South Downs at Butser Hill (270m). **Butser Hill** (see Map 10, p87) is another National Nature Reserve, earning its status for its fine chalk grassland. The only blot on the landscape here is the car park at the top of the hill and the less than attractive A3 dual carriageway that slices through the lower flanks. However, see box p47.

(cont'd on p88)

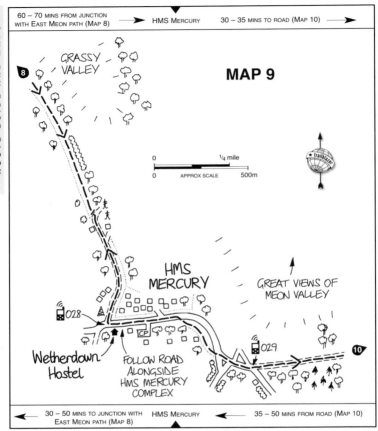

GRASSY VALLEY

8

MAP 9

0   ¼ mile
0   APPROX SCALE   500m

★ trailblazer

028

Wetherdown Hostel

HMS MERCURY

FOLLOW ROAD ALONGSIDE HMS MERCURY COMPLEX

GREAT VIEWS OF MEON VALLEY

029

10

❏ Butser Hill

Butser Hill (Map 10), on the western side of the A3, is another National Nature Reserve and is managed by Natural England (see pp41-5). It is also the highest point on the South Downs at 270m and is home to over thirty species of butterfly including the tiny, difficult-to-spot but exquisite Chalkhill blue (see opposite p49). As a consequence it is considered one of the most important areas of chalk grassland on the Downs. It was also the original starting point for the South Downs Way before it was decided to extend the path all the way to Winchester.

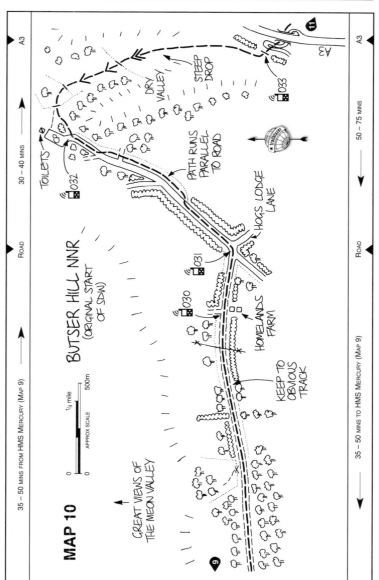

MAP 10

BUTSER HILL NNR
(ORIGINAL START
OF SDW)

GREAT VIEWS OF
THE MEON VALLEY

¼ mile

500m

APPROX SCALE

TOILETS

☎ 032

☎ 031

☎ 030

HOMELANDS
FARM

KEEP TO
OBVIOUS
TRACK

HOGS LODGE
LANE

PATH RUNS
PARALLEL
TO ROAD

DRY
VALLEY

STEEP
DROP

☎ 033

A3

35 – 50 MINS FROM HMS MERCURY (MAP 9)

30 – 40 MINS

ROAD

A3

50 – 75 MINS

ROAD

35 – 50 MINS TO HMS MERCURY (MAP 9)

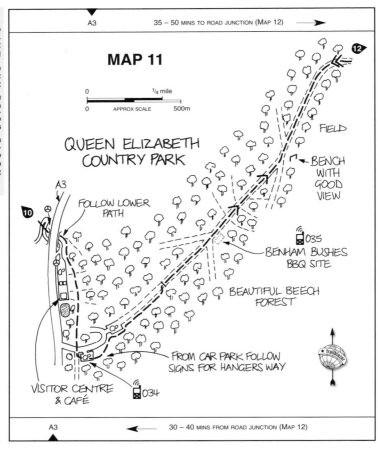

(cont'd from p85) Once past the din of racing traffic the path climbs steadily back to the top of the downland escarpment above Buriton, passing through the **Queen Elizabeth Country Park** (see box on p90 and Map 11 above), a magnificent natural mixed woodland that covers the rolling Downs for miles around, just as it has done through the centuries. If the accommodation in **Buriton** is booked up head into the old market town of **Petersfield**, where there are a couple of places offering B&B.

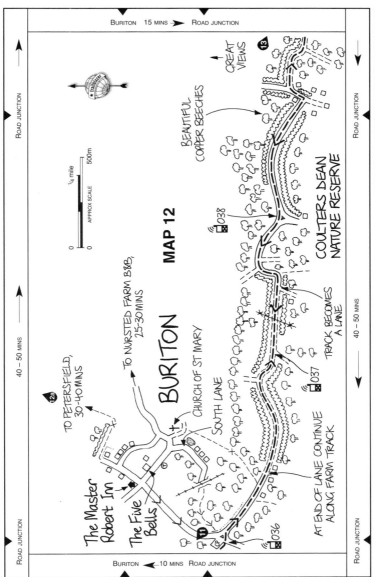

MAP 12

BURITON

BURITON   15 MINS →   ROAD JUNCTION

ROAD JUNCTION

ROAD JUNCTION

40 – 50 MINS

APPROX SCALE

¼ mile

500m

0

0

GREAT VIEWS ←

BEAUTIFUL COPPER BEECHES

COULTERS DEAN NATURE RESERVE

038

037

036

TO NURSTED FARM B&B, 25–30 MINS

TO PETERSFIELD, 30–40 MINS

CHURCH OF ST MARY

SOUTH LANE

The Master Robert Inn

The Five Bells

TRACK BECOMES A LANE

40 – 50 MINS

AT END OF LANE CONTINUE ALONG FARM TRACK

BURITON ← 10 MINS   ROAD JUNCTION

ROAD JUNCTION

❑ Queen Elizabeth Country Park

The South Downs Way cuts right through the heart of this vast protected area which includes the chalk downland of Butser Hill. To the east of the hill the park is dominated by one of the largest expanses of unbroken woodland cover in the South-East, comprised of both ancient broadleaved wood as well as beech and conifer plantations.

The park (🖳 www.hants.gov.uk/qecp; open all the time) is popular with daytrippers and picnickers largely thanks to its proximity to the main A3 road. If you prefer to escape the crowds it is worth exploring some of the smaller trails that criss-cross the park. The **Visitor Centre** (Map 11; ☎ 023-9259 5040, 🖳 www.hants.gov .uk/countryside/qecp; Mar-Oct daily 10am-5.30pm, Nov-mid Dec & early Jan-Feb daily 10am-4.30pm) can provide maps and guides to the park. The centre houses a **shop** and **café** offering a selection of cakes and snacks.

Stagecoach's No 37 (Liss to Havant) **bus** stops on the A3. The northbound stop lies just beyond the slip road under the A3 (the slip road needs to be used with care). Access to the park from the stop on the south side is no problem. Either way make sure you let the driver you know you want to stop here and also if you are waiting at the bus stop make sure you can be seen. See the public transport map and table pp38-40 for further details.

BURITON   MAP 12, p89

Buriton is yet another pretty village commanding an enviable position at the foot of the wooded downland escarpment.

The **Church of St Mary** by the duck pond is of particular interest as the interior dates back to the 12th century.

Country Liner Coaches **bus** No 95 runs between Buriton and Petersfield (see public transport map and table, pp38-40).

Where to stay and eat

In the village there's *The Master Robert Inn* (☎ 01730-267275, www.masterrobert inn.co.uk; 4D/2T all en suite, food Mon-Sat noon-2pm & 6.30-9.30pm, Sun carvery open approx noon-4pm) with B&B from £50 (£40 for single occupancy). It also serves traditional pub grub and the bar is open all day at weekends.

However, a better choice if you can bear the walk is *Nursted Farm* (☎ 01730-264278; 1D or F/2T, all with private facilities), a magnificent old farmhouse about a mile and a half up the lane with B&B from £30. There is plenty of wildlife to spot in the garden and the owner has lived there all his life so he knows a thing or two about the area.

The Five Bells (☎ 01730-263584; food Mon-Sat noon-2.30pm & 6.30-9.30pm, Sun noon-3.30pm & 5.30-8.30pm) is a great pub with friendly staff and good food. The pub is open all day at the weekends but closes in the afternoon during the week.

PETERSFIELD   MAP 12a

The centre has been redeveloped to incorporate a small shopping arcade and supermarket. But luckily, despite this attempt to turn it into something bland and modern, the town still retains some of its charms.

Petersfield Museum (☎ 01730-262601, 🖳 www.petersfieldmuseum.co.uk; Mar-Nov Tue-Sat 10am-4pm; admission free), behind The Square, has old newspaper cuttings, photos and antique maps of the local area. The museum has also taken over the running of the **Flora Twort Gallery** (Mar-Nov Tue-Sat 12.30-4pm) which will exhibit paintings by Flora Twort as well as historic costumes from the Bedales collection.

Services

The **library** (☎ 01730-263451; Mon, Tue, Wed and Fri 9.30am-5pm, Thur 9.30am-1pm, Sat 9.30am-4pm), 27 The Square,

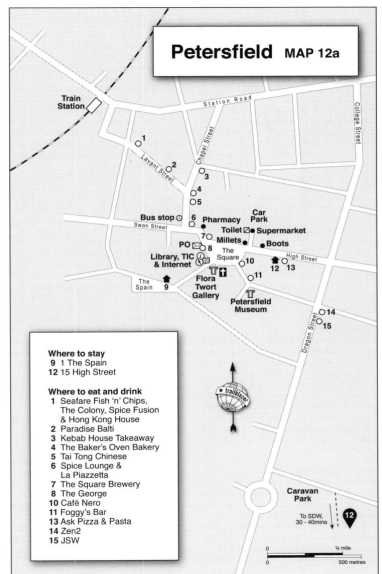

Petersfield MAP 12a

Train Station

Station Road

College Street

1

Lavant Street

2

Chapel Street

3

4

5

Bus stop 6 Pharmacy

Swan Street

7

PO 8

Library, TIC & Internet

The Spain 9

Flora Twort Gallery

Car Park

Toilet Supermarket

Millets Boots

The Square

10

High Street

12 13

11

Petersfield Museum

Dragon Street

14

15

trailblazer

Where to stay
9 1 The Spain
12 15 High Street

Where to eat and drink
1 Seafare Fish 'n' Chips,
  The Colony, Spice Fusion
  & Hong Kong House
2 Paradise Balti
3 Kebab House Takeaway
4 The Baker's Oven Bakery
5 Tai Tong Chinese
6 Spice Lounge &
  La Piazzetta
7 The Square Brewery
8 The George
10 Café Nero
11 Foggy's Bar
13 Ask Pizza & Pasta
14 Zen2
15 JSW

Caravan Park

To SDW,
30 - 40mins

12

0   ¼ mile
0   500 metres

offers free **internet access** for one hour.

The **Tourist Information Centre** (☎ 01730-268829; Mon-Wed & Fri 9.30am-5pm, Thurs 9.30am-1pm, Sat 9.30am-4pm) is also in the library. The **post office** (Mon, Wed-Fri 9am-5.30pm, Tues 9.30am-5.30pm, Sat 9am-12.30pm) is located on the edge of The Square.

On the High St there are various banks with ATMs, as well as a branch of the **camping shop** Millets (Mon-Sat 9am-5.30pm, Sun 10am-4pm) if your boots have already worn through, while round the corner is Day-Lewis **Pharmacy** (Mon-Fri 9am-5.30pm, Sat 9am-5pm). On the High St is a Boots and just off it is a large **supermarket**.

There are regular **trains** from here to both London Waterloo and Portsmouth. National Express's London to Portsmouth No 30 **coach** service stops here and **buses** leave from the town centre with Countryliner's No 54 (to Chichester) and Nos 91 & 92 (to Midhurst), Stagecoach's No 67 (to Winchester) and Brijan Tours' No 17 (to Bishops Waltham) being the most useful; see the public transport map and table, pp38-40.

Where to stay

Halfway along the High St, *15 High Street* (☎ 01730-263925, 🖳 www.number15.net; 1S/1D/1T, all with en suite showers) offers B&B for £65 (£35 for the single).

At the end of Sheep St, *1 The Spain* (☎ 01730-263261, 🖳 www.1thespain.com; 2D/1T) is a well-kept 18th-century townhouse with B&B from £60 to £62, or £40-5 for single occupancy. One of the doubles and the twin are en suite, the other double has a private bathroom.

Where to eat and drink

Petersfield is replete with eating places. On The Square is *The George* (☎ 01730-233343; food Mon-Fri 8am-4pm, Sat noon-6pm), where the bar is open all day.

Just off The Square on St Peter's Rd looking onto the church is probably the best pub in town: *Foggy's Bar* (☎ 01730-263411; food Mon-Thur noon-2.30pm &

6.30-10pm, Fri & Sat noon-3pm). Monday night is pizza night and Wednesday is steak night with both these evenings offering a 'buy one get one free' meal deal.

More pub food can be found at *The Square Brewery* (☎ 01730-264291; food daily 10am-4pm, also Wed 6-9.30pm) with live music on Wednesday evenings when the only food they serve is curry.

For cheap eats head down Chapel St and its offshoot Lavant St, where you'll find such gustatory joys as *Kebab House Takeaway* (Sun-Thur 11.30am-midnight, Fri & Sat 11am-1am), on Chapel St, open late for burgers, kebabs and chips. On Lavant St there's *Seafare Fish and Chip Shop* (☎ 01730-265702; Mon-Thur 5-10pm, Fri & Sat 4.30-10pm), the Indian takeaway *Spice Fusion* (☎ 01730-333334; daily 5-11pm), as well as the Chinese rivals *The Colony* (☎ 01730-233323; open Wed-Mon 5pm to late) and the superior *Hong Kong House* (☎ 01730-265256; Tue, Thur & Sun 5-11pm, Fri & Sat noon-1.30pm & 5pm-midnight).

Going more upmarket, *Paradise Balti* (☎ 01730-262748; Wed, Thurs, Sat & Sun noon-2.30pm, Sun-Thur 5.30-11.30pm, Fri & Sat 5.30pm-midnight) is a smart Indian restaurant with chicken dansak for £7.50 (£6.50 takeaway).

The *Spice Lounge* (☎ 01730-303303; daily noon-2.30pm & 6-11.30pm) is another Indian restaurant and they serve a delicious trout bhuna for £6.95. Sharing the same building is *La Piazzetta* (☎ 01730-260006, 🖳 www.lapiazzetta.co.uk; Mon-Sat 11.30am-11pm, Sun noon-10pm), with pizzas from £5.70.

Another option for Italian food is *Ask Pizza & Pasta* (☎ 01730-231113; Sun-Thur noon-11pm, Fri & Sat noon-11.30pm) with a large range of dishes including the vegetarian penne el giardino (penne, courgettes, peppers, cherry tomatoes and onions) at £7.45.

On Chapel St is *Tai Tong Chinese Restaurant* (☎ 01730-263216; Wed-Sun noon-2pm & 6-11.30pm, Tue 6-11.30pm) with typical Chinese fare such as roasted duck with cashew nuts (£7.90), to eat-in or take away.

At the other end of the High St on Dragon St are several classy restaurants such as the rather small, swish and exclusive *JSW* (☎ 01730-262030; Tue-Sat noon-1.30pm & 7-9pm) with wicker chairs and virgin-white tablecloths. The very small seating capacity makes booking essential. A two-course meal which could include sea bass, suckling pig belly, lamb or guinea fowl costs £19.50 at lunch, £25 for dinner (Tue-Thur only), though there is an á la carte menu too. If you really want to splash out their eight-course tasting menu is £40 at lunch and £50 in the evening. At 14 Dragon St, another quality joint is *Zen2* (☎ 01730-

267077, 🖳 www.zen2.co.uk; Mon-Sat noon-2.30pm & 6.30-10.30pm), a pan-Asian restaurant with an all-you-can-eat buffet for £10 (Mon-Thur) and £12 (Fri & Sat); they also do takeaway.

For a relaxing coffee on the town square the Italian-style *Café Nero* (☎ 01730-261783; Mon-Sat 7.30am-6.30pm, to 6pm in winter, Sun 8.30am-5.30pm) is just the place. They also serve a variety of light lunches.

If you are looking for takeaway lunch ingredients or a tasty pasty head for *The Baker's Oven Bakery* (☎ 01730-263450; Mon-Sat 8am-5pm) on Chapel St.

BURITON TO COCKING

MAPS 12-16

The route from Buriton follows tracks and lanes along the top of the South Downs escarpment for **11 miles/18km**. It is very wooded before reaching South Harting (Map 13, p95) so although the views are limited there is plenty of beautiful shady woodland to enjoy.

About ten minutes south of the Way where it crosses the B2146 is **Uppark House**.

❏ **Uppark House**
Uppark House (off Map 13, p95; ☎ 01730-825857, 🖳 www.nationaltrust.org.uk/uppark; late Mar to late Oct daily except Fri & Sat, gardens open 11.30am-5pm, house 12.30-4.30pm) is a magnificent 17th-century country home perched high on a hill with extensive views across the Downs and beyond. The Georgian interior and gardens can be toured for just £8.20; visiting the garden costs only £4.

One of the most remarkable things about Uppark is the near-perfect restoration of the building after it was all but gutted by a rampant fire in 1989.

SOUTH HARTING   MAP 13, p95

From the top of Harting Down the village of South Harting with its distinctive church steeple is clearly visible and looks very inviting.

It's not a long walk to the village from the Way but you do have to climb back up the hill through the woods on the return. This can be a bit of a strain especially if you have been sampling the very fine ales in either of the village's two pubs.

Services

The **post office** (Mon, Tue, Thur & Fri 9am-1pm & 2-5.30pm, Wed 9am-1pm only) is on The Square and there is a small **shop** (☎ 01730-825219; Mon-Fri 7am-7pm, Sat 7.30am-1pm, Sun 8am-noon) on North Lane which sells a wide variety of provisions.

Countryliner has a couple of useful **bus** services passing through: the No 91 will take you to either Petersfield or

ROUTE GUIDE AND MAPS

Midhurst and their No 54 service runs between Petersfield and Chichester; see the public transport map and table, pp38-40.

Where to stay

The most beautiful B&B in the village is the spectacular old timber-framed, thatched *South Gardens Cottage* (☎ 01730-825040, 🖳 julia@randjhomes.plus.com; 2D, one en suite and one with a private bathroom), with a garden that's ablaze with flowers in the summer. B&B in this wonderful place is from £32 per person.

At the other end of South Harting is certainly the most unusual B&B: *Pyramids* (☎ 01730-825398; 1S/1T, both en suite), on the right-hand side as you walk up North Lane, is a modern house and it is probably unique in that the ceiling of each room goes up into a pyramid. The tiles on the 'pyramids' are cedar-wood shingle and the views of the Downs from the house, particularly from the single room, are magnificent; the garden is also full of interest. The rate is from £35 per person.

A few minutes further up North Lane, *Shotgun Cottage* (☎ 01730-826878, 🖳 qe joy@hotmail.com; 3D or T/2F) charges from £25-30; £40 single occupancy. One of

the doubles/twins and the family rooms are in a self-contained building so are ideal for groups of up to five people. One of the rooms in the house is en suite, the other has a private bathroom. To reach the cottage turn right into Pays Farm, which, like Pyramids, is on the right-hand side of the road.

There is also bed and breakfast at *10 The Square* (☎ 01730-825178; 1D en suite/ 1T private bathroom), a small whitewashed cottage in the centre of the village. A bed here costs from £25 per person.

Where to eat and drink

There are two pubs serving food and real ale. The first one you come to as you walk into the village from the Downs is *The White Hart Inn* (☎ 01730-825355; food daily noon-2.30pm & 6.30-9pm except Monday evening) with good pub food from an extensive menu. The bar is open all day.

A stone's throw away is *The Ship* (☎ 01730-825302; food daily noon-2pm & 7-9.30pm, except Sun & Tue eve), so called because it was constructed using old ships' timbers. It is a traditional country pub with plenty on the menu including a delicious home-made fish pie (£10); the bar is open all day.

After South Harting the trees begin to thin out as the Way passes over **Harting Down**. The views open up over the patchwork fields below and the path climbs even higher onto **Beacon Hill** (Map 14, p96).

There then follows another wooded section, the **Monkton Estate**, where it's worth listening out for peacocks before the path continues through the pastureland of **Cocking Down** down to the main road leading to Cocking. There is an interpretation board (see Map 16, p99) in the car park there.

❏ **Glorious Goodwood – not so glorious for walkers**
Goodwood (🖳 www.goodwood.co.uk), near Singleton, has long been associated with country pursuits such as horse-racing and shooting but is also host to sports such as flying and motor racing. The Festival of Speed, held every July, celebrates the history of motor sport and is one of many events held here around the year. Whilst these are probably not of interest to walkers of the South Downs Way, the relevance is that accommodation in the area is often booked up months in advance so it is probably worth checking the dates for events (see the Goodwood website) before you set off.

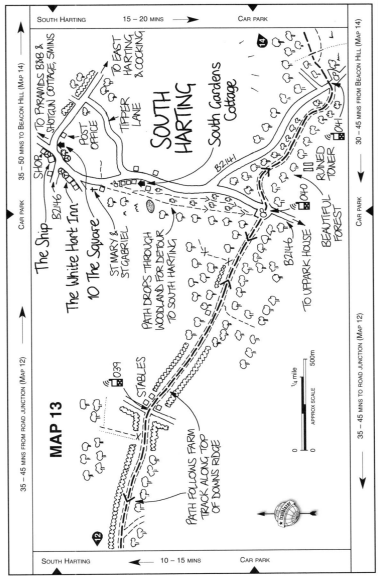

SOUTH HARTING   15 – 20 MINS →   CAR PARK

35 – 50 MINS TO BEACON HILL (MAP 14) ←

CAR PARK

35 – 45 MINS FROM ROAD JUNCTION (MAP 12) ←

30 – 45 MINS FROM BEACON HILL (MAP 14) →

CAR PARK

35 – 45 MINS TO ROAD JUNCTION (MAP 12) →

TO PYRAMIDS B&B & SHOTGUN COTTAGE, 5MINS

TO EAST HARTING & COCKING

TIPPER LANE

POST OFFICE

SOUTH HARTING

South Gardens Cottage

B2141

SHOP

B2146

The Ship

The White Hart Inn

10 The Square

ST MARY & ST GABRIEL

PATH DROPS THROUGH WOODLAND FOR DETOUR TO SOUTH HARTING

RUINED TOWER

BEAUTIFUL FOREST

TO UPPARK HOUSE

B2146

STABLES

039

MAP 13

PATH FOLLOWS FARM TRACK ALONG TOP OF DOWNS RIDGE

¼ mile

APPROX SCALE

500m

0

0

SOUTH HARTING   ← 10 – 15 MINS   CAR PARK

Trailblazer

ROUTE GUIDE AND MAPS

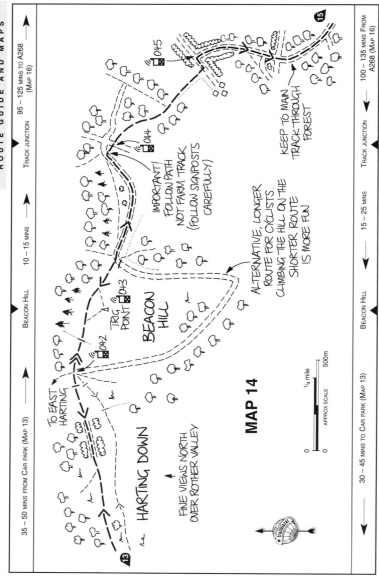

35 – 50 MINS FROM CAR PARK (MAP 13)

Beacon Hill

10 – 15 MINS

Track Junction

95 – 125 MINS TO A268 (MAP 16)

To EAST HARTING

☒ 042

TRIG POINT ☒ 043

BEACON HILL

☒ 044

☒ 045

HARTING DOWN

FINE VIEWS NORTH OVER ROTHER VALLEY

IMPORTANT! FOLLOW PATH NOT FARM TRACK (FOLLOW SIGNPOSTS CAREFULLY)

ALTERNATIVE, LONGER ROUTE FOR CYCLISTS. CLIMBING THE HILL ON THE SHORTER ROUTE IS MORE FUN

KEEP TO MAIN TRACK THROUGH FOREST

MAP 14

13

15

APPROX SCALE

0   ¼ mile
0   500m

30 – 45 MINS TO CAR PARK (MAP 13)

Beacon Hill

15 – 25 MINS

Track Junction

100 – 135 MINS FROM A268 (MAP 16)

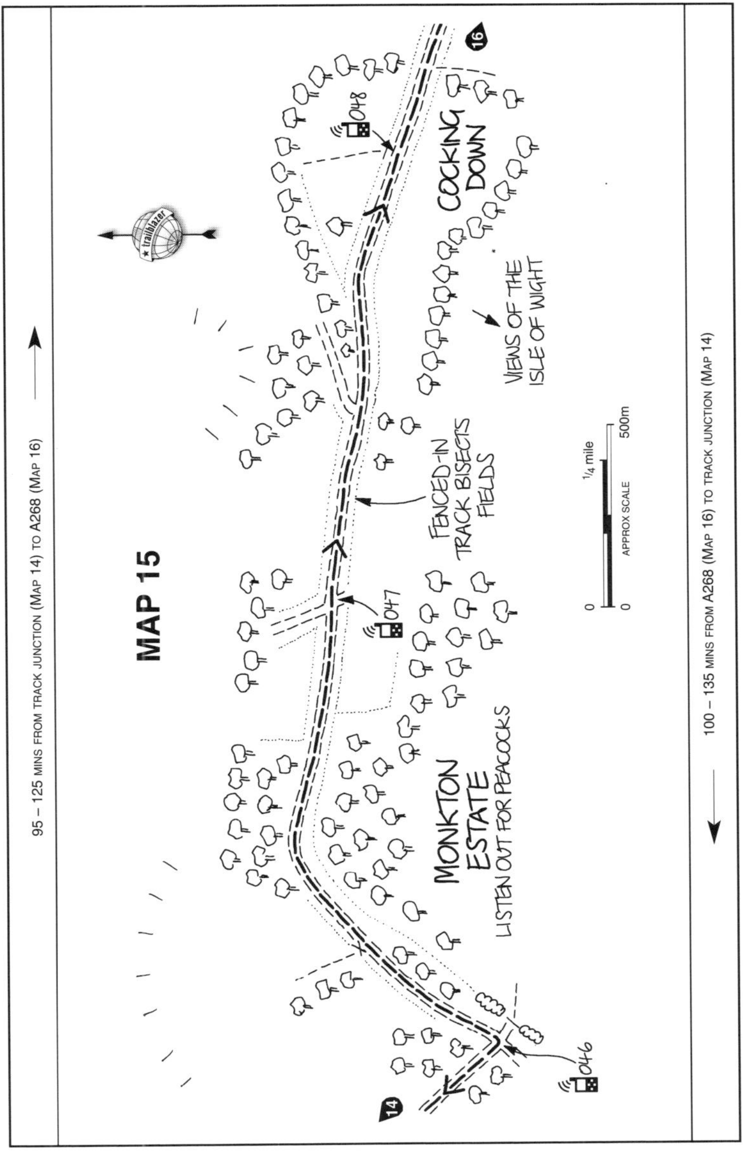

MAP 15

95 – 125 MINS FROM TRACK JUNCTION (MAP 14) TO A268 (MAP 16)

100 – 135 MINS FROM A268 (MAP 16) TO TRACK JUNCTION (MAP 14)

048

047

046

14

16

MONKTON ESTATE
LISTEN OUT FOR PEACOCKS

FENCED-IN TRACK BISECTS FIELDS

COCKING DOWN

VIEWS OF THE ISLE OF WIGHT

trailblazer

¼ mile

500m

0

0

APPROX SCALE

COCKING   MAP 16

Cocking is pleasant enough but the busy main road that slices the village in two has rather taken the soul out of the place despite one or two pretty old cottages.

If you do find yourself drawn to the village the consolation is that it is not too far from the Way. It is best reached by ignoring the obvious route down the busy main road and continuing, instead, to the farm buildings ten minutes east of this road and following the farm track north down the hill which ends up by the post office in the village.

Services

The **post office/shop** (☎ 01730-817867; post office Mon-Fri 8am-5pm, Sat 8am-noon; shop Mon-Fri 7am-6.30pm, Sat 7am-4pm, Sun 8am-4pm) is on the corner of the main road with Mill Lane. Under new ownership, the new people are enthusiastic and helpful and serve tea, coffee and sandwiches – which you can eat on one of their benches outside.

The **bus stop** is on the main road and Stagecoach's No 60 passes through regularly on its route between Chichester and Midhurst; see the public transport map and table, pp38-40.

Where to stay, eat and drink

The most convenient place to stay is *Hilltop Cottages* (☎ 01730-814156; 1D/1T), part of Manor Farm, because it is right on the Way; it offers B&B from £29 per person, with one bathroom (no shower) shared between the two rooms. Packed lunches (about £3) are available on request. They now have a farm shop (Fri-Sun) selling produce from the farm, including their home-made sausages. When the shop is open they sell sandwiches, drinks and

snacks and at the time of writing were hoping to develop part of the shop premises into an actual café.

If this place is full you will need to go down to the village where there are several places to choose from: *Manor Farm Cottage* (☎ 01730-812784; 1D/1T shared bathroom) is run by the parents of the owners of Hilltop Cottages, a sweet and very helpful couple who will aid you in finding alternative accommodation if they are full (and are thus very useful people to contact during the Goodwood Festival of Speed; see box p94). They charge £27.50 per person, up to £30 for single occupancy.

There is always a warm welcome for walkers at *Moonlight Cottage Tea Rooms* (☎ 01730-813336, 🖳 www.moonlightcot tage.co.uk; 1D/1T/1F sleeping up to 8 in a chalet £30 per person) with B&B from £70, or £40 for single occupancy. The double and twin share a bathroom and the family room, which is in a separate building, has en suite facilities. As the name suggests, there is a **tea room** here too: they are open for light lunches and afternoon teas (Mar-Oct, Wed-Sun 10.30am-5.30pm, weekends only in winter).

On Bell Lane there's also *Downsfold* (☎ 01730-814376, 🖳 www.downsfold.co .uk; 1D/1T, shared bathroom), with B&B for £29, or £35 for single occupancy. Packed lunches (£4) are available if requested in advance.

The Blue Bell Inn closed in December 2008 and it was not certain what would happen to the premises. If it is not serving meals it may be worth going to *The Greyhound* which is a mile away on the road towards Midhurst. It is on Stagecoach's No 60 bus route.

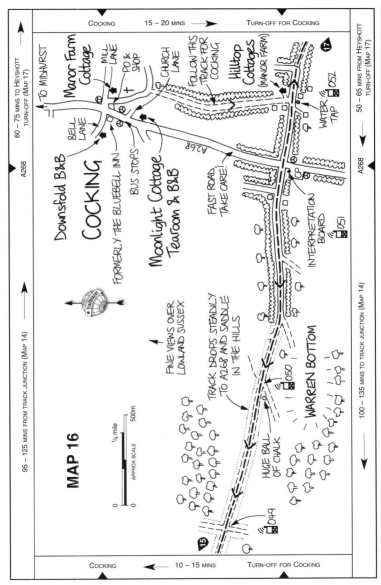

COCKING   15 – 20 MINS ⟶   TURN-OFF FOR COCKING

60 – 75 MINS TO HEYSHOTT TURN-OFF (MAP 17)

50 – 65 MINS FROM HEYSHOTT TURN-OFF (MAP 17)

A268

95 – 125 MINS FROM TRACK JUNCTION (MAP 14)

100 – 135 MINS TO TRACK JUNCTION (MAP 14)

A268

TO MIDHURST

Manor Farm Cottage

MILL LANE

PO & SHOP

CHURCH LANE

FOLLOW THIS TRACK FOR COCKING

Hilltop Cottages (MANOR FARM)

17

WATER TAP

052

BELL LANE

Downsfold B&B

COCKING

FORMERLY THE BLUEBELL INN

BUS STOPS

A268

Moonlight Cottage Tearoom & B&B

FAST ROAD, TAKE CARE!

INTERPRETATION BOARD

051

trailblazer

FINE VIEWS OVER LOWLAND SUSSEX

TRACK DROPS STEADILY TO A268 AND SADDLE IN THE HILLS

WARREN BOTTOM

050

MAP 16

¼ mile

500m

0

0

APPROX SCALE

HUGE BALL OF CHALK

049

15

COCKING   ⟵ 10 – 15 MINS   TURN-OFF FOR COCKING

MIDHURST off MAP 16, p99

If everywhere in Cocking is booked up you can take the bus (see public transport map and table pp38-40) to Midhurst about two to three miles to the north where there is a wider choice of accommodation including the friendly *Pear Tree Cottage* (☎ 01730-817216; 1T/1D/1D or F) on Lamberts Lane. B&B is from £30 per person or from £40 for single occupancy. All the rooms are en suite and self contained and they contain a fridge, microwave and kettle. The owner leaves the ingredients for a continental breakfast outside the door the night before so guests are free to do what they want for their meals.

Failing that try the **tourist information centre** (☎ 01730-817322, 🖳 www.visitmidhurst.com; Apr-Sep Mon-Sat 9.15am-5.15pm, Sun 11am-3.30pm, Mar & Oct Mon-Sat 9.15am-5.15pm, Nov-Feb Mon-Sat 9.15am-4.15pm). They have an accommodation-booking service and charge £2 per booking and also take a 10% deposit for the first night's accommodation at the time of booking.

Midhurst also has a range of eating places, a Tesco Express, Barclays Bank and other services should you find yourself here.

COCKING TO AMBERLEY MAPS 16-22

It is **13½ miles/21.5km** from Cocking to Amberley. From the main road south of Cocking the Way follows a chalk lane, climbing steadily through fields to rejoin the high escarpment. There is a drinking-water tap by the farm buildings (see Map 16). Just after that you will notice that the window frames on the cottages here, including Hilltop Cottages (see p98), are painted yellow; this shows they are part of the Cowdray Estate (see box below).

The track here used to be bordered on one side by dense woodland and on the other by a high hedge so the view was somewhat obscured in parts but the South Downs Joint Committee and Graffham Down Trust have created a wildlife corridor in order to link up two rich grassland sites – Heyshott Down (Map 17) and Graffham Down (Map 18). **Heyshott Down** is one of the nature reserves in this area which is managed by the Murray Downland Trust (see pp45-6) – making it easier for a lot of the flora and fauna here to survive. The best view is probably from the trig point (Map 17), about 50m off the path.

❏ The two Cowdray Gold Cups

The Cowdray Estate is probably best known for the Polo Club and the polo matches (both national and international) held there during the year; the main event is the Gold Cup which is held in July.

The second Gold Cup refers to the colour of the paint seen on the window frames and doors of cottages and buildings that are part of the estate, particularly around Midhurst. The 'cowardy custard' yellow, as some locals call it, was first used on the cottages by the 2nd Viscount Cowdray who was a Liberal MP (yellow being the colour particularly associated with the Liberal Party), thus it was a good way of promoting the Liberal party. The paint was made specially for the Viscount and was originally called Cowdray Gold but is now called Gold Cup, though it is not exactly the same shade as the original colour.

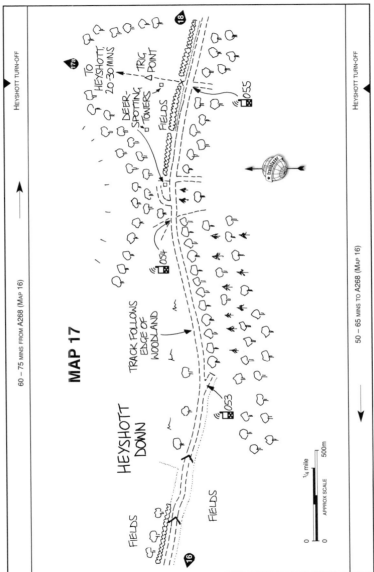

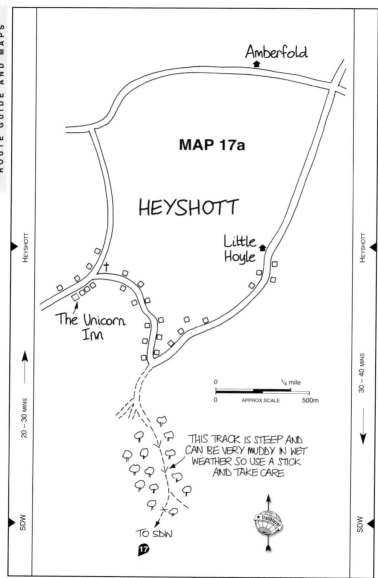

Amberfold

MAP 17a

HEYSHOTT

Little
Hoyle

The Unicorn
Inn

HEYSHOTT

HEYSHOTT

30 – 40 MINS

20 – 30 MINS

SDW

SDW

0   ¼ mile
0   APPROX SCALE   500m

THIS TRACK IS STEEP AND
CAN BE VERY MUDDY IN WET
WEATHER SO USE A STICK
AND TAKE CARE

TO SDW

17

HEYSHOTT   MAP 17a

There are a couple of B&Bs here: *Amberfold* (☎ 01730-812385; 1S/3D/1T, all en suite) with rooms from £85 (the single costs £50) and *Little Hoyle* (☎ 01798-867359, 🖳 www.littlehoyle.co.uk; 1D en suite) on Hoyle Lane with B&B at £70 for the room, with a reduction for single occupancy. Packed lunches (from £3.50) are available if requested in advance and they have a drying room.

A little way to the west of the village is *The Unicorn Inn* (☎ 01730-813486, 🖳 www.unicorn-inn-heyshott.co.uk; food Tue-Sat noon-2pm & 7-9pm, Sun noon-2.30pm), a smart country pub with excellent food. Main dishes, which include ale-battered cod with chips and peas, cost £10-12 but the great views across the hay meadows to the Downs escarpment are free. The pub is closed on Sunday evenings and all day on Mondays.

The path then continues past a **Bronze Age burial ground** (Map 18; see box below) with tumuli clearly visible among the tussocks of grass. The track continues on through a mixture of woodland and grassland, passing the turn-off for Graffham.

GRAFFHAM   MAP 18a, p105

There is little to see in Graffham but it has a lazy, peaceful air about it, being well away from any major roads. The **post office**/well-stocked village **shop** (Mon-Fri 8.30am-5.30pm, Sat 9am-4pm) is next to the village hall.

B&B can be found on Selham Rd at *Brook Barn* (☎ 01798-867356; 1D en suite) for £85, or £55 for single occupancy. Discounts are available for stays of more than one night and a camp bed can be put in the room for a third person. Dogs are welcome.

In the centre of the village, *The Foresters Arms* (☎ 01798-867202, 🖳 www.forestersgraffham.co.uk; 2D en suite) has two comfortable doubles and charges £98 for each room, continental breakfast included.

Campers should head up the road for about a mile to the *Great Bury Caravan &*

Camping Site (☎ 01798-867476; end Mar-end Oct) where a pitch is £7.60 per person in high season.

There are two good pubs serving food: the first, *The White Horse* (☎ 01798-867331; food Tue-Fri noon-2pm & 6-9pm, Sat noon-2.30pm & 6-9pm, Sun noon-2.30pm) is just outside the village close to the Downs. It's a friendly place with some interesting real ales, a quiet garden and spectacular views onto the hills. It's open all day at weekends, evening only on Mondays, and is closed between 3 and 6pm during the week.

The Foresters Arms (see above; food Tue-Sat noon-2.30pm & 6.30-9.30pm, Sun noon-2.30pm) has a lunchtime and evening menu in their cosy restaurant area. They serve locally-sourced homemade food and have a constantly changing range of dishes to reflect the seasons. They also have good real ales on tap.

❏ Tumuli

All along the crest of the Downs are numerous burial mounds known as tumuli. These are in the region of 4000 to 4500 years old. Some are overgrown or are not particularly distinct but many are surprisingly well preserved. A glance at an Ordnance Survey map of the area will indicate exactly where they are. Next time you stop for lunch on that nice grassy hump just remember you may be sitting on the grave of someone who has been dead for 4500 years.

ROUTE GUIDE AND MAPS

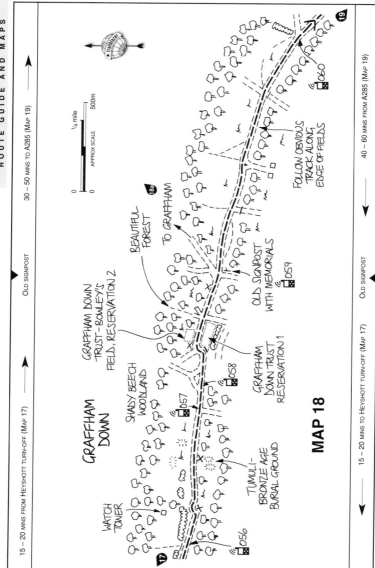

15 – 20 MINS FROM HEYSHOTT TURN-OFF (MAP 17)

30 – 50 MINS TO A285 (MAP 19)

OLD SIGNPOST

15 – 20 MINS TO HEYSHOTT TURN-OFF (MAP 17)

OLD SIGNPOST

40 – 60 MINS FROM A285 (MAP 19)

GRAFFHAM DOWN

WATCH TOWER

SHADY BEECH WOODLAND

GRAFFHAM DOWN TRUST – BOWLEY'S FIELD, RESERVATION 2

BEAUTIFUL FOREST

TO GRAFFHAM

18a

¼ mile
500m
APPROX SCALE

TUMULI-BRONZE AGE BURIAL GROUND

GRAFFHAM DOWN TRUST RESERVATION 1

OLD SIGNPOST WITH MEMORIALS

FOLLOW OBVIOUS TRACK ALONG EDGE OF FIELDS

056

057

058

059

060

MAP 18

17

19

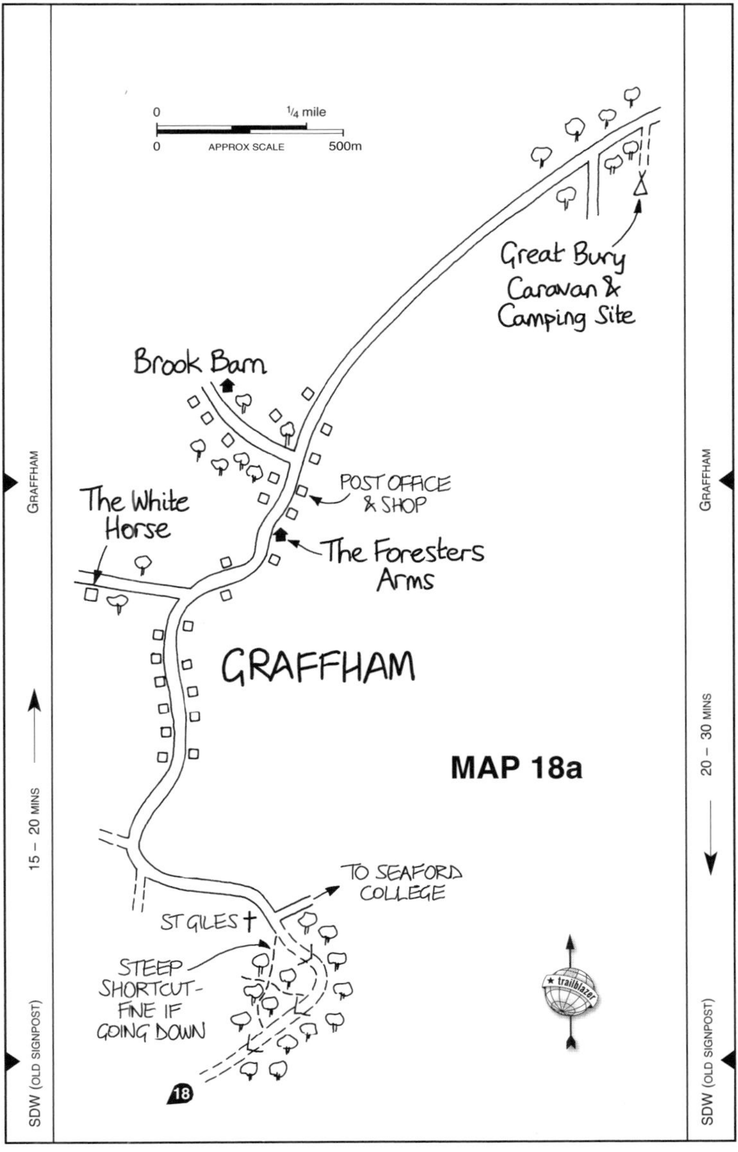

0   ¼ mile

0   APPROX SCALE   500m

Great Bury
Caravan &
Camping Site

Brook Barn

POST OFFICE
& SHOP

The White
Horse

The Foresters
Arms

GRAFFHAM

GRAFFHAM

GRAFFHAM

MAP 18a

15 – 20 MINS

20 – 30 MINS

TO SEAFORD
COLLEGE

ST GILES †

STEEP
SHORTCUT-
FINE IF
GOING DOWN

18

trailblazer

SDW (OLD SIGNPOST)

SDW (OLD SIGNPOST)

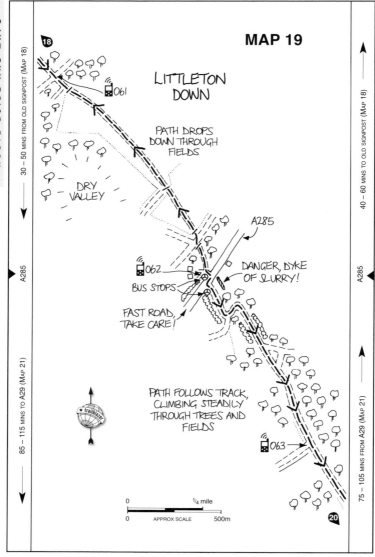

ROUTE GUIDE AND MAPS

30 – 50 MINS FROM OLD SIGNPOST (MAP 18)

A285

85 – 115 MINS TO A29 (MAP 21)

MAP 19

LITTLETON DOWN

061

PATH DROPS DOWN THROUGH FIELDS

DRY VALLEY

A285

062

DANGER, DYKE OF SLURRY!

BUS STOPS

FAST ROAD, TAKE CARE!

PATH FOLLOWS TRACK, CLIMBING STEADILY THROUGH TREES AND FIELDS

063

40 – 60 MINS TO OLD SIGNPOST (MAP 18)

A285

75 – 105 MINS FROM A29 (MAP 21)

trailblazer

0   ¼ mile

0   500m
APPROX SCALE

After the Graffham turn-off the Way eventually drops down across pasture to the A285 main road (Map 19). Compass's No 99 **bus** service calls here if booked in advance; see public transport map and table, pp38-40.

Climbing back up towards Bignor Hill the views open out spectacularly to the south. The rather outlandish-looking tent structure visible by the coast is the Butlins holiday complex at Bognor Regis. Of far greater interest is **Stane St** (Map 20, p108), the Roman road built around 500AD to connect Noviomagus (Chichester) with Londinium (London).

Close to Bignor Hill, a mile south of the Way, is the excellent National Trust camping barn *Gumber Bothy* (see Map 20; ☎ 01243-814484; open Mar-Oct) which has simple accommodation for £10. They also allow **camping** here for the same price. Facilities include showers, toilets, a basic kitchen and a pay phone. Booking in advance is preferred and indeed recommended.

The Way follows part of the old Roman road over **Bignor Hill**. Look out for the signpost in Latin in the car park (not actually of Roman origin!) and look out, too, for any Roman coins that may be buried among the flint and chalk. Continuing down the hill along the Way, there are sensational views to the east along the length of the Downs.

SUTTON & BIGNOR   MAP 20a, p109

There are only two reasons for dropping off the hills to these twin villages. One is to stay at or get fed at *The White Horse Inn* (☎ 01798-869221, www.whitehorse-sutton .co.uk; 5D all en suite, food Tue-Sat noon-2pm & 7-9pm, Sun noon-3pm), a magnificent isolated country pub with B&B (£85 for a double, single occupancy £65, and £110 for the room with a four poster)

and a large restaurant. The food is exquisite: all home cooked and sourced locally, with the bread, sausages and ice cream all made on the premises. Packed lunches are available on request. The pub is closed between 3pm and 6pm. The premises were completely refurbished in 2008.

The other reason for the detour is to visit **Bignor Roman Villa**.

❏ **Bignor Roman Villa**   **Map 20a, p109**

Just off the old Roman road of Stane Street are the remains of Bignor Roman Villa (☎ 01798-869259, 🖳 www.bignorromanvilla.co.uk; Mar & Apr Tue-Sun & Bank hols 10am-5pm, May daily 10am-5pm, June-Aug daily 10am-6pm, Sep-Oct daily 9.30am-4.30pm; admission £5.50). It was discovered by a farmer ploughing his field in 1811.

Believed to date from the 3rd century AD, Bignor Villa was one of the biggest in England and probably home to a wealthy farmer considering its enviable position on fertile land close to the main road between Chichester and London. Bignor is perhaps most famous for the stunning floor mosaics, said to be some of the world's best-preserved examples, many in near perfect condition.

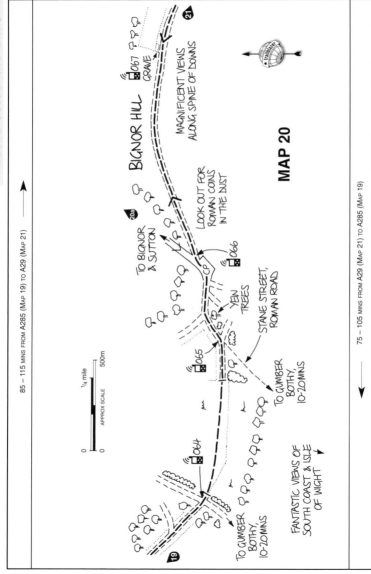

85 – 115 MINS FROM A285 (MAP 19) TO A29 (MAP 21)

75 – 105 MINS FROM A29 (MAP 21) TO A285 (MAP 19)

MAP 20

BIGNOR HILL

MAGNIFICENT VIEWS ALONG SPINE OF DOWNS

067 GRAVE

LOOK OUT FOR ROMAN COINS IN THE DUST

066

TO BIGNOR & SUTTON

YEW TREES

STANE STREET, ROMAN ROAD

TO GUMBER BOTHY, 10-20 MINS

065

064

TO GUMBER BOTHY, 10-20 MINS

FANTASTIC VIEWS OF SOUTH COAST & ISLE OF WIGHT

¼ mile

500m

APPROX SCALE

0

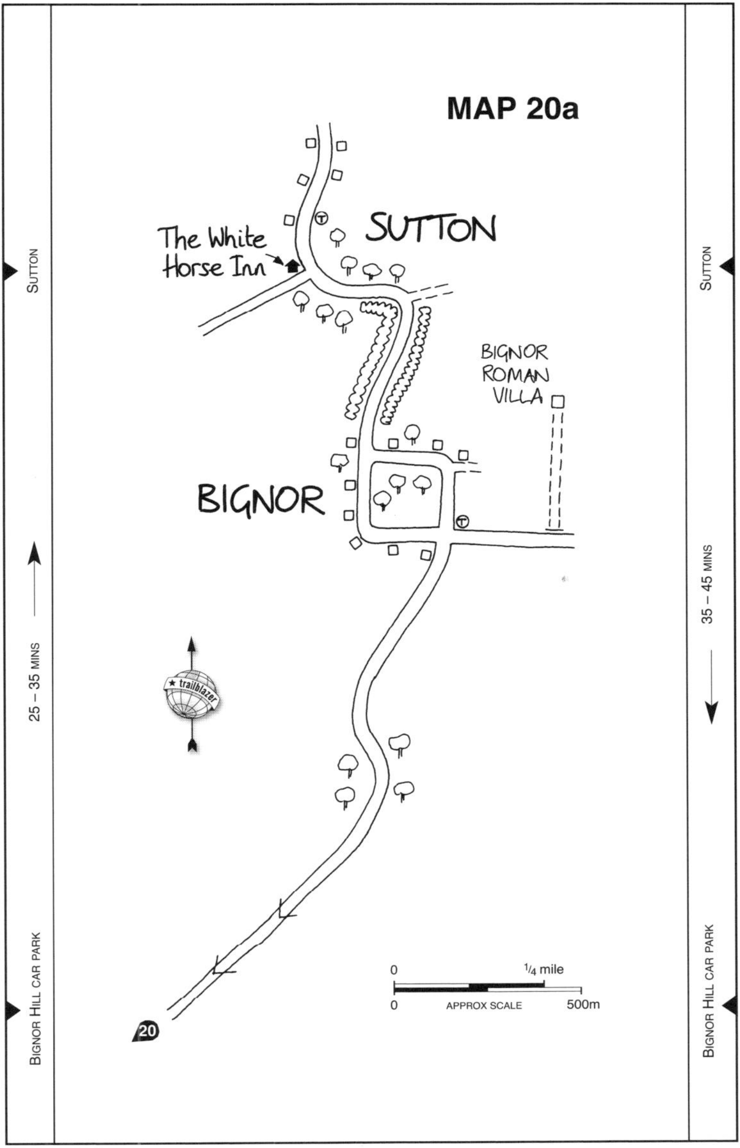

MAP 20a

The White
Horse Inn

SUTTON

BIGNOR
ROMAN
VILLA

BIGNOR

★ trailblazer

0   ¼ mile
0   APPROX SCALE   500m

20

SUTTON

SUTTON

25 – 35 MINS

35 – 45 MINS

BIGNOR HILL CAR PARK

BIGNOR HILL CAR PARK

BURY   MAP 21

This unassuming village offers accommo-dation, food and a **post office**.

Harkaway (☎ 01798-831843, 🖳 www .harkaway.freeuk.com; 2S/1D/1T), on Houghton Lane, offers B&B: a room for two sharing costs from £55 or £50 for more than one night, or it's £60/55 in the en suite double and £25 in a single. The singles and the twin room share a bathroom.

The Squire & Horse Inn (☎ 01798-831343; food Mon-Sat noon-2pm & 6-9pm, Sun noon-2pm & 6-8.30pm), by the main road, has a variety of good pub meals.

Follow the route across the main road and down into the Arun valley for the villages of Houghton Bridge and Amberley. If you have time it is well worth visiting Arundel, about a mile further south along the River Arun. You can reach it by following the riverside footpath but the easier route is to jump on the train at Houghton Bridge.

HOUGHTON BRIDGE   MAP 22, p113

The village of Houghton Bridge can easily be reached from the SDW as the trail almost passes through it. The **train station** (called, a little confusingly, Amberley Station) has regular services to London Victoria and south to Arundel and beyond; see the public transport map and table, pp38-40. There are, however, no useful bus services.

Right by the station you'll find the entrance to **Amberley Working Museum** (☎ 01798-831370, 🖳 www.amberleymuse um.co.uk; open mid Feb to end Oct, Tue-Sun & Bank hols, plus every day during school holidays 10am-5.30pm, last entry 4.30pm; admission £9.30; call for details), situated in an old chalk pit. This extensive museum features a blacksmith's and foundry, as well as workshops producing traditional items such as brooms, clay pipes and walking sticks.

You can get teas, light lunches and B&B at *Riverside Café & Bistro* (☎ 01798-831558, 🖳 gwenriverside@yahoo.co.uk; 2D/2T; mid-Mar to Oct daily 10am-5pm, to 6 or 7pm at weekends; Nov to mid-Mar Fri, Sat & Sun only from 10am). Riverside is also known as Houghton Bridge Tea Gardens & B&B. This café is especially popular when the weather is good as they have a riverside garden where they serve breakfasts, jacket spuds and cakes amongst other items on the menu, all of which are home-made. The premises are licensed for people sitting inside. In winter their hours depend partly on the weather and also on how busy they are. One of the double rooms is en suite and the other rooms share a bath/shower room. The friendly owners charge from £35-45 per person – there is no single supplement.

Then there is *Cherry Tree Cottage* (☎ 01798-831052 ☎ 07814-944110; 1T), right by the railway bridge, with just one room with private bathroom. A stay in this family home costs £35 per person. They have dogs but at the time of writing can't accept visiting dogs.

Just across the road is *The Bridge Inn* (☎ 01798-831619; food Mon-Fri noon-2.30pm & 6-9pm, Sat noon-4pm & 6-9pm, Sun noon-4pm & 5.30-8pm) which, as you'd expect, is also near the river. It's relaxed but busy on summer evenings and serves hearty meals.

Opposite is *The Boathouse Brasserie* (☎ 01798-831059; Mon-Sat noon-2pm & 7-9pm, Sun two sittings, noon & 2pm) which caters for a more upmarket crowd with a 3-course lunch with coffee during the week costing £21 (£23 for dinner).

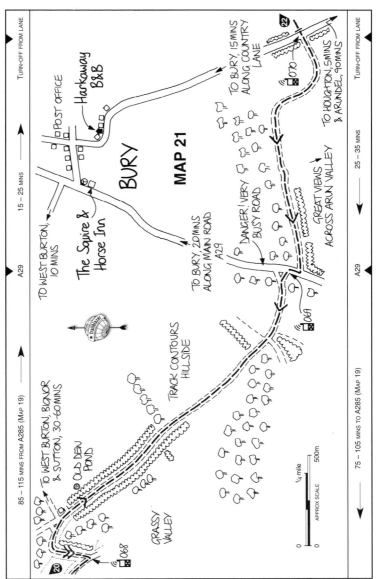

AMBERLEY   MAP 22

Perched on a sandstone ridge below the chalk Downs with the wild marshland of **Amberley Brooks** (see p45) stretching to the north, Amberley claims to be the prettiest village on the Downs and it would be hard to argue otherwise.

The quiet lane leading to the church and castle is lined with thatched cottages; hollyhocks and foxgloves bloom in the small front gardens in the summer months. Unlike other downland villages where local flint is prominent in the architecture, many of Amberley's cottages were built using local sandstone, making the village distinctive.

There are records referring to Amberley dating back to 680AD. The pretty **church** was built by Bishop Luffa between 1091 and 1125. Next to the church is the **castle** (now a hotel, see Where to stay) which used to be the bishop's residence until it was recognised as a castle upon completion of the walls in 1377. More information on the history of the village and the local area can be found at Amberley Working Museum (see p110).

There is a small community-run village **shop** (Mon-Sat 7am-5pm, Sun 8am-4pm) **and post office** (Mon, Thur & Fri 9am-1pm, Tue 9am-noon), near the Black Horse pub.

In term time Compass Travel operate two school **buses**, Nos 601 and 619, that the public are welcome to use: in the morning buses go from Houghton/Amberley to Thakeham/ Steyning via Storrington and in the afternoon from Steyning/Thakeham to Houghton via Storrington/Amberley.

Where to stay and eat

At the top of the scale is *Amberley Castle* (☎ 01798-831992, 🖳 www.amberleycastle .co.uk; 19D all en suite) where a double room with a Jacuzzi bathroom will cost from around £200 for a room, though it is always worth enquiring about special offers. Some rooms have four-poster beds. The restaurant has a dress code with jacket and tie required for men so it is unlikely many walkers will be eating there.

Away from the village, about a mile down the lane at Crossgates, is *Woody Banks* (☎ 01798-831295, 🖳 www.woody banks.co.uk; 1D/1T private bathroom) with B&B from £30 per person (single occupancy bookings are unlikely in the summer months); packed lunches are available for £3.50. Not very far away there's *The Sportsman Inn* (☎ 01798-831787, 🖳 thesportsmaninn@btconnect .co.uk; 1T/3D/1F, all en suite; food Mon-Thur noon-2pm & 7-9pm, Fri noon-2pm & 7-9.30pm, Sat noon-2.30pm & 7-9.30pm, Sun noon-2.30pm & 7-9pm), a pleasant place which offers B&B for £70, or £50 for single occupancy, and has a wide choice of pub food: they serve cream teas (3-5pm).

The Black Horse (☎ 01798-831700; food Mon-Thur noon-3pm & 6-8.30pm, Fri & Sat noon-3pm & 6-9.30pm, Sun noon-8pm) in the centre of the village is an eccentric place full of quirky curiosities. There are some mouthwatering dishes including various daily specials (around £10) and they also have some vegetarian options. They may stay open all day on Saturday in the peak season but check in advance.

❏ **Important note – walking times**

Unless otherwise specified, **all times in this book refer only to the time spent walking**. You will need to add 20-30% to allow for rests, photography, checking the map, drinking water etc. When planning the day's hike count on 5-7 hours' actual walking.

(Opposite) Top: Thatched cottage in the attractive village of East Meon (see p83) which dates back 1600 years. **Bottom**: Swan nesting by the Cuckmere (see p158) near Alfriston.

(Overleaf) Top: Said to be haunted, the Chanctonbury Ring (see p122) is an Iron Age fort. **Bottom**: With its castle and cathedral, Arundel (see p114) makes an interesting place for a rest day if you're walking the entire South Downs Way.

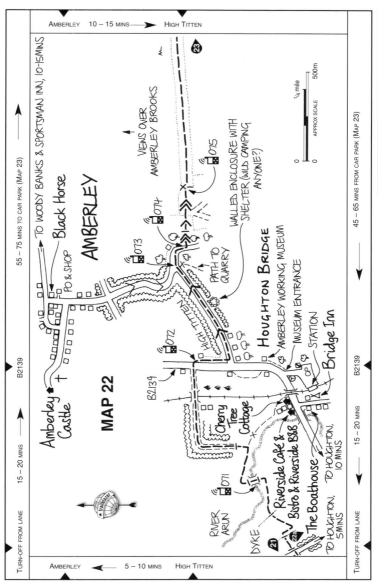

AMBERLEY 10 – 15 MINS → HIGH TITTEN

TURN-OFF FROM LANE | B2139 | 15 – 20 MINS ↑ | 55 – 75 MINS TO CAR PARK (MAP 23) ↑

VIEWS OVER AMBERLEY BROOKS

23

🏠 015

WALLED ENCLOSURE WITH SHELTER (WILD CAMPING ANYONE?)

TO WOODY BANKS & SPORTSMAN INN, 10-15MINS

Black Horse

PO & SHOP

AMBERLEY

🏠 014

🏠 013

PATH TO QUARRY

Amberley Castle †

MAP 22

HIGH TITTEN

B2139

HOUGHTON BRIDGE

Amberley Working Museum

MUSEUM ENTRANCE

STATION

Bridge Inn

🏠 012

Cherry Tree Cottage

Riverside Café & Bistro & Riverside B&B

🏠 011

The Boathouse

TO HOUGHTON, 10 MINS

TO HOUGHTON, 5 MINS

21

22

RIVER ARUN

DYKE

APPROX SCALE

0 ¼ mile 500m

TURN-OFF FROM LANE | B2139 | 15 – 20 MINS ↓ | 45 – 65 MINS FROM CAR PARK (MAP 23)

AMBERLEY ← 5 – 10 MINS HIGH TITTEN

ARUNDEL   MAP 22a

The town of Arundel is about an hour and a half from the South Downs Way via the riverside path from Houghton Bridge or a five-minute train ride from Amberley station. Those who are walking the entire South Downs Way in one trip will find that a visit to this historic town makes an ideal rest day.

Arundel boasts a fine cathedral but it is the perfectly preserved castle with its grand turreted walls that really catches the eye. **Arundel Festival** (see p23) is held in the castle in August.

What to see and do

This gothic **cathedral** (🖳 www.arundel cathedral.org) is somewhat upstaged by the immense castle down the road but is still a fine building in its own right. Founded by Henry, the 15th Duke of Norfolk, the cathedral is relatively new, dating back to 1873. A good time to visit is during the annual Corpus Christi festivities in early June when the main aisle of the cathedral is covered in a spectacular carpet of flowers.

The **castle** (☎ 01903-882173, 🖳 www .arundelcastle.org; Easter to early Nov Tue-Sun 10am-5pm, plus Mon during Aug and bank holidays) is the centrepiece of this historical town. Rising grandly from the trees it looms over the Arun Valley and is everything you imagine an English castle to be, complete with imposing walls, turrets and winding stone staircases. Of Norman origin it is now home to the dukes of Norfolk but is open to the public most of the year.

There are four levels of ticket ranging from Bronze (grounds and chapel only £7) to Gold Plus (castle rooms and bedrooms, castle keep, chapel and grounds £15).

Whilst in the castle area it's worth calling in at **Arundel Museum** (☎ 01903-882456, 🖳 www.arundelmuseum.org.uk; Easter-Oct daily 11am-3pm, Nov-Easter 11am-3pm subject to both the availability of volunteers and the weather; free admission), which has been forced to move from its previous home in a Grade 2 listed building on the High St to a portakabin in the castle's Mill Road car park. They hope that a new, permanent home will have been completed, on a site next to the portakabin, by 2010. The museum's exhibits focus on local history, archaeology and agriculture. Of particular interest are the fine old photographs portraying local life through the years. However, whilst in the portakabin, they can exhibit only part of their collection at a time. Contact them for further details and also for information about their guided walks around Arundel or their notes for self-guided walks.

The **Arundel Wildfowl and Wetlands Trust Centre** (☎ 01903-883355, 🖳 www .wwt.org.uk; late Mar to late Oct daily 9.30am-5.30pm, rest of year 9.30am-4.30pm; admission £8.50, free for WWT members) is a natural wetland site bordered by ancient woodland and is a perfect diversion for anyone interested in birds. The hides provide opportunities for viewing a variety of warblers and waders as well as the odd buzzard circling above the oak trees.

Services

The **TIC** (☎ 01903-882268, 🖳 www.sussex bythesea.com; Apr-Oct Mon-Sat 10am-5pm, Sun 10am-4pm, Nov-Mar daily 10am-3pm), sits just off River Rd at the entrance to the car park. It offers an accommodation-booking service (they charge £1.50 per booking) which can prove a lot easier than looking for a bed yourself since rooms get booked up quickly in the summer.

There are two places in town with public **internet** access: the **library** (Mon 10am-1pm, Tue 10am-1pm & 2-7pm, Thurs-Sat 10am-1pm & 2-5pm; £1.25 for 30mins) at the western end of Tarrant St, and there's also a terminal on the bar at the Arundel Park Hotel (£1 for 30mins), by the train station.

Food supplies can be found at the small **shop**, the Minimart, near the bridge at the bottom of the High St, while across the bridge is a Co-op. The **post office** lies just across the road from the Minimart, while **Lloyds Pharmacy** sits further up the hill on the same street, and there are several **banks** on the same strip. Chocoholics will be pleased to know that Arundel is home to

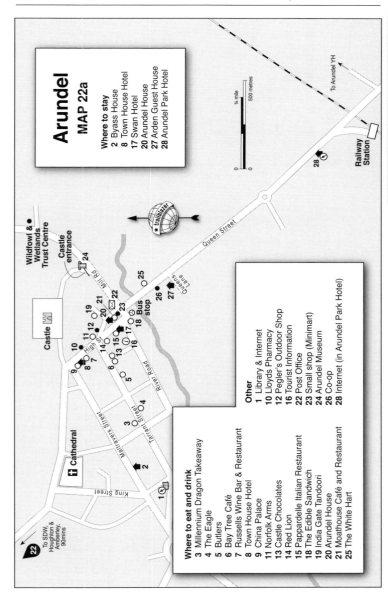

Arundel
MAP 22a

Where to stay
2 Byass House
8 Town House Hotel
17 Swan Hotel
20 Arundel House
27 Arden Guest House
28 Arundel Park Hotel

Where to eat and drink
3 Millennium Dragon Takeaway
4 The Eagle
5 Butlers
6 Bay Tree Café
7 Russells Wine Bar & Restaurant
8 Town House Hotel
9 China Palace
11 Norfolk Arms
13 Castle Chocolates
14 Red Lion
15 Pappardelle Italian Restaurant
18 The Edible Sandwich
19 India Gate Tandoori
20 Arundel House
21 Moathouse Café and Restaurant
25 The White Hart

Other
1 Library & Internet
10 Lloyds Pharmacy
12 Pegler's Outdoor Shop
16 Tourist Information
22 Post Office
23 Small shop (Minimart)
24 Arundel Museum
26 Co-op
28 Internet (in Arundel Park Hotel)

¼ mile
500 metres

Wildfowl &
Wetlands
Trust Centre

Castle
entrance

Castle

Cathedral

King Street

Maltravers Street

Tarrant Street

River Road

High St

Mill Rd

Queen Street

Queens Lane

Bus stop

Railway
Station

To Arundel YH

To SDW,
Houghton &
Amberley,
90mins

Castle Chocolates (☎ 01903-884419; Thur-Mon 9.30am-5.30pm, Tue & Wed 10am-5pm), 11 Tarrant St, who claim to produce what is 'probably the finest confectionery, chocolate and fudge in the South of England'. Tuck in.

Arundel is also home to **Pegler's Outdoor Shop and Expedition Advisers** (☎ 01903-883375, 🖳 www.peglers.co.uk; daily 9am-6pm), a local family-run business. They have shops throughout the town, each one specialising in a different aspect of outdoor adventure from canoeing to trekking. The main shops are on the High St and are well worth a visit. However, if you need another pair of walking boots you will need to go to their branch at 69 Tarrant St. Overall there is a vast range of stock and the staff really know what they are talking about.

Those coming to Arundel by **train** from Amberley will find that the **station** is a ten-minute walk from the town centre; other rail services from here are to London, Pulborough and Chichester. One route on Stagecoach's No 700 Coastliner service runs from here to Brighton. Compass Travel's **bus** No 85 is the best choice for travel to Chichester; see the public transport map and table, pp38-40. The bus stop is near the bridge.

Where to stay

The cheapest accommodation is at **Arundel Youth Hostel** (☎ 0845-371 9002, 🖳 arundel@yha.org.uk; members £13.95, breakfast included, 62 beds), which is not far from the train station but a good 15-minute walk from the town centre. In addition to the standard facilities (kitchen, drying room, showers) this hostel has a restaurant, internet access and a games room with table tennis, a pool table and bar football.

On the road leading from the town centre to the train station is **Arundel Park Hotel** (☎ 01903-882588, 🖳 www.arundel parkhotel.co.uk; 1S/9D/3T/2F, all en suite); it has plenty of rooms and a laid-back unpretentious style. Prices start at £75 for a double room, £55 for the single and from £100 for a family room. All rates include breakfast.

In the town centre there are several options but all are likely to be heavily booked. **Arundel House** (☎ 01903-882136, 🖳 www.arundelhouseonline.com; 5D all en suite), near the post office at 11 High St, is an intimate little boutique guesthouse: a good location and a gorgeous place though you do pay for it. B&B costs from £80 to £160 for a room; there is no discount for single occupancy. Nearby is the elegant **Swan Hotel** (☎ 01903-882314, 🖳 www .fullershotels.com; 2S/3T/8D/1F, all en suite) with prices from £65, for a single room, to £115 depending on the day of the week and the size of the room.

The Town House Hotel (☎ 01903-883847, 🖳 www.thetownhouse.co.uk; 4D, all en suite) opposite the castle at the top of the High St (No 65) is a very attractive place with immaculate and stylish rooms equipped with flat-screen TVs. Prices start at around £85 for two sharing. It also has an excellent restaurant (see opposite).

On Queen's Lane, a few minutes from the centre, is **Arden Guest House** (☎ 01903-882544, 🖳 www.ardenguesthouse.net; 1S/4D/2T/1T or D). Some rooms are en suite but the others share a shower room. B&B costs £58-67 (single occupancy £40-48).

Finally, **Byass House** (☎ 01903-882129, 🖳 www.byasshouse.com; 1D private bathroom/1D, T or F en suite) is a beautiful red-brick Georgian townhouse at 59 Maltravers St; B&B is from £70, or £45 for single occupancy.

Where to eat and drink

Arundel is bursting with excellent pubs and restaurants. The best place to start looking is on the High St where you will find decent, filling, cheap snacks at the bottom of the hill in **The Moathouse Café and Restaurant** (☎ 01903-883297; Mon-Sat 8am-5pm, to 3pm on Thur in winter, Sun 9am-5pm) at 9 High St.

Arundel House (see above; Mon-Sat noon-2pm & 7-9.30pm) is a smart, bijou place which charge £18 for three courses at lunch and £28 for the same in the evening: the menu changes almost every month.

On the other side of the road there's a line of eateries starting with **The Red Lion**

(☎ 01903-885255; food daily noon-9pm) at No 45, a large no-nonsense pub with rear garden serving cheap and filling dishes.

The **White Hart** (☎ 01903-884422; food daily noon-2pm, Thur-Sat & Mon 6-9.30pm) also produces standard but tasty pub food. At the time of writing they did not serve any food on Tuesdays or on Sunday evenings though this may change so check in advance.

A short stagger from The Red Lion is **Pappardelle Italian Restaurant** (☎ 01903-882025, 🖥 www.pappardelle.co.uk; Mon 6.30-10pm, Tue-Fri noon-2pm & 6.30-10pm, Sat noon-2pm & 6-10.30pm), at 41 High St, which serves excellent pizzas and pasta. **India Gate Tandoori** (☎ 01903-882140; daily noon-2.30pm & 5.30-11.30pm), just off the High St at 3 Mill Lane, has all the usual curries. Chinese food can be found at the other end of the High St at No 67: **China Palace** (☎ 01903-883702; daily noon-2.15pm & 6pm-midnight) is a smarter than average Chinese (Cantonese) restaurant.

Expensive but excellent food is served in the rather swanky **Russells Wine Bar & Restaurant** (☎ 01903-883029; bar Sun-Thur noon-11pm, Fri & Sat noon-12.45am, food daily noon-8.30pm), nearby at No 63.

Those who want to find out how good English food can be should aim for **The Norfolk Arms** (☎ 01903-882101; food Mon-Thur 7-9.30pm, Fri & Sat 7-9.30pm, Sun noon-3pm & 7-9.30pm), at 22 High St, which has a traditional restaurant serving English dishes.

More top-notch food can be found at the **Town House Hotel** (see Where to stay, food Tue-Sat noon-2pm & 7-9.30pm) which has a smart restaurant where two courses at lunchtime/in the evening will set

you back £14/22 and three courses cost £18/27.50.

Rivalling the Town House for service, friendliness and good-quality food is **The Bay Tree Café** (☎ 01903-883679, 🖥 www .thebaytreearundel.com; Tue-Fri 10.30am-4pm & 6.45-9.15pm, Sat 10.30am-4.30pm & 6.45-9.30pm, Sun 10.30am-4.30pm, closed Mon except Bank Holiday Mon – when it may be closed the following day) at 21 Tarrant St, serving contemporary British food. Mains at lunchtime cost around £10 and in the evening around £17.

The Eagle (☎ 01903-882304; daily 11am-11pm), on Tarrant St, serves an excellent array of beers and sometimes has live music at weekends. It is one of the best pubs in town and regularly has locals spilling out onto the pavement on warm summer evenings. They also now boast a Cellar Restaurant (Fri-Mon 7-9pm), an atmospheric spot to savour dishes such as venison steak (£14.95). They do bar snacks every day at lunchtime and a roast on Sunday which costs about £12.

After supping the final pint most punters stumble over the road to **The Millennium Dragon Takeaway** (☎ 01903-883017; Mon, Wed, Thurs 5-11.30pm, Fri & Sat 5pm-midnight, Sun 5.30-11pm), at 32 Tarrant St.

Butlers (☎ 01903-882222; Mon-Sat noon-2.15pm & 7-9pm, Sun noon-2pm) is the place for a glass of wine but the food is slightly pricey.

Good places for sandwiches and pastries for lunch include the **Edible Sandwich** (☎ 01903-885969; Mon-Fri 5.30am-dark, Sat 7am-dark, Sun 8am-dark) just off River Rd by the big car park. They have found an amazing variety of ways to fill a sandwich.

AMBERLEY TO STEYNING   MAPS 22-27a

The first half of this **12-mile/19.5km** stretch is an easy stroll along the high crest of the Downs with great views over the swamp-like **Amberley Wild Brooks** and the Low Weald. The quickest way to Storrington (Map 24) is along the path leading off the Way at GPS Waypoint 079. Alternatively take the road leading off from the Rackham Hill car park.

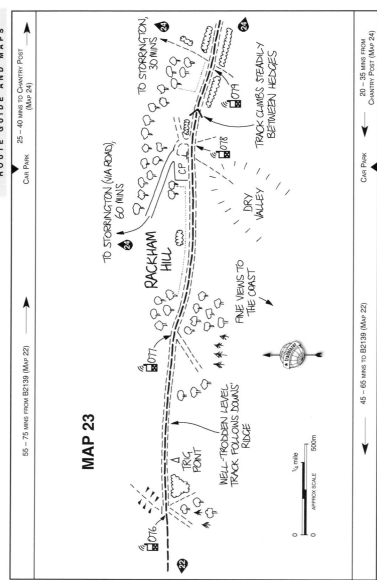

MAP 23

55 – 75 MINS FROM B2139 (MAP 22)

25 – 40 MINS TO CHANTRY POST (MAP 24)

CAR PARK

45 – 65 MINS TO B2139 (MAP 22)

20 – 35 MINS FROM CHANTRY POST (MAP 24)

CAR PARK

TO STORRINGTON, 30 MINS

079

TRACK CLIMBS STEADILY BETWEEN HEDGES

TO STORRINGTON, 30 MINS

078

CP

DRY VALLEY

TO STORRINGTON (VIA ROAD), 60 MINS

RACKHAM HILL

FINE VIEWS TO THE COAST

077

WELL-TRODDEN LEVEL TRACK FOLLOWS DOWNS' RIDGE

TRIG POINT

076

22

¼ mile

500m

APPROX SCALE

0

0

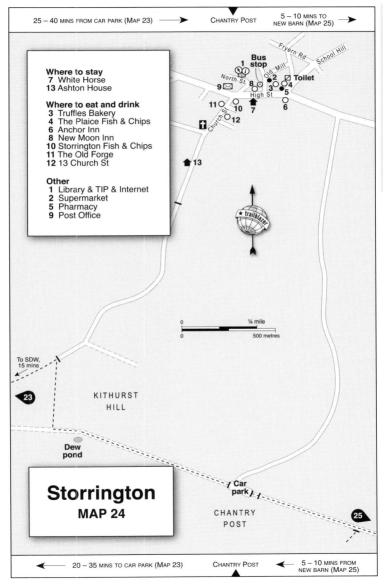

ROUTE GUIDE AND MAPS

Where to stay
7 White Horse
13 Ashton House

Where to eat and drink
3 Truffles Bakery
4 The Plaice Fish & Chips
6 Anchor Inn
8 New Moon Inn
10 Storrington Fish & Chips
11 The Old Forge
12 13 Church St

Other
1 Library & TIP & Internet
2 Supermarket
5 Pharmacy
9 Post Office

Bus stop

1

North St   Old Mill   Fryern Rd   School Hill

2   Toilet

9 ⊠   8   3   4

High St   5

11   10   7   6

Church St

12

13

★ trailblazer

0   ¼ mile
0   500 metres

To SDW,
15 mins

23

KITHURST
HILL

Dew
pond

Car
park

Storrington
MAP 24

CHANTRY
POST

25

STORRINGTON   MAP 24, p119

In comparison to many of the other towns and villages along the Downs the busy little town of Storrington is functional rather than attractive. It is a convenient place for topping up on supplies, getting a bite to eat or for finding a bed for the night but apart from that there is little reason to make the detour.

Services

Storrington has everything you would expect in a prosperous town. The reception at the **library** (☎ 01903-743075; Mon, Thur & Sat 9.30am-5pm, Tue & Fri 9.30am-7pm, Wed 9.30am-1pm) doubles up as the **tourist information** point and they also have **internet** access (£1.25 for 30 mins). The all-important **supermarket** (Mon-Sat 7am-9pm, Sun 10am-4pm) is in a small shopping arcade just off the High St, and nearby is a **pharmacy** (Mon & Fri 9am-5.30pm, Tue, Wed & Thur 9am-6.30pm, Sat 9am-5pm). At the other end of the High St is the **post office** (Mon-Sat 9am-5.30pm). There are also three banks with **ATMs** on this street.

Compass's **Bus** No 100 goes to Burgess Hill and their No 74 service stops here en route between Ashington and Horsham; see the public transport map and table, pp38-40.

Where to stay

There is a much wider choice of places to stay in Arundel (see p114) and Steyning (see p125) but if you do find yourself looking for a bed in Storrington the most accessible B&B from the Way is *Ashton House* (☎ 01903-746661, 🖳 http://freespace .virgin.net/ted.howl; 2D/1T, all en suite) on the lane leading from the Downs into the town. One of the three rooms is actually a studio with kitchen facilities. B&B in any room starts from £70 for one night, or it's £45 single occupancy.

Much more central, the *White Horse* (☎ 01903-745831, 🖳 www.thewhitehorse .biz; 10D/2F, all en suite) charges from £85 per room, or £75 for single occupancy.

Where to eat and drink

The short High St has several cafés and pubs including *The Anchor Inn* (☎ 01903-742665; food Mon-Sat noon-2.30pm, Sun noon-5pm), at the eastern end, with jacket spuds from £4.75, and the marginally more attractive *New Moon Inn* (☎ 01903-744773; food Mon-Sat noon-2.30pm & 6-9.30pm, Sun noon-5pm) where the menu includes a range of pizzas and Tex-Mex food; they have live music once a month, usually at the beginning, on Thursday evenings.

The best restaurant in town is the 15th-century *Old Forge* (☎ 01903-743402, 🖳 www.oldforge.co.uk; Thur, Fri & Sun lunch from 12.30pm, last reservation 1.15pm, Thur, Fri & Sat dinner from 7.15pm, last reservation 8.45pm) where the quality of the food justifies the prices. A two-course lunch costs £15.50 (including one glass of wine and coffee) and a two-course evening meal costs £26 (including coffee). It is popular with locals and tourists alike; book in advance. They have also opened a **deli** (Mon & Wed 9.30am-1pm, Tue, Thur & Sat 9.30am-5.30pm) which serves home-made soups and sandwiches.

The main rival for fine dining in Storrington sits just across the road: *13 Church Street* (☎ 01903-746964, 🖳 www .thirteenchurchstreet.co.uk; Mon-Sat 11am-10.30pm) is a coffee house but it serves Thai food at lunch and in the evening (noon-3pm & 6-10.30pm), with unusual dishes such as roast monkfish tail (£16.50).

For a quick, cheap snack you could try *Truffles Bakery* (☎ 01903-742459; Mon-Sat 8am-5.30pm), one of a chain of bakeries, this one sitting next to the supermarket in the small shopping arcade. For something more filling, *Storrington Fish and Chip Shop* (☎ 01903-742216; Mon-Thur & Sat 11.30am-2pm & 5-10pm, Fri 11.30am-2pm & 4.30-10pm, Sun 5-9pm) is the better of the two chippies in town.

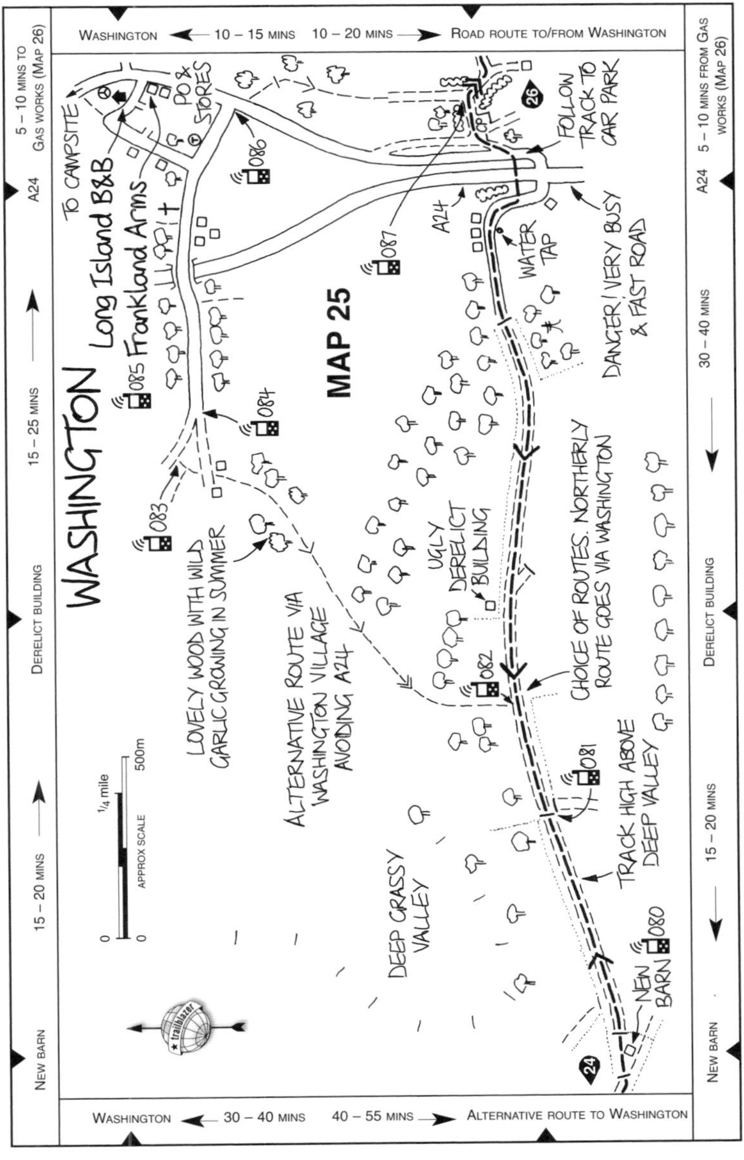

WASHINGTON ← 10 – 15 MINS   10 – 20 MINS → ROAD ROUTE TO/FROM WASHINGTON

5 – 10 MINS TO GAS WORKS (MAP 26)

A24

15 – 25 MINS

DERELICT BUILDING

15 – 20 MINS

A24   5 – 10 MINS FROM GAS WORKS (MAP 26)

30 – 40 MINS

DERELICT BUILDING

15 – 20 MINS

NEW BARN

WASHINGTON

TO CAMPSITE

Long Island B&B

085 Frankland Arms

PO & STORES

084

083

MAP 25

086

087

A24

WATER TAP

26

FOLLOW TRACK TO CAR PARK

DANGER! VERY BUSY & FAST ROAD

UGLY DERELICT BUILDING

082

CHOICE OF ROUTES. NORTHERLY ROUTE GOES VIA WASHINGTON

LONELY WOOD WITH WILD GARLIC GROWING IN SUMMER

ALTERNATIVE ROUTE VIA WASHINGTON VILLAGE AVOIDING A24

081

TRACK HIGH ABOVE DEEP VALLEY

DEEP GRASSY VALLEY

NEW BARN 080

24

¼ mile

500m

APPROX SCALE

0

0

NEW BARN

WASHINGTON ← 30 – 40 MINS   40 – 55 MINS → ALTERNATIVE ROUTE TO WASHINGTON

WASHINGTON MAP 25, p121

Despite the proximity of the busy A24 dual carriageway this village is a peaceful place with most of the traffic noise being absorbed by the trees. There is an alternative South Downs Way path which leads the walker directly into the village.

Next to the **post office and village stores** (Mon-Fri 9am-1pm) there's good food in the welcoming, rather civilised *Frankland Arms* (☎ 01903-892220, 🖳 www.frankland arms.co.uk; food Mon-Thur noon-2.30pm & 6-9pm, Fri noon-2.45pm & 6-9.30pm, Sat noon-3pm & 6-9.30pm, Sun noon-4pm). The bar here is open all day and they serve a wide range of dishes from sandwiches and jacket potatoes (from £4) to meals such as wild duck (£10.95) and lasagne (£7.25).

For accommodation there's *Long Island B&B* (☎ 01903-892237; 🖳 b_stur gess@sky.com; 1D/1T/1F, shared bathroom) just around the corner; beds start at £27 per person and there is no single supplement. Packed lunches (£5-6) are available.

Finally, north of the village on London Rd, *Washington Caravan & Camping Park* (☎ 01903-892869, 🖳 www.wash camp.com) charges £6 per tent plus £4 per person.

Stagecoach's **bus** No 1 stops here en route between Midhurst and Worthing as does Compass's No 100 (Burgess Hill to Storrington). Metrobus's No 23 (Crawley to Worthing) service also stops here. See public transport map and table, pp38-40.

The A24 dual carriageway (Map 25) is something of a blot on the landscape but it is soon forgotten once the steep climb up Chanctonbury Hill (Map 26) begins.

At the top there are the somewhat storm-ravaged remains of **Chanctonbury Ring**, a beautiful circle of beech trees that was shaken into a ragged mess during the famous storm of October 1987.

The descent to Botolphs Lane (Map 28, p129) for access to the beautiful small town of Steyning (Map 27a, p127) is a leisurely one with fine views over Steyning Bowl and down to the coastal towns of Worthing and Lancing.

❑ Chanctonbury Ring Map 26

This exposed hilltop is one of the great viewpoints of the South Downs but more significantly it is the site of an Iron Age hill-fort believed to date back to the sixth century BC. Today it is equally famous for the copse of beech trees that were planted on the site of the fort by Charles Goring in 1760 and which grew to become one of the most famous landmarks in Sussex. Sadly, the copse was badly damaged by the storm of October 1987 and despite a replanting programme the skyline has not yet recovered its distinctive crown of trees.

Chanctonbury Ring is also known for its folklore, tales of witchcraft, fairies and other mysterious goings-on. Perhaps the most famous story goes that while Satan was digging the nearby Devil's Dyke valley, spadefuls of earth landed here creating the hill you see today. The ring is also said to be haunted. It may be a beauty spot by day but it takes a brave person to spend the night there.

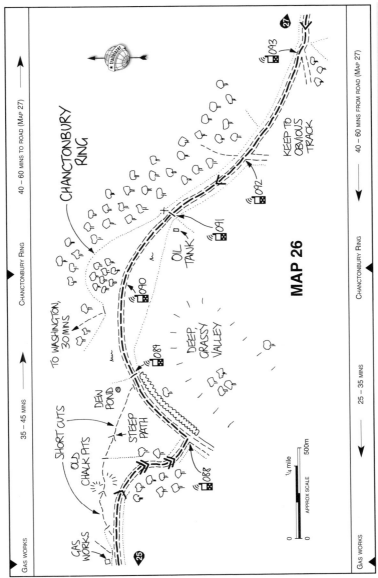

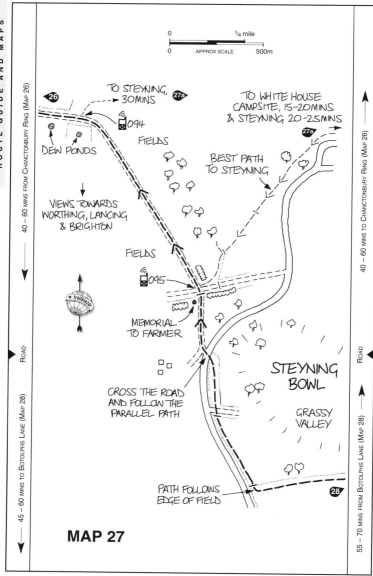

MAP 27

TO STEYNING, 30MINS

TO WHITE HOUSE CAMPSITE, 15-20MINS & STEYNING 20-25MINS

094

FIELDS

DEW PONDS

BEST PATH TO STEYNING

VIEWS TOWARDS WORTHING, LANCING & BRIGHTON

FIELDS

095

MEMORIAL TO FARMER

STEYNING BOWL

CROSS THE ROAD AND FOLLOW THE PARALLEL PATH

GRASSY VALLEY

PATH FOLLOWS EDGE OF FIELD

trailblazer

0   ¼ mile

0   APPROX SCALE   500m

STEYNING   MAP 27a, p127

Steyning, about one mile north of the path, is well worth the minor detour and not just to replenish supplies and energy. This small town has retained all the charm of a downland village and it is worth taking an afternoon off to wander around and maybe visit one or two of the sights. There are some beautiful old buildings, particularly along Church St where the **Brotherhood Hall Grammar School**, dating from 1614, really catches the eye with its black timber framing.

Next to the library is the small **Steyning Museum** (☎ 01903-813333, 🖳 www .steyningmuseum.org.uk; open Tue, Wed, Fri & Sat 10.30am-12.30pm & 2.30-4.30pm, Sun 2.30-4.30pm only, closes at 4pm Oct-Mar, open Bank Hol Mons) with displays on local history. Entrance is free.

Services

There is an **information point** in the **library** (☎ 01903-812751; Mon, Tue, Wed & Sat 9.30am-1pm & 2-5pm, Fri 9.30am-1pm & 2-7pm) which has **internet** access for £1.25/2.50 for half an hour/an hour.

The Chequer Inn (see Where to stay) has wi-fi for those carrying their own laptop. The High St has plenty of **banks** and **cash machines** and there's a **post office** (Mon-Fri 9am-5.30pm, Sat 9am-12.30pm) too. The main **supermarket**, Somerfield (Mon-Sat 8am-8pm, Sun 9am-6pm) is also on the High St and there is a smaller Co-op further along the same street. Further down is a **chemist** and, virtually opposite, there is also a good **bookshop** on the High St that sells maps.

Compass's **bus** No 100 (Burgess Hill to Storrington) continues to Pulborough (for trains to London and the south coast) and the towns in-between. Brighton & Hove Buses' services Nos 2a and 20 head in the other direction to Brighton via Upper Beeding; see the public transport map and table, pp38-40.

Where to stay

Just to the south-west of town off Newham Lane is the *White House Caravan and Campsite* (☎ 01903-813737; open end

Mar-Oct) with camping pitches from £6 for up to two people. Note that there is no shower block and only one toilet here. The walk into town takes about eight minutes.

A good hotel to try is *Springwells Hotel* (☎ 01903-812446, 🖳 www.spring wells.co.uk; 2S/5D/2D or T, two with four posters), 9 High St, built in 1772, with B&B from £72/42 for the double and single that share a bathroom; the other single is en suite and costs £61, and the other rooms, with shared facilities, cost from £80. Packed lunches are available if booked in advance.

If you can bear the noise from the bar, *The Chequer Inn* (☎ 01903-814437, 🖳 www.chequerinnsteyning.co.uk; 1D/1T/1F, all en suite), at 41 High St, offers comfortable B&B from £70, or £45 for single occupancy. A cheaper option a little further from the centre is *5 Coxham Lane* (☎ 01903-812286; 1S/2T, shared bathroom) charging from £23 per person.

Where to eat and drink

The High St is the place for food. Cheap eats can be had at *Truffles* (☎ 01903-816140; Mon-Sat 8am-5.30pm, Sun 8.30am-5.30pm; the café open 30 mins later than the shop, and during the week closes an hour earlier), a chain bakery offering cooked breakfasts from £4.14.

A classier café is *Michael's Country Kitchen* (Mon-Fri 8.30am-5pm, Sat & Sun 8.30am-6pm, Mon 9am-6pm), with two-filling sandwiches from £2.50 and jacket potatoes with various fillings from £3.50. You will find it hidden away inside the small Cobblestones Arcade opposite the main car park.

For lunch packs there are takeaway buns, cakes and savouries at the *Model Bakery* (☎ 01903-813785; Mon-Fri 8.30am-5pm, Sat 8.30am-1pm), on Church St, with a second branch (☎ 01903-13126; Mon-Fri 8.30am-5pm, Sat 8.30am-3pm) at the northern end of the High St.

For more substantial meals there are a couple of good pubs including the prominent, ivy-clad *The White Horse* (☎ 01903-812347, 🖳 www.the-whitehorse.com;

food: bar daily noon-9.30pm; restaurant noon-2.30pm & 6-9.30pm, closed Sun eves), also known as Whites, at the crossroads on the High St. Although the pub can get quite lively in the evening there is a quieter restaurant section which serves up cheap but tasty meals. Just two minutes up the High St is *The Chequer Inn* (see Where to stay; food Mon-Sat noon-2pm & 6.30-9pm, Sun noon-2.30pm), another cheery local serving a wide range of dishes. The filling steak and ale pie (made with the local Dark Star ale) with chips is £10.

At the top end of the High St there is a good place, serving more interesting food: *The Star Inn* (☎ 01903-813078; food Wed-Sun noon-3pm) serves traditional pub food

BRAMBER & UPPER BEEDING
MAP 27a

Almost acting as suburbs of Steyning, the twin villages of Bramber and Upper Beeding lie either side of the River Adur.

The main attraction is **Bramber Castle** (free, dawn to dusk). It was built by William de Broase in 1073 on a prominent knoll behind the village. In truth there is not much left of it, save for a few old ramparts and some collapsed sections of wall but the old moat, despite now having no water and having been taken over by trees, is still clearly visible. The only surviving part of the castle that's still in use is the **Church of St Nicholas** which was built around the same time.

St Mary's House (☎ 01903-816205, 🖳 www.stmarysbramber.co.uk; open May-Sep Thur, Sun & bank holidays 2-6pm; admission £7, concessions £6.50) is a magnificent place which claims to be the finest example of a 15th-century (built c1470) timber-framed house in Sussex. The perfectly manicured front garden, with its topiary and fish ponds, only adds to the charm.

Despite the house being a private residence the owners do allow visitors to admire the antiques, an Elizabethan *trompe l'oeil* painted room, four-poster beds, a 'mysterious, ivy-clad monks' walk' and octagonal dining-room. It is a popular location for TV dramas, most notably *Dr Who*.

with dishes such as sausage and mash, pies, or liver and bacon for around £8.

There is also an Indian restaurant in the village: *Saxons* (☎ 01903-813533; Sun-Thur noon-2pm & 5.30-11pm, Fri & Sat noon-2pm & 5.30-11.30pm) serves all the usual Indian and Nepali dishes with the vegetable dansak (£5.95) being particularly tasty. There's also a *fish and chip shop*, though it's open two days a week only (Wed & Fri noon-2pm & 5-9pm).

Finally, for a straightforward pint of real ale away from diners, head to *The Norfolk Arms* (☎ 01903-812215) at 18 Church St. It sits almost opposite the Brotherhood Hall Grammar School and does not serve food.

Services

On the main street in Upper Beeding there is a **newsagent** (Mon-Fri 5.30am-5pm, Sat 5.30am-1pm, Sun 6am-noon) as well as a **chemist** (Mon-Fri 9am-1pm & 2-5.30pm, Sat 9am-12.30pm) and small **post office** (Mon-Fri 9am-5.30pm, Sat 9am-12.30pm). There's also a small Spar **supermarket** (daily 6am-10pm), part of the garage on the way out of town near The Rising Sun (see Where to stay).

Brighton & Hove Buses' **bus** Nos 2a and 20 pass through Bramber and Upper Beeding on their way to Brighton from Steyning, and Compass Bus No 100 calls in at both on its way between Storrington and Burgess Hill; see the public transport map and table, pp38-40.

Where to stay

In **Upper Beeding** close to the Downs is *The Rising Sun* (☎ 01903-814424; 4S/1D/1D, T or F, shared bathroom), an inn with simple, clean and newly renovated rooms with B&B from just £25 for a single or £45 for a double.

In **Bramber**, *The Castle Inn Hotel* (☎ 01903-812102, 🖳 cjmitchell44@hotmail.com; 7D/5T all en suite) has B&B from £80, or £60 if you're on your own. It can get a little noisy in the evenings as the drinkers stagger home but the rooms are comfortable.

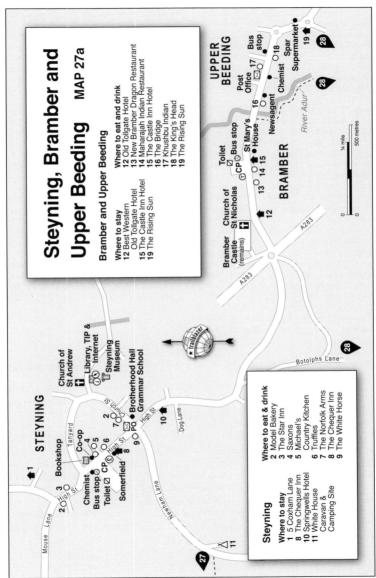

Steyning, Bramber and Upper Beeding   MAP 27a

Bramber and Upper Beeding

Where to stay
12 Best Western
    Old Tollgate Hotel
15 The Castle Inn Hotel
19 The Rising Sun

Where to eat and drink
12 Old Tollgate Hotel
13 New Bramber Dragon Restaurant
14 Maharajah Indian Restaurant
15 The Castle Inn Hotel
16 The Bridge
17 Khushbu Indian
18 The King's Head
19 The Rising Sun

UPPER BEEDING

Bus stop
Post Office
19   28
Spar Supermarket
18
Chemist
Newsagent
16   28
St Mary's House
Toilet
CP   Bus stop
13   14 15
12

BRAMBER

Bramber Castle (remains)
Church of St Nicholas

River Adur

¼ mile
500 metres

A283
A283

Botolphs Lane

28

STEYNING

Church of St Andrew
Library, TIP & Internet
Steyning Museum
Brotherhood Hall Grammar School
Bookshop
Tanyard
Co-op
Church St
2
7
4
5
6
8
9   PO
High St
10
Dog Lane
Chemist
Bus stop
Toilet   CP
CP
Somerfield
Mouse Lane
High St
2   3
Newham Lane
11
27

Trailblazer

Where to eat & drink
2 Model Bakery
3 The Star Inn
4 Saxons
5 Michael's
  Country Kitchen
6 Truffles
7 The Norfolk Arms
8 The Chequer Inn
9 The White Horse

Steyning

Where to stay
1 5 Coxham Lane
8 The Chequer Inn
10 Springwells Hotel
11 White House
   Caravan &
   Camping Site

If you have cleaned the mud from your boots you could splash out on the extravagant *Best Western Old Tollgate Hotel* (☎ 01903-879494, 🖥 www.oldtoll gatehotel.com; 34D, two with four posters/ 4T, all en suite) which incorporates a smart restaurant and lots of pristine rooms and charges from £95 per room.

Where to eat and drink

In **Bramber** there are a surprising number of food outlets for such a small village. One of the best places is *The Castle Inn Hotel* (see p126; food Apr to late Oct Mon-Sat noon-2.30pm & 6.30-9.30pm, Sun noon-4pm; late Oct to Mar Tue-Sat noon-2pm & 6.30-9.30pm, Sun noon-3pm); they serve standard pub food and also have a specials board which changes daily – most specials cost around £10.

Eating at the *Old Tollgate Hotel* (see above; food: Mon-Fri 7.30-9.30am, Sat & Sun 8-10am; Mon-Sat noon-2pm, Sun 11.45am-3pm; daily 6.30-9.30pm) is a classy experience with the three-course Total Tollgate Experience dinner (including dessert and a cheeseboard) for £24.50.

For a cheaper night out head for *New Bramber Dragon Restaurant* (☎ 01903-812408; daily noon-2.30pm & 5.30-11.30pm) where a typical Chinese dish such as sweet and sour pork will cost £5.70.

The *Maharajah Indian Restaurant* (☎ 01903-814746; Mon-Fri noon-2pm & 5.30-11.30pm, Fri & Sat 5.30pm-midnight) claims to be the 'largest and most famous Indian restaurant in Sussex'. The chicken dopiaza is only £5.95 while the speciality balti and patila dishes start at £9.45.

Moving into **Upper Beeding** there is more food from the Indian subcontinent to take away at *Khushbu* (☎ 01903-816646; daily 5.30-11pm), with masala (or 'mossol-la' as they spell it here) dishes from £7.95.

For more of an English flavour try *The Bridge* (☎ 01903-812773; food Mon-Fri noon-2pm & 5-9pm, Sat & Sun noon-9pm), which is where the name suggests. *The King's Head* (☎ 01903-812196; food Mon-Fri noon-2.30pm & 6-9pm, Sat & Sun noon-3pm & 6-9pm) does some fine grub too, including lamb braised in red wine and rosemary (£9.95).

There is also pub grub at *The Rising Sun* (see p126; food daily noon-2.30pm, Thurs-Sat 6-9pm) at the far end of the village. Scampi and chips cost £6.95, steak £11.95.

STEYNING TO PYECOMBE   MAPS 27a-32

The going is easy for most of this **9¹/₂ mile/15.5km** section with a good track leading the way along the level escarpment of the Downs. There are, once again, great views in all directions but particularly to the north across the Weald.

Despite the ugly pub and car park at the top of the hill the highlight of this stretch has to be **Devil's Dyke** (Map 31, p133), a spectacular dry valley said to have been carved out by Satan himself in order to let the sea flood over the low-land Weald and destroy all the churches. Geologists have blown this theory out of the water by proving that it is in fact a result of folding of the chalk strata due to pressure building between the African and Eurasian plates.

After leaving Devil's Dyke the Way drops down to a farm and then over the flanks of **Newtimber Hill**, a National Trust property and a veritable oasis of calm after the crowds that flock to Devil's Dyke.

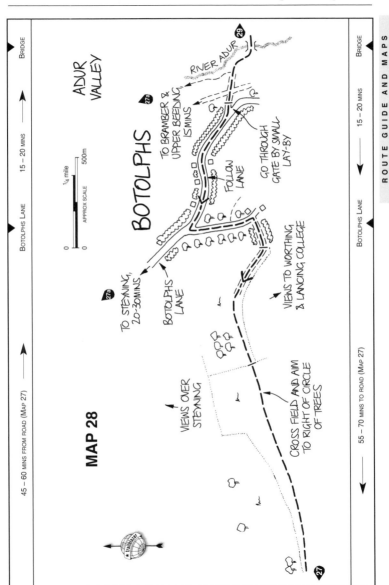

BRIDGE

15 – 20 MINS

BOTOLPHS LANE

15 – 20 MINS

45 – 60 MINS FROM ROAD (MAP 27)

ADUR VALLEY

BOTOLPHS

29

27b

RIVER ADUR

TO BRAMBER & UPPER BEEDING 15 MINS

GO THROUGH GATE BY SMALL LAY-BY

FOLLOW LANE

TO STEYNING, 20-30MINS

27a

BOTOLPHS LANE

VIEWS TO WORTHING & LANCING COLLEGE

1/4 mile

500m

0

0

APPROX SCALE

MAP 28

VIEWS OVER STEYNING

CROSS FIELD AND AIM TO RIGHT OF CIRCLE OF TREES

55 – 70 MINS TO ROAD (MAP 27)

27

BRIDGE

15 – 20 MINS

BOTOLPHS LANE

15 – 20 MINS

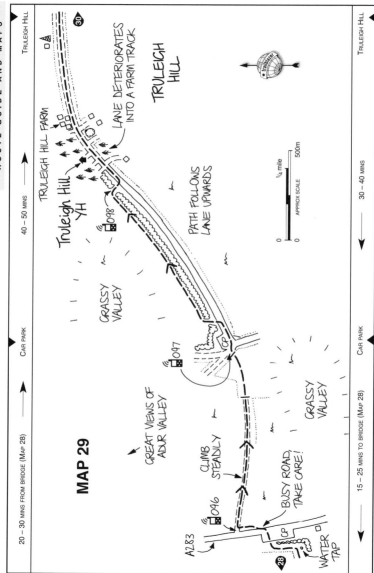

20 – 30 MINS FROM BRIDGE (MAP 28) ▶ CAR PARK ▶ 40 – 50 MINS ▶ TRULEIGH HILL

15 – 25 MINS TO BRIDGE (MAP 28) ◀ CAR PARK ◀ 30 – 40 MINS ◀ TRULEIGH HILL

MAP 29

GREAT VIEWS OF ADUR VALLEY

CLIMB STEADILY

BUSY ROAD, TAKE CARE!

A283

WATER TAP

GRASSY VALLEY

096

097

PATH FOLLOWS LANE UPWARDS

Truleigh Hill YH

098

GRASSY VALLEY

Truleigh Hill Farm

LANE DETERIORATES INTO A FARM TRACK

TRULEIGH HILL

30

APPROX SCALE

0   ¼ mile

0   500m

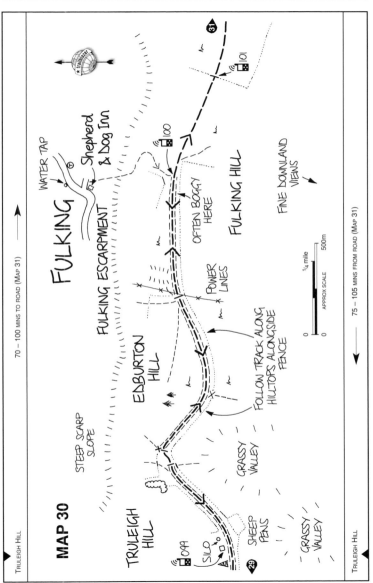

MAP 30

TRULEIGH HILL

SILO

SHEEP PENS

GRASSY VALLEY

GRASSY VALLEY

FOLLOW TRACK ALONG HILLTOPS ALONGSIDE FENCE

EDBURTON HILL

POWER LINES

STEEP SCARP SLOPE

FULKING ESCARPMENT

FULKING

WATER TAP

Shepherd & Dog Inn

OFTEN BOGGY HERE

FULKING HILL

FINE DOWNLAND VIEWS

0   ¼ mile
0   APPROX SCALE   500m

70 – 100 MINS TO ROAD (MAP 31)

75 – 105 MINS FROM ROAD (MAP 31)

TRULEIGH HILL

TRULEIGH HILL

TRULEIGH HILL   MAP 29, p130

By the South Downs Way is *Truleigh Hill Youth Hostel* (☎ 0845-371 9047, 🖳 truleigh@yha.org.uk; members £13.95, 56 beds). The purpose-built hostel has all the usual facilities and serves breakfast, packed lunches and evening meals but also has a shop and kitchen for those preferring to self cater.

FULKING   MAP 30, p131

Fulking is a tiny village with little of specific interest to the walker except for the delightful *Shepherd & Dog Inn* (☎ 01273-857382; food Mon-Sat noon-9.30pm, Sun noon-8pm). It's everything that a proper country pub should be with plenty of real ales and good food and, what's more, the bar is open all day everyday. They also hold a pub quiz on the last Sunday of every month. The pub gets its name from Fulking's reputation for having a rather large population of sheep: in the early 19th century the village was home to ten times as many sheep as people and the pub was the place where the shepherds would meet after a hard day's shearing to spend their earnings on the local brew.

Next to the pub car park is the locally famous **Victorian fountain** installed in memory of John Ruskin, the man responsible for installing the village's water supply.

POYNINGS   MAP 31

The hidden leafy village of Poynings sits at the foot of the escarpment away from the hustle and bustle high above at the beauty spot of Devil's Dyke. Poynings is a scenic two-mile walk from the Dyke.

Brighton & Hove Buses' **bus** service No 77 from Devil's Dyke to Brighton is the most convenient public transport link from this village; see the public transport map and table, pp38-40.

Where to stay and eat

Dyke Lane Cottage (☎ 01273-857335, 🖳 jakeamber@dykelane.freeserve.co.uk; 1T shared bathroom/2D en suite) is walker and cyclist friendly and offers B&B from £25 per person with a supplement for single occupancy.

Or there is *Poynings Manor Farm* (☎ 01273-857371, 🖳 www.poyningsmanorfarm.co.uk; 1D/2T, all en suite), open May to October, which is a working farm and provides huge breakfasts. B&B is £35 a night per person (£45 single occupancy).

Set in the heart of the village, *The Royal Oak* (☎ 01273-857389; food daily noon-9.30pm) serves fabulous food, not least the deep-fried fish.

If descending to The Royal Oak does not appeal, the only other choice is the characterless and completely out-of-place *Devil's Dyke* pub (☎ 01273-857256; food Mon-Sat 11.30am-10pm, Sun noon-10pm) at the top of the hill, whose only redeeming feature is its proximity to the Way. Main courses cost £6-10.

❏ **Important note – walking times**
Unless otherwise specified, **all times in this book refer only to the time spent walking.** You will need to add 20-30% to allow for rests, photography, checking the map, drinking water etc. When planning the day's hike count on 5-7 hours' actual walking.

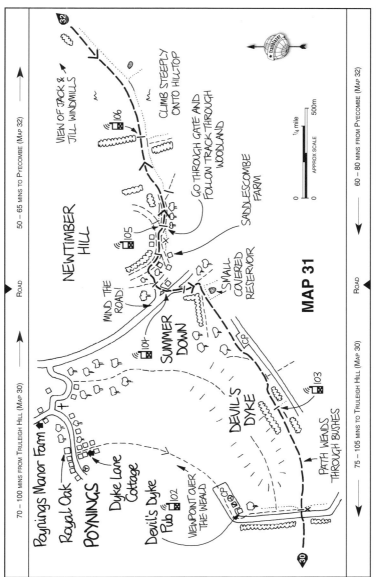

70 – 100 MINS FROM TRULEIGH HILL (MAP 30)

ROAD

50 – 65 MINS TO PYECOMBE (MAP 32)

ROAD

75 – 105 MINS TO TRULEIGH HILL (MAP 30)

60 – 80 MINS FROM PYECOMBE (MAP 32)

VIEW OF JACK & JILL WINDMILLS

CLIMB STEEPLY ONTO HILLTOP

GO THROUGH GATE AND FOLLOW TRACK THROUGH WOODLAND

SADDLESCOMBE FARM

NEWTIMBER HILL

106

105

WIND THE ROAD!

SMALL COVERED RESERVOIR

MAP 31

SUMMER DOWN

104

Poynings Manor Farm

Royal Oak

POYNINGS

Dyke Lane Cottage

Devil's Dyke Pub 102

VIEWPOINT OVER THE WEALD

DEVIL'S DYKE

103

PATH WENDS THROUGH BUSHES

APPROX SCALE
¼ mile
0   500m
0

TrailBlazer

PYECOMBE MAP 32

Pyecombe, like many a downland village, has some very pretty ivy-clad flint houses but the peace and tranquillity that this place evidently once had has been somewhat spoilt by the constant hum of traffic from the A23 which converges with the equally unappealing A273 just below the village. The trees hide the roads from view but struggle to do the same with the constant drone. Nevertheless, a little wander through the lanes of Pyecombe is pleasant enough. Just keep your fingers in your ears.

Metrobus's No 273 (Brighton to Crawley) stops here; see the public transport map and table, pp38-40.

Where to stay and eat

The White House (☎ 01273-846563, 🖵 lou loua@onetel.net; 1S/1D shared bathroom) is the only option in town. They charge £30 for the single and £55 for two in the double. In addition to the rooms they also have a **caravan** (£50 for two) outside for smokers or those who want to come in late without disturbing the owner. Both walker and dog friendly, this is a nice place.

For **food**, the only pub in the vicinity is *The Plough Inn* (☎ 01273-842796; food Mon-Fri 11.30am-10pm, Sat & Sun noon-10pm) located at the southern end of the village and commanding unenviable views of the commuter traffic hurtling down the A23 to and from Brighton. Despite this it is a good pub with tasty pub meals and the bar is open all day, every day.

PYECOMBE TO SOUTHEASE MAPS 32-38

This reasonably long stretch, **14¹/₂ miles/23.5km**, provides sweeping views north. The high ground in the distance is the High Weald, a large area of sandstone incorporating Ashdown Forest, the home of Winnie the Pooh, while to the south is Brighton and the English Channel.

The high point of this section is **Ditchling Beacon** (Map 33, p137). The name refers to the pyres that were burnt here and at other sites along the Downs such as Beacon Hill (see p79) in Hampshire. The beacons were lit to warn of impending attack, most notably during the time of the Spanish Armada. More recently they were used for celebrating Millennium Eve. Ditchling Beacon is another National Nature Reserve but is also a popular tourist spot. Access is made particularly easy by the road that winds in hairpins up the escarpment from Ditchling village; Brighton & Hove Buses bus No 79 runs between the car park at Ditchling Beacon and Brighton Railway station; see public transport map and table, pp38-40.

After leaving the hustle and bustle of the Beacon the route continues towards **Black Cap** (Map 34, p139) where the track takes a sharp right-hand turn. Those wishing to visit Lewes should head straight on at this point: however, it is important to note that it is at least an hour's walk from here.

For those continuing on the Way, once over the A27 dual carriageway the path returns to the ridge of the Downs before crossing the Greenwich Meridian to reach the villages of **Rodmell** and **Southease** (Map 38, p149) where the smell of the sea will probably be prevalent and the chalk cliffs of Seaford Head can be seen in the distance.

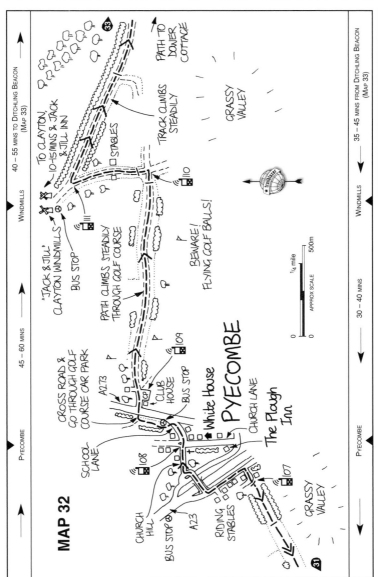

MAP 32

← PYECOMBE → 45 – 60 MINS → WINDMILLS → 40 – 55 MINS TO DITCHLING BEACON (MAP 33) →

PYECOMBE → 30 – 40 MINS → WINDMILLS → 35 – 45 MINS FROM DITCHLING BEACON (MAP 33)

CROSS ROAD &
GO THROUGH GOLF
COURSE CAR PARK

A273

SCHOOL
LANE

108

CHURCH
HILL

BUS STOP

A23

RIDING
STABLES

31

GRASSY
VALLEY

CLUB
HOUSE

BUS STOP

109

White House

PYECOMBE

Church Lane

The Plough
Inn

107

GRASSY
VALLEY

PATH CLIMBS STEADILY
THROUGH GOLF COURSE

BEWARE!
FLYING GOLF BALLS!

¼ mile

APPROX SCALE

0   500m

"JACK & JILL"
CLAYTON WINDMILLS

BUS STOP

111

TO CLAYTON,
10-15 MINS & JACK
& JILL INN

STABLES

110

TRACK CLIMBS
STEADILY

PATH TO
DOWER
COTTAGE

GRASSY
VALLEY

33

❏ Jack and Jill Windmills

The twin windmills above Clayton, known as Jack and Jill (Map 32), are famous local landmarks that can be seen for miles around. There is evidence that suggests the first windmill was erected way back in 1765. The names of the windmills are said to originate from the 1920s when tourists first came to visit. The post mill Jill, the white windmill, has been fully restored and occasionally grinds out some wholemeal flour. It is the only one of the two that is open to the public (🖥 www.jillwindmill.org.uk; May-Sep, most Sun & bank hols 2-5pm). Admission is free and there is a tea shop.

CLAYTON   off MAP 32, p135

The main attraction of Clayton is not the small village at the foot of the hill but the two windmills (see box above) sitting conveniently at the top just two minutes from the path. There's no B&B in the village itself but out on the bend on the main road, about five minutes' walk away, is the *Jack & Jill Inn* (☎ 01273-843595; 3T/1D all en suite; food Mon-Thur noon-2pm & 6-9pm, Fri, Sat & Sun noon-9pm) with B&B for £65, or £40 for single occupancy. The bar is open all day, every day.

A better place to rest your head is *Dower Cottage* (Map 33; ☎ 01273-843363, 🖥 www.dowercottage.co.uk; 1S/3D/1T) about a mile along Underhill Lane at the foot of the Downs. The single room is £50-55 and the twin £80 and they share a shower room. An en suite double is £85-90, and it's £80-85 in the double with a private shower. They do not accept bookings for just one night at weekends.

DITCHLING   MAP 33a, p138

It is about a mile from the Downs to this village but if you are trying to decide on a place to spend the night this is a good choice and worth the short detour. Ditchling is among the prettiest of the pretty, perhaps bettered only by Alfriston and Amberley. There is a multitude of historic buildings centred around the crossroads but the oldest of all is the fine 13th-century Norman **church**.

Opposite the church you can still see the house, **Wings Place**, bought by Henry VIII for his fourth wife, Anne of Cleves (see Plumpton p138 and pp140-1), as part of a 'pay off' at the end of their marriage.

Not far from the church, in the old Victorian village school, is **Ditchling Museum** (☎ 01273-844744, 🖥 www.ditchling-museum.com; mid Mar-Dec, Tue-Sat & bank holidays 10.30am-5pm, Sun 2-5pm; £3.50/children free) which has a wealth of information on local history.

The emphasis, however, is put on Ditchling's renown as the home of famous artists such as the sculptor Eric Gill and the painter Sir Frank Brangwyn.

Services

There are two small **village shops** with limited provisions. One is a short way up the High St next to Church Lane while the other, incorporating the **post office** (☎ 01273-842736; post office Mon-Fri 9am-1pm & Sat 9am-12.30pm, shop Mon-Fri 8am-1pm & 2.15pm-6pm, Sat 8am-1pm), is at the crossroads in the centre of the village. Close by is **Ditchling Pharmacy** (Mon-Thur 9am-1pm & 2-5.30pm, Fri 9am-1pm & 2-6.30pm).

Where to stay and eat

The wonderful old *Bull Inn* (☎ 01273-843147, 🖥 www.thebullditchling.com; 4D en suite, food Mon-Fri noon-2.30pm & 6-9.30pm, Sat noon-9.30pm, Sun noon-9pm), on the High St, has B&B from £100, rising to £120 at weekends. However, if staying in a pub does not appeal to you – especially as

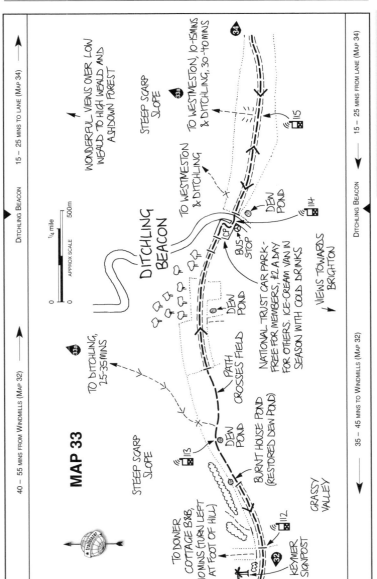

MAP 33

WONDERFUL VIEWS OVER LOW WEALD TO HIGH WEALD AND ASHDOWN FOREST

STEEP SCARP SLOPE

¼ mile

500m

0

0

APPROX SCALE

DITCHLING BEACON

TO WESTMESTON & DITCHLING

TO WESTMESTON, 10-15MINS & DITCHLING, 30-40MINS

STEEP SCARP SLOPE

34

33b

115

114

DEW POND

CP

BUS STOP

NATIONAL TRUST CAR PARK – FREE FOR MEMBERS, £2 A DAY FOR OTHERS. ICE-CREAM VAN IN SEASON WITH COLD DRINKS

VIEWS TOWARDS BRIGHTON

DEW POND

TO DITCHLING, 25-35MINS

33a

PATH CROSSES FIELD

STEEP SCARP SLOPE

113

DEW POND

BURNT HOUSE POND (RESTORED DEW POND)

GRASSY VALLEY

TO DOWER COTTAGE B&B, 10 MINS (TURN LEFT AT FOOT OF HILL)

112

KEYMER SIGNPOST

32

the bar here is open all day, every day – there are a couple of more peaceful options away from the busy main road that runs through the village centre.

There are beds from £35 at *2 South Cottage* (☎ 01273-846636, 🖳 soniastock@btinternet.com; 1S/2D, shared bathroom) which can be found down a rough track known as The Drove.

Or there is the *White Barn* (☎ 01273-842920, 🖳 blakewhitebarn@hotmail.com; 1D private bathroom), on Lodge Hill Lane near the museum, with B&B from £70, single occupancy £45.

For breakfast and lunch try *Dolly's Pantry and Bakery* (☎ 01273-842708; summer daily 9am-5.30pm, winter 9am-4.30pm), where you can pick up a filled baguette from £2.75 as well as more substantial fare like minced beef and ale pie (£7.95). For an evening meal *The White Horse* (☎ 01273-842006; food Tue-Sat noon-3pm & 6-9pm, Sun noon-6pm) offers

sandwiches for £4.95 or pub fare such as beef chilli or fish & chips for £6.95. They do a roast on Sundays for £7.95.

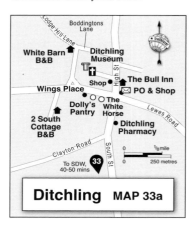

Ditchling MAP 33a

PLUMPTON MAP 34

Famous for its agricultural college, Plumpton is also the location for the privately owned **Plumpton Place**, a 16th-century mansion complete with moat, once owned by Anne of Cleves after it was given to her by Henry VIII. The best view of the mansion is from the Way on the top of the hill.

Countryliner's **bus** No 166 will take you to Lewes or Haywards Heath from here; see the public transport map and table, pp38-40.

Campers will find pitches at *Hackman's Farm* (☎ 01273-890348) between February and October for £6 per two-man tent. Campers can use the toilet at the back of the farm and there's also a water tap there.

For lunch or an evening meal there is *The Half Moon* (☎ 01273-890253; food Mon-Fri noon-3pm & 6-9pm, Sat noon-10pm, Sun noon-3pm) which has a selection of delicious lunches including locally made sausage and mash with Sussex ale onion chutney (£8.50); they have specials of the day. All their meat and fish is sourced locally. There are also some excellent real ales on tap which are locally brewed and changed on a regular basis. The bar is open all day on Saturdays but closes at 6pm on Sundays. The landlord allows walkers to **camp** in the beer garden but bear in mind that the toilets are closed from 11pm until 9am the next morning!

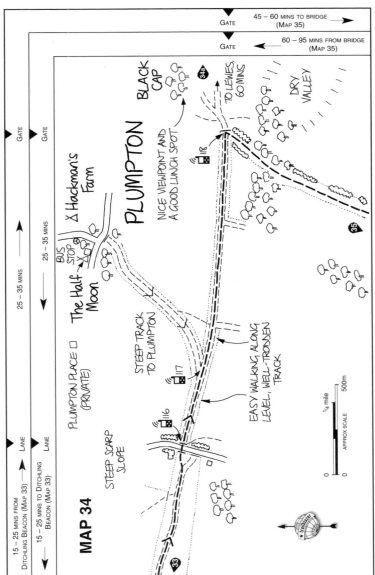

MAP 34

15 – 25 MINS FROM
DITCHLING BEACON (MAP 33)

15 – 25 MINS TO DITCHLING
BEACON (MAP 33)

LANE

LANE

GATE

GATE

25 – 35 MINS

25 – 35 MINS

45 – 60 MINS TO BRIDGE
(MAP 35)

60 – 95 MINS FROM BRIDGE
(MAP 35)

GATE

GATE

BLACK
CAP

34a

TO LEWES,
60 MINS

DRY
VALLEY

PLUMPTON

✗ Hackman's
Farm

NICE VIEWPOINT AND
A GOOD LUNCH SPOT

118

35

The Half
Moon

BUS
STOP

PLUMPTON PLACE ☐
(PRIVATE)

STEEP TRACK
TO PLUMPTON

117

EASY WALKING ALONG
LEVEL, WELL-TRODDEN
TRACK

116

STEEP SCARP
SLOPE

¼ mile

500m

APPROX SCALE

0

0

33

33

LEWES   MAP 34a, p142

'Lewes ... lying like a box of toys under a great amphitheatre of chalky hills'

William Morris

Lewes, the county town of East Sussex, lies in a strategic position by the River Ouse with Mount Caburn (see p151) rising steeply to the west. This did not go unnoticed by William the Conqueror who had

William de Warrene fortify the town soon after the Battle of Hastings in 1066.

The town's focal point is **Lewes Castle** (see box opposite), which sits proudly at the very highest point on a grassy bluff. Down the hill from the castle, **Anne of Cleves House** (☎ 01273-474610, 🖳 www.sussexpast.co.uk/anneofcleves; Mar-Oct Tue-Sat 10am-5pm, Sun & Mon

---

❏ The Lewes Pound

In 2008, Lewes town took the unusual step of issuing its own currency, to be used alongside sterling.

The idea behind the 'Lewes Pound' is to encourage demand for local goods and services, and the logic behind it is simple: money spent in shops in the town that are merely another branch of a national chain does not stay in the local economy; but money spent in shops owned by locals or on local services does. So while the Lewes Pound would not be accepted in, for example, the local outlet of a nationwide superstore, of which there are several in Lewes, it would be accepted by a local trader – who would then spend it locally with another local trader, and so on and so on. Thus, by ensuring that money is spent locally and so stays within the community, the wealth of the locals is safeguarded.

The founders of the Lewes Pound argue that there are environmental benefits, too, for by supporting local businesses one reduces the need to transport goods over many miles, thus minimising one's carbon footprint. There is also a social case to be made too, as the Pound could be seen to strengthen the relationship between shopkeepers and the local community.

The actual practicalities of circulating the pound are simple: people buy Lewes Pounds (with sterling) at one of three issuing points – Lewes Town Hall, Mays General Store on Cliffe High St, and Richards & Son, Butchers, on Western Rd – then spend them with participating traders.

Whilst the establishing of a new currency may seem like a highly bizarre step to take, it isn't without precedent; indeed, Lewes itself had its own currency for over a century between 1789 and 1895. The issuers of the latest Lewes Pound, however, admit that their currency is not actually legal tender, in that there is no obligation on the part of retailers to accept the pound. Nevertheless, with its own watermarks, serial numbers and other hidden security features, the current Lewes Pound note certainly looks like money.

Initially this new Lewes Pound enjoyed some success. Indeed, such was the demand for the new currency that more had to be produced. The demand for the currency was due not only to people wishing to buy local produce, but also from souvenir hunters; and some of the currency even appeared for sale on eBay.

Some residents of the town, however, see the Lewes Pound as an unnecessary complication. They argue, rightly, that they can support local traders by buying from them using good old-fashioned sterling, and don't see the need for this new currency.

At the moment, it is too early to judge whether the scheme will be a success. Some will argue that the publicity brought about by the new currency, and the issues it has raised, means that it is *already* a success. But whether the currency can establish itself as a long-term, viable alternative to sterling in the town remains to be seen.

❏ **Lewes Castle**
This Norman castle (☎ 01273-486290, 💻 www.sussexpast.co.uk/lewescastle; Apr-Oct Tue-Sat 10am-5.30pm, Sun & Mon 11am-5.30pm, Nov-Mar opening hours as for summer but the castle closes at dusk or 5.30pm and the museum at 5.30pm, closed on Mon in Jan; admission £5.20 or combined ticket for Anne of Cleves House £7.75) was built by Lieutenant William de Warenne shortly after the Battle of Hastings in 1066. The well-preserved castle gate and walls can be explored and the ticket also gives access to the **Barbican House Museum** opposite, which contains artefacts from the castle and an interactive display covering the history of the town and castle. At the time of writing the castle and museum were closed as they were undergoing extensive refurbishment: the displays and interpretation boards were being replaced as were the stairs. The work should be completed by April 2009.

11am-5pm; Nov-Feb Tue-Sat 10am-5pm, admission £3.90, or £7.75 with combined Lewes Castle ticket) is open to the public – unlike Plumpton Place (see p138) and Wing's Place (see p136) which were also given as a gift from Henry VIII to his fourth wife Anne of Cleves. This house is well worth visiting for its beautiful interior with timber beams and oak furnishings. The herb garden is also interesting.

Today Lewes is famed for its profusion of bookshops, the oldest of which, the **Fifteenth Century Bookshop**, can be found at the top of the High St opposite the castle entrance. The timber-framed building that houses the shop is worth a visit in itself.

At the same end of the High St is **Bull House** where Thomas Paine, the founder of American Independence, lived between 1768 and 1774. During his time in Lewes he acted as the local tobacconist and exciseman. A commemoration plaque can be seen on the outside wall.

Real-ale drinkers cannot go to Lewes without visiting **Harvey's Brewery** and **Harvey's Shop**. The brewery (☎ 01273-480209, 💻 www.harveys.org.uk) runs tours by appointment only. The tours are run Mondays to Thursdays, 6.30-8.45pm, between June and July, and September to November. The tours are very popular so it is best to book as far in advance as possible: bookings are taken from June onwards and the charge (£2.50) is taken at the time of booking. It's the oldest brewery in Sussex

and has been producing real ales for well over 200 years using hops from Sussex and Kent and water from their own spring. The company is still run by the same family that founded it seven generations ago. The shop (☎ 01273-480217; Mon-Sat 9.30am-4.45pm) sells a vast array of Harvey's related paraphernalia.

Services
The **tourist information centre** (☎ 01273-483448, 💻 lewes.tic@lewes.gov.uk; Apr-Sep Mon-Fri 9am-5pm, Sat 9.30am-5.30pm, Sun & Bank hols 10am-2pm; Oct-Mar Mon-Fri 9am-5pm, Sat 10am-2pm, closed Sun) is on the corner of Fisher St and the High St at No 187. There is no charge for accommodation booked in the Lewes area for visitors to the centre though a 10% deposit towards the cost of the first night's accommodation is taken.

The **post office** (Mon-Fri 9am-5.30pm, Sat 9am-12.30pm) is on the High St where there is also a **chemist** and there are plenty of **banks** with **cash machines**. Morrisons **supermarket** is on Eastgate St and walking equipment can be found at **The Outdoor Shop** (☎ 01273-487840; Mon-Sat 9am-5.30pm) at the lower end of the High St near the river.

Taxis can be called on ☎ 01273-483232. Convenient and regular **trains** from Lewes run south to Seaford, Eastbourne and Brighton and north to Gatwick Airport and London Victoria. There are also several useful **bus** services: Brighton and Hove

ROUTE GUIDE AND MAPS

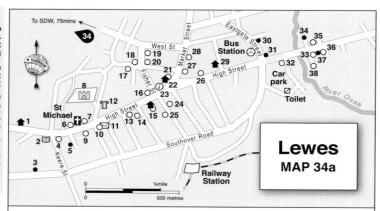

Lewes
MAP 34a

KEY

Where to eat and drink
4 Full of Beans
6 Castle Sandwich Bar
7 Panda Garden Chinese
9 Shanaz Indian Restaurant
10 Beckworths
13 Charcoal Grill
14 Pelham House
15 Carvery Restaurant at
      White Hart Hotel
16 Ask Pizza & Pasta
17 Lewes Arms
18 The Friar Fish and Chips
19 Carnival Chinese Takeaway
20 Dilraj Indian
21 Crown Inn
24 The Royal Oak
25 The Snack Shop
26 Seasons of Lewes
27 Fillers Sandwich Shop
28 Lazzati's Italian Restaurant
32 Forfars Bakery
33 Bill's Produce Store
35 Doorsteps Sandwich Bar
36 Gardener's Arms
38 John Harvey Tavern

Where to stay
1 Millers
15 White Hart Hotel
22 The Crown Inn
29 Berkeley House Hotel

Other
2 15th Century Bookshop
3 Anne of Cleves House
5 Bull House
8 Castle
11 Post Office
12 Barbican Museum
23 TIC
30 Supermarket
31 Chemist
34 Harvey's Brewery and shop
37 The Outdoor Shop

Buses' No 28 runs to Brighton and their No 29/29a service stops here en route between Brighton and Tunbridge Wells; for Plumpton or Haywards Heath you'll need to use Countryliner's No 166 and for Alfriston their No 125 service. For Rodmell, Southease and Newhaven take Renown's No 123; see the public transport map and table, pp38-40. The bus station is on Eastgate St.

Where to stay

There is no shortage of rooms in Lewes but as with any other popular tourist town booking in advance is advised. Close to the town centre is *Millers* (☎ 01273-475631, 🖳 www.millersbedandbreakfast.com; 3D, all en suite), at 134 High St, with B&B for £85 per person or £75 for single occupancy. It features four-poster beds in a 16th-century timber-framed house.

Even closer to the action is *Berkeley House* (☎ 01273-476057, 🖳 www.berkeley houselewes.co.uk; 2D/1T or F, all en suite), a Georgian townhouse where B&B is from £75 for two sharing (£55 single occupancy).

The Crown Inn (☎ 01273-480670, 🖳 www.crowninnlewes.co.uk; 4D/3T/1F) has been around for nearly 400 years. In a prominent position on the High St, it charges from £38 for single occupancy and £70 for two sharing. The rooms are all en suite apart from one of the twins which has a shared bathroom.

The smartest place in town, for those wishing to indulge in a little luxury, has to be the *White Hart Hotel* (☎ 01273-476694, 🖳 www.whitehartlewes.co.uk; 3S/21T/27D/2F, all en suite) at 55 High St, a 16th-century inn with a leisure centre boasting a magnificent indoor swimming pool complete with palm trees, marble pillars and a Jacuzzi. There are also a couple of rooms with four-poster beds if you really fancy pushing the boat out. All this luxury will set you back at least £109 for a double room or £75 for a single.

Where to eat and drink

Most of Lewes's cafés, pubs and restaurants can be found on or just off the upper High St. A classy place is *Pelham House* (☎ 01273-488600, 🖳 www.pelhamhouse .com; daily noon-2.30pm & 6.30-9.30pm) located inside the hotel of the same name, where grilled sea bass with crushed new potatoes and caper butter will set you back £12.

For Italian food you could try *Ask Pizza & Pasta* (☎ 01273-479330; Mon-Sat 11am-midnight, Sun noon-11pm) where all the usual pizza and pasta dishes are served in a relaxed atmosphere. Mains cost around £7-11.

The Lewes Arms (☎ 01273-473152; food Mon-Fri noon-3pm & 5.30-8.30pm, Sat & Sun noon-5pm) is a lovely traditional pub with snugs and quiet corners where you can enjoy a beer; they serve standard pub fare.

On Station St there's a selection of real ales and more pub grub at *The Royal Oak* (☎ 01273-474803; food from the menu daily noon-3pm, pizzas served until 11pm) with ham, egg and chips (£6.30) and a rather tasty chicken salad (£5.75) as well as daily specials. Live folk music is played in their upstairs function room on Thursday nights.

There are several small cafés and takeaways. The *Charcoal Grill* (☎ 01273-471126; Sun-Thur noon-midnight, Fri & Sat noon-1am) has takeaway pizzas, kebabs and burgers. For cheap homemade pizzas, sandwiches or cakes try *Beckworths* (☎ 01273-474502; Mon-Sat 9am-5pm) which is set in a tiny timber-framed house at 67 High St: it is also a deli which serves a variety of cold meats. Further along is *Full of Beans* (☎ 01273-472627; Mon-Fri 9.30am-4.30pm, Sat 9.30am-5pm), a vegetarian food outlet where the 70p flapjacks are well worth tasting. In the vicinity *Castle Sandwich Bar* (☎ 01273-478080; Mon-Fri 9.30am-3pm, Sat 11am-2pm) has very reasonably priced sandwiches (from £1.90). *Seasons of Lewes* (☎ 01273-473968; Wed-Sat 10am-5pm) is a cosy and informal café with the emphasis on organic foods.

For a little bit more luxury try *The Carvery Restaurant* in the White Hart

Hotel (see Where to stay; food served daily 12.30-10pm), said to be a local hangout of Thomas Paine, the founder of American Independence, who lived in Bull House (see p141).

There is a very good Italian restaurant, *Lazzati's* (☎ 01273-479539; Mon-Fri 5-10pm, Sat & Sun noon-10pm) on Market St; it's small, cheerful and informal and the pizzas start at £5.95.

For more exotic cuisine there are a few choices along Fisher St such as the *Carnival Chinese Takeaway* (☎ 01273-474221; Wed-Mon 5-11pm). In the same area is *Dilraj Indian Restaurant* (☎ 01273-479279; daily noon-2pm & 6-11.30pm), where chicken jalfrezi costs £6.25.

Back on the High St is the classy *Shanaz Indian Restaurant* (☎ 01273-488028; daily noon-2pm & 6-11pm) which has an extensive range of authentic Indian dishes such as chicken korma for £6.95. Opposite is a Chinese restaurant, *Panda Garden House* (☎ 01273-473235; Mon-Fri noon-2pm & 6-10.30pm, Sat 6-10.30pm), while for fish try *The Friar Fish and Chip Shop* (☎ 01273-472016; Tue-Sat noon-1.45pm & 5-9.30pm) on the aptly named Fisher St.

Lewes has some good sandwich shops and bakers. *The Snack Shop* (☎ 01273-475633; Mon-Fri 7.15am-3pm, Sat 9am-2pm), on Station St, has takeaway sandwiches from £1.50 and there's also *Fillers Sandwich Shop* (☎ 01273-477042; Mon-Fri 7am-3pm, Sat 8am-2.30pm) on Market St.

Another place to find something quick to eat is on the lower High St by the river where *Forfars Bakery* (☎ 01273-474827;

Mon-Sat 7am-5pm) has sandwiches and jacket potatoes from £2. Also worth visiting is *Bill's Produce Store* (☎ 01273-476918, 🖥 www.billsproducestore.co.uk; Mon-Sat 8am-5pm, Sun 10am-4pm) a fantastic place with tables outside on the cobbled street. The store incorporates a very colourful fruit and veg shop as well as a café and is always deservedly busy with locals and tourists alike. This place is a must.

On the other side of the road towards the church is the tiny *Doorsteps Sandwich Bar* (☎ 01273-487544; Mon-Sat 7.30am-4pm, Sun 10.30am-3pm) with sandwiches from £1.80.

There is also the *John Harvey Tavern* (☎ 01273-479880; food Mon-Sat noon-2.30pm & 6-9.30pm, Sun noon-4.30pm), part of the famous brewery, just off the High St. The menu is full of tasty-looking dishes and there is also, of course, plenty of Harveys Ale to wash it all down.

Another good spot for a pint of the local brew is *The Gardener's Arms* (☎ 01273-474808; food daily noon-2.30pm) which is conveniently situated a short way down the High St; it is a popular place with locals wanting a quiet drink. There is no menu as such; they offer a changing selection of locally made pies and, if there are any left, they will serve them in the evening too. Wash them down with one or two pints of some 'blinding real ales' (as they described them).

The Crown Inn (see Where to stay; food daily 11.30am-3pm) has an elegant dining-room and conservatory for diners. Meals, with many of the ingredients sourced locally, are also served in the bar.

(Opposite) Top left: Lewes Castle (see p141) was built shortly after the Battle of Hastings in 1066. **Top right**: Famous local landmarks, the two windmills above Clayton (see p136) are known as Jack and Jill. The latter, shown here, can be visited. **Bottom**: The Fifteenth Century Bookshop, the oldest in Lewes.

(Overleaf) A peaceful place to rest your legs: St Peter's Church in Southease (see p150). The church has an unusual round tower dating from the middle of the 12th century.

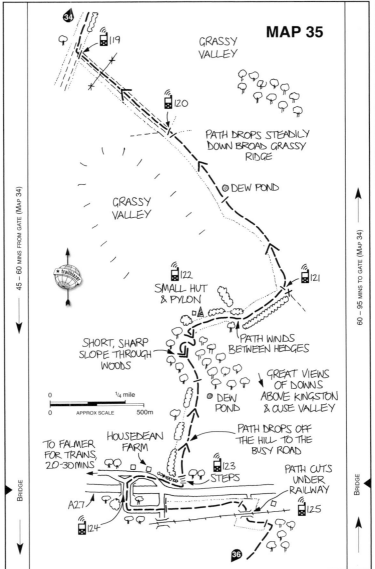

MAP 35

GRASSY
VALLEY

119

120

PATH DROPS STEADILY
DOWN BROAD GRASSY
RIDGE

DEW POND

GRASSY
VALLEY

45 – 60 MINS FROM GATE (MAP 34)

60 – 95 MINS TO GATE (MAP 34)

122

SMALL HUT
& PYLON

121

SHORT, SHARP
SLOPE THROUGH
WOODS

PATH WINDS
BETWEEN HEDGES

GREAT VIEWS
OF DOWNS
ABOVE KINGSTON
& OUSE VALLEY

0   1/4 mile
0   APPROX SCALE   500m

DEW
POND

PATH DROPS OFF
THE HILL TO THE
BUSY ROAD

HOUSEDEAN
FARM

TO FALMER
FOR TRAINS,
20-30 MINS

123
STEPS

PATH CUTS
UNDER
RAILWAY

A27

BRIDGE

BRIDGE

124

125

36

ROUTE GUIDE AND MAPS

❏ Paragliding

At certain points on the Downs, particularly around the Lewes area, colourful canopies can be seen floating effortlessly, high above the hilltops. These paragliders are attracted to the scarp slope of the Downs by thermal updrafts which develop through the course of warm summer days. Anyone can try paragliding with the following companies offering expert tuition to help fledgling fliers take their first flight. The sensation of running along a hilltop only for your feet to leave the ground and find yourself floating like a weightless feather in a cool breeze is certainly a unique way to appreciate the countryside. Popular spots for paragliding include Ditchling Beacon and Mount Caburn near Lewes.

● **Airsports Paragliding** (☎ 01903-879241, 🖳 www.airsports.co.uk) Offers five-day beginners' courses at their private site near Steyning from £495 per person.

● **Freeflight Paragliding** (☎ 01273-628793, 🖳 www.freeflightbrighton.co.uk) Offers day tuition for £125 and four-day courses from £450 near Steyning.

● **Airworks Paragliding Centre** (☎ 01273-858108, 🖳 www.airworks.co.uk) One-, five- and ten-day courses for £150, £550 and £990 respectively, operated from their base at Glynde. They can also give tuition in hang-gliding.

KINGSTON-NEAR-LEWES   MAP 36

Kingston-near-Lewes is one of the larger downland villages. From the top of the hill the rather out-of-place housing estate is all too obvious but once down in the village it is well hidden. The main street, lined with pretty cottages, comes as a pleasant surprise.

There are two B&Bs in the village. On The Avenue *Nightingales* (☎ 01273-475673, 🖳 nightingalesbandb@google .com; 2D, both en suite) offers B&B for about £65-75, £45 for single occupancy.

Bethel (☎ 01273-478658, 🖳 www .bethelbandb.co.uk; 1D/1T, both en suite) is on Kingston Ridge and charges £75 or £45 for single occupancy.

The only place to eat is *The Juggs* (☎ 01273-472523; food Mon-Fri noon-2.30pm & 6-9pm, Sat noon-9pm, Sun noon-4pm), an excellent pub, open all day, with a pretty front garden. There are plenty of vegetarian options on the menu. The unusual name refers to the baskets once used for carrying fish from Brighton to the market in Lewes.

The only **bus** service is Renown Coaches' **bus** No 123, between Lewes and Newhaven; see the public transport map and table, pp38-40.

TELSCOMBE   off MAP 38, p149

Telscombe Youth Hostel (☎ 0845-371 9663, 🖳 reservations@yha.org.uk; members £13.95, 22 beds) is best reached by leaving the South Downs Way at the farm buildings at the bottom of the steep path down Mill Hill. The hostel itself is self-catering only but there is a shop selling basic provisions.

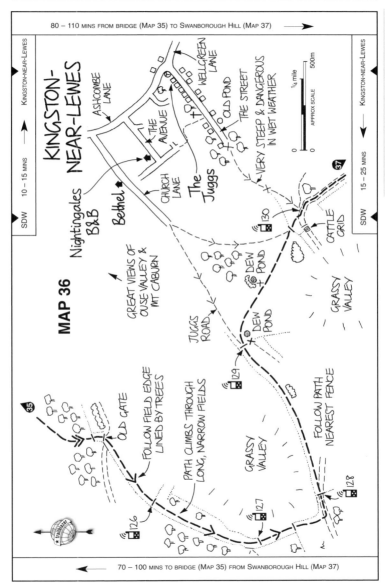

80 – 110 MINS FROM BRIDGE (MAP 35) TO SWANBOROUGH HILL (MAP 37)

KINGSTON-NEAR-LEWES

SDW 10 – 15 MINS

KINGSTON-NEAR-LEWES

ROUTE GUIDE AND MAPS

SDW 15 – 25 MINS

KINGSTON-NEAR-LEWES

KINGSTON-NEAR-LEWES

ASHCOMBE LANE

WELLGREEN LANE

OLD POND

THE STREET

THE AVENUE

The Juggs

VERY STEEP & DANGEROUS IN WET WEATHER

¼ mile

APPROX SCALE

0   500m

37

130

CHURCH LANE

Bethel

Nightingales B&B

MAP 36

GREAT VIEWS OF OUSE VALLEY & MT CABURN

CATTLE GRID

DEW POND

GRASSY VALLEY

JUGGS ROAD

DEW POND

OLD GATE

FOLLOW FIELD EDGE LINED BY TREES

129

PATH CLIMBS THROUGH LONG, NARROW FIELDS

GRASSY VALLEY

FOLLOW PATH NEAREST FENCE

126

127

128

70 – 100 MINS TO BRIDGE (MAP 35) FROM SWANBOROUGH HILL (MAP 37)

35

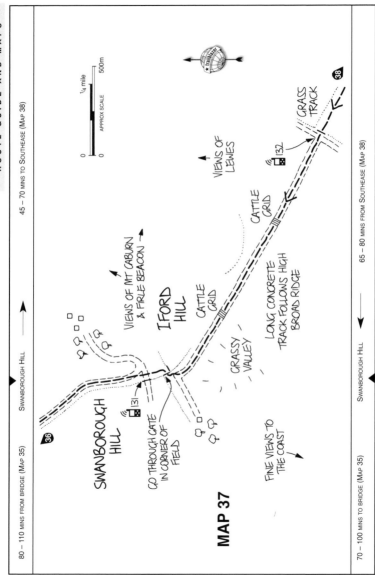

MAP 37

SWANBOROUGH HILL

IFORD HILL

GO THROUGH GATE IN CORNER OF FIELD

VIEWS OF MT CABURN & FIRLE BEACON →

CATTLE GRID

GRASSY VALLEY

LONG CONCRETE TRACK FOLLOWS HIGH BROAD RIDGE

FINE VIEWS TO THE COAST

CATTLE GRID

VIEWS OF LEWES

GRASS TRACK

APPROX SCALE

0 — ¼ mile
0 — 500m

80 – 110 MINS FROM BRIDGE (MAP 35)   SWANBOROUGH HILL   45 – 70 MINS TO SOUTHEASE (MAP 38)

70 – 100 MINS TO BRIDGE (MAP 35)   SWANBOROUGH HILL   65 – 80 MINS FROM SOUTHEASE (MAP 38)

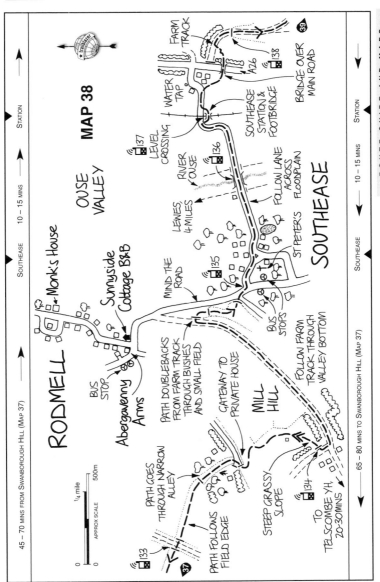

45 – 70 MINS FROM SWANBOROUGH HILL (MAP 37)

SOUTHEASE 10 – 15 MINS STATION

MAP 38

OUSE VALLEY

¼ mile
500m
APPROX SCALE
0
0

RODMELL

Monk's House

Sunnyside Cottage B&B

BUS STOP

Abergavenny Arms

PATH DOUBLEBACKS FROM FARM TRACK THROUGH BUSHES AND SMALL FIELD

GATEWAY TO PRIVATE HOUSE

MILL HILL

FOLLOW FARM TRACK THROUGH VALLEY BOTTOM

PATH GOES THROUGH NARROW ALLEY

STEEP GRASSY SLOPE

TO TELSCOMBE YH, 20-30MINS

PATH FOLLOWS FIELD EDGE

133

37

134

65 – 80 MINS TO SWANBOROUGH HILL (MAP 37)

MIND THE ROAD

135

LEWES, 4 MILES

ST PETER'S

BUS STOP

SOUTHEASE

SOUTHEASE 10 – 15 MINS STATION

136

RIVER OUSE

FOLLOW LANE ACROSS FLOODPLAIN

137

LEVEL CROSSING

WATER TAP

SOUTHEASE STATION & FOOTBRIDGE

FARM TRACK

A26

138

BRIDGE OVER MAIN ROAD

39

★ trailblazer

RODMELL   MAP 38, p149

Rodmell is famous for having been home to Virginia Woolf (see box below) and her husband Leonard who achieved new-found fame in 2002 in the Hollywood film, *The Hours*. Their old home, **Monk's House** (☎ 01323-870001, Apr-Oct Wed & Sat 2-5.30pm, £3.80 or free to NT members) is owned by the National Trust and open to the public. It can be found by walking towards the end of the dead-end lane. Whilst down there it is also a good idea to follow the loop in the road to admire the pretty thatched cottages.

The only **bus** service is Renown Coaches' **bus** No 123, between Lewes and Newhaven; see the public transport map and table, pp38-40.

Where to stay, eat and drink

Opposite the pub, is the friendly *Sunnyside Cottage B&B* (☎ 01273-476876; 1T en suite), complete with its own goat, and B&B at £30 per person (with no extra charge for single occupancy). The accommodation is like a separate flat though the entrance is through the main house and the breakfast is mainly organic.

The Abergavenny Arms (☎ 01273-472416, 🖳 www.abergavennyarms.com; food Tue-Thur noon-2pm & 6-9pm, Fri noon-2.30pm & 6-9.30pm, Sat noon-3pm & 6-9.30pm, Sun noon-3.30pm; closed completely on Mondays Jan to Easter) is a great place to take a break and maybe dry wet socks by the log fire. The bar is open all day at weekends only and real ales and tasty meals are a speciality – their honey roast ham with two eggs and chips (£7.95) is particularly delicious; they also do jacket potatoes (£4.95-5.95). There is a well in the pub which was once the main source of water for the entire village. In the 1970s the pub was called The Holly after the then-landlord's daughter but its current name refers to Lord Abergavenny who owned much of the land in this area.

SOUTHEASE   MAP 38, p149

Not far from Rodmell and actually lying on the route of the Way is Southease. This is a very small settlement, tucked away from any main roads, with a tiny Saxon church, **St Peter's**, incorporating an unusual Norman round tower. This round tower is

---

❏ Virginia Woolf and the Bloomsbury Group

Born in 1882 in London, Virginia Woolf began writing essays in her early twenties. She soon earned respect as a highly accomplished novelist, penning such titles as *The Voyage Out*, *Night and Day*, and *Jacob's Room*. In 1912 she married Leonard Woolf. Their links with Sussex began in 1919 when they moved to the 18th-century **Monk's House** in Rodmell. Their friends included a number of famous artists and writers of the time, not least Virginia's sister the artist Vanessa Bell. Along with the poet TS Eliot and the artists Duncan Grant, Roger Fry and Clive Bell they were known collectively as the Bloomsbury Group.

Many of the paintings from the Bloomsbury Group can be seen in the gallery at the former home of Vanessa Bell and Duncan Grant, **Charleston Manor** (see opposite), and also in the small church of St Michael and All Angels at **Berwick** (see p154).

Woolf's life was beset by frequent and sometimes enduring spells of mental breakdown. On one occasion she tried to kill herself through defenestration (ie throwing herself from a window) before finally, on 18 March 1941, filling her pockets with stones and drowning herself in the nearby River Ouse. Her husband Leonard was left with a suicide note in which she spells out the depths of her love for him: 'If anybody could have saved me it would have been you. Everything has gone from me but the certainty of your goodness'.

one of three in Sussex, all in the Ouse Valley and all built in the first half of the 12th century. Inside the church are the remains of some wall paintings which date from the 13th century and which used to cover the whole church; they were revealed again in the 1930s. The triangular village green surrounded by cottages makes an excellent lunch stop.

Because Southease is on the **train** line between Lewes and Seaford it's an ideal place to start or end a day walk; services operate approximately once an hour. Renown Coaches **bus** No 123, between Lewes and Newhaven, stops here; see the public transport map and table, pp38-40.

SOUTHEASE TO ALFRISTON   MAPS 38-42

Continuing along the crest of the escarpment, with the high point at Firle Beacon (Map 40), this stretch affords easy walking for **8 miles/13km** with fine views to the coast and across the lowlands to **Mount Caburn**, probably the most grandiose name for any hill of 150 metres altitude.

Once past **Bostal Hill** (Map 41) the path drops steadily down to pretty wee Alfriston.

WEST FIRLE   off MAP 40, p153

This small village among the trees at the foot of the Downs escarpment has few facilities to attract the walker but there is **Firle Stores & Post Office** (☎ 01273 858219; Mon-Sat 9am-5.30pm, closed for lunch 1-2pm, Sat 9am-1pm), which offers plenty of choice for your lunchbox.

Perhaps more tempting is the **The Ram Inn** (☎ 01273-858222; Mon noon-3pm, Tue-Fri noon-3pm & 6.30-9.30pm, Sat noon-3.30pm & 6.30-9.30pm, Sun noon-4pm & 6-8.30pm), a Grade II listed building where one can eat in the Court Room where judges once passed sentence on misbehaving villagers. The pub grub is filling

if unfancy. However, the real ales are worth the detour and the bar is open 11.30am-11pm every day.

About a mile from the village is **Charleston Manor** (☎ 01323-811626, 🖥 www.charleston.org.uk; Apr-Oct Wed-Sun daily 1-6pm, July & Aug from noon Mon-Sat, admission £7.50) which houses a gallery of work by the Bloomsbury group of artists (see box opposite), and hosts a festival each May (see p22). Charleston is a stop on Cuckmere Community Bus's No 40 service; see public transport map and table, pp38-40.

ALCISTON   off MAP 41, p155

Alciston is yet another beautiful but tiny downland village but there is little to draw the walker here apart from **Rose Cottage Inn** (☎ 01323-870377, 🖥 www.therosecot tageinn.co.uk; 1D, food Mon-Sat noon-2pm & 7-9.30pm, Sun noon-2pm & 7-9pm), a genuine country pub that has been around for over 350 years. Timber framing and open fires add to the charm and there is also a good choice of locally brewed ales

though the bar is closed in the afternoons (3-6pm). There is a mouthwatering menu based on locally sourced produce: the restaurant menu contains a wide selection of fish dishes as well as standard pub fare. They offer **B&B** in a self-contained flat with a kitchen, lounge diner, toilet and shower room at £120 for a minimum of two nights.

ROUTE GUIDE AND MAPS

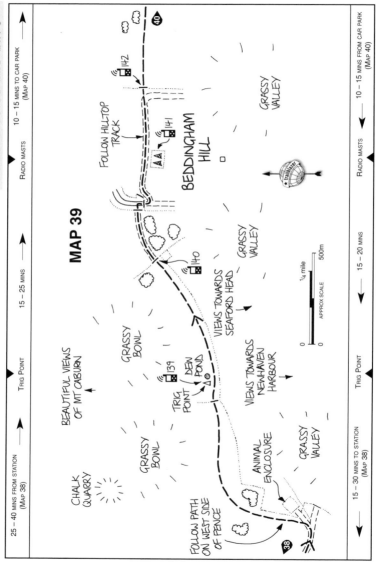

MAP 39

25 – 40 MINS FROM STATION (MAP 38) ▶ TRIG POINT ◀ 15 – 25 MINS ▶ RADIO MASTS ◀ 10 – 15 MINS TO CAR PARK (MAP 40) ▶

15 – 30 MINS TO STATION (MAP 38) ▶ TRIG POINT ◀ 15 – 20 MINS ▶ RADIO MASTS ◀ 10 – 15 MINS FROM CAR PARK (MAP 40) ▶

CHALK QUARRY

BEAUTIFUL VIEWS OF MT CABURN

GRASSY BOWL

GRASSY BOWL

TRIG POINT

139

DEW POND

FOLLOW PATH ON WEST SIDE OF FENCE

ANIMAL ENCLOSURE

GRASSY VALLEY

VIEWS TOWARDS NEWHAVEN HARBOUR

VIEWS TOWARDS SEAFORD HEAD

140

GRASSY VALLEY

GRASSY VALLEY

FOLLOW HILLTOP TRACK

141

BEDDINGHAM HILL

142

GRASSY VALLEY

¼ mile
APPROX SCALE
0   500m

trailblazer

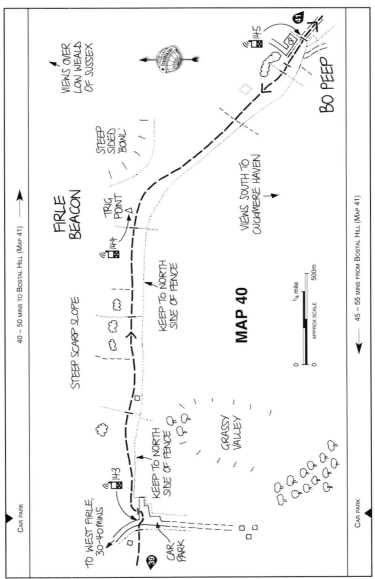

40 – 50 MINS TO BOSTAL HILL (MAP 41)

CAR PARK

VIEWS OVER LOW WEALD OF SUSSEX

STEEP SIDED 'BOWL'

FIRLE BEACON

TRIG POINT

144

145

41

BO PEEP

VIEWS SOUTH TO CUCKMERE HAVEN

STEEP SCARP SLOPE

KEEP TO NORTH SIDE OF FENCE

MAP 40

¼ mile

500m

APPROX SCALE

0

0

GRASSY VALLEY

KEEP TO NORTH SIDE OF FENCE

143

TO WEST FIRLE, 30–40 MINS

CAR PARK

39

CAR PARK

45 – 55 MINS FROM BOSTAL HILL (MAP 41)

ROUTE GUIDE AND MAPS

BERWICK   off MAP 41

Berwick is famous for the Bloomsbury Group of Victorian artists which included Vanessa Bell, Roger Fry and Duncan Grant. Some of Vanessa Bell's work can be seen in the small **church** on the edge of the village.

For food head to *The Cricketer's Arms* (☎ 01323-870469, 🖳 www.cricketersberwick.co.uk; food May-mid Sep daily noon-9pm, mid Sep-Apr Mon-Fri noon-2.15pm & 6-9pm, Sat & Sun noon-9pm; open all day at Easter and on bank holidays). The bar is open all day at weekends only and they serve a large range of dishes; the locally produced pork and herb sausages (£8.25) are particularly good.

Berwick is a stop on the London to Eastbourne **train** line and Cuckmere Community **bus** operates several routes (see public transport map and table, pp38-40), most of which connect with train arrivals here, making it an ideal place to start or end a day walk.

ALFRISTON   MAP 42, p157

Alfriston is another candidate for 'prettiest village on the South Downs Way'. However, this small collection of Tudor wood-beamed buildings slung higgledy-piggledy along a narrow main street is far from a well-kept secret. In high season coachloads of tourists come to 'ooh' and 'ahh' at the sights and have cream teas. Nevertheless, it is worth planning on spending a few hours to take it all in at a leisurely pace.

Whilst here make sure you take a look around the **church** and the **Clergyman's House** (see box below) by the church and the village green.

Services

The **post office** (Mon-Fri 9am-5.30pm, Sat 9am-noon) on The Square doubles up as the village **shop** (Mon-Fri 9am-5.30pm, Sat 9am-6pm, Sun 10am-5pm). Even if you have nothing to buy it is worth a visit just to take in its almost authentic 'Olde Worlde' atmosphere. If you are suffering from sore feet or blisters the **apothecary** may have a remedy or two.

For those with a sweet tooth there is **Not Just Chocolate** (☎ 01323-871505; daily 10am-5pm), a shop selling a bewildering array of chocolate; anything from Columbian to organic. They sell ice creams in the summer months and also have traditional sweets if you fancy something for the next day of walking.

Cuckmere Community Bus's Nos 26, 42 & 47 services stop here as does Countryliner's No 125 service (Alfriston to Lewes) and Renown's No 126 service (Eastbourne to Seaford); see public transport map and table, pp38-40.

Where to stay

Youth hostel members should walk south out of the village to *Alfriston Frog Firle Youth Hostel* (☎ 0845-371 9101, 🖳 alfriston@yha.org.uk; members £13.95, 68 beds) about a mile down the road. The hostel has all the usual facilities, offers meals and internet access is available.

Campers should also head to the southern extreme of the village where a sign

---

❑ Alfriston Church and Clergyman's House

The 14th-century flint church by the river sits in the middle of a well-groomed lawn and is worth a look, as is the Clergyman's House (☎ 01323-870001, 🖳 www.nationaltrust.org.uk; daily except Tue & Fri late Feb-mid Mar & Nov-mid Dec 11am-4pm, mid Mar-end Oct 10.30am-5pm; £4.30) next door. This beautiful 14th-century, timber-framed thatched house was the first property the National Trust bought thanks to the local vicar who in 1896 suggested the building be safeguarded for the nation. Apart from anything else it's a good spot for lunch.

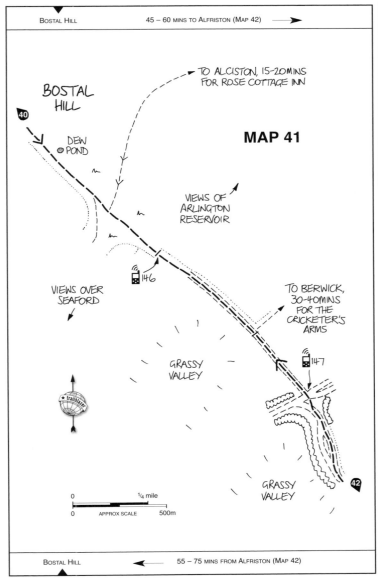

BOSTAL HILL   45 – 60 MINS TO ALFRISTON (MAP 42) ⟶

TO ALCISTON, 15-20MINS
FOR ROSE COTTAGE INN

BOSTAL
HILL

40

DEW
POND

MAP 41

VIEWS OF
ARLINGTON
RESERVOIR

146

VIEWS OVER
SEAFORD

TO BERWICK,
30-40MINS
FOR THE
CRICKETER'S
ARMS

147

GRASSY
VALLEY

★ trailblazer

0   ¼ mile
0   APPROX SCALE   500m

GRASSY
VALLEY

42

BOSTAL HILL   ⟵ 55 – 75 MINS FROM ALFRISTON (MAP 42)

points down a track to **Pleasant Rise Farm Campsite** (☎ 01323-734265; Mar-Sep); pitches cost £6 per person; bookings taken for Friday and Saturday nights only.

More or less next to the trail, on the way into the village, is **5 The Broadway** (☎ 01323-870145; 1D/1T, both en suite) where beds are from £35 per person. If requested in advance the owner can provide a packed lunch (£5) for the next day.

In the village itself there are few cheap options though **Chestnuts B&B** (☎ 01323-870298, 🖳 www.chestnuts-alfriston.co.uk; 1D/2T shared bathroom), which also has a tearoom (see Where to eat) on the ground floor, is from £60 in the twin, £70 in the double (single occupancy is £45/50 in the twin/double).

Though more expensive, a good choice would be **Rose Cottage** (☎ 01323-871534, 🖳 www.rosecott.uk.com; 2D, en suite) on North St. This tastefully restored Georgian house has spacious rooms and charges £75-85 (£60-70 for single occupancy) for B&B. The friendly owners can also provide packed lunches (£5) and a lift to the top of the Downs if arranged in advance.

The Star Inn (☎ 01323-870495, 🖳 www .thestaralfriston.co.uk; 2S/21D/14T, all en suite) is one of the oldest inns in England, said to date back to 1345 (see box p166). B&B costs £115-145 for two sharing a double or twin and £80-105 in a single.

The George Inn (☎ 01323-870319, 🖳 www.thegeorge-alfriston.com; 1S/5D, all en suite) is a magnificent old building with oak beams. The rates for B&B here reflect the fact that the rooms were fully renovated in 2005; from £90 upwards for two in a double and the single is £60.

At the southern end of the village is the large **Deans Place Hotel** (☎ 01323-870248, 🖳 www.deansplacehotel.co.uk; 3S/29D or T/4F, all en suite) a smart 14th-century country house hotel set in a big garden with manicured lawns. Prices start from £115 for a double room or £71 for a single but contact them on the day to enquire if they have any special deals.

Where to eat and drink

For such a small village Alfriston does well for pubs and cafés, many of which have long histories. **Chestnuts Tearoom** (see Where to stay; daily 10am-5pm, Sat & Sun 10am-5.30pm, to 5pm in winter) is a no-frills place with cheap but tasty food, all homemade, while on the main street are several old pubs serving very good pub meals. One of the best is undoubtedly **The George Inn** (see Where to stay; Mon-Thur noon-2.30pm & 7-9pm, Fri, Sat & Sun noon-2.30pm & 7-9.30pm) where a rack of lamb costs £17.95.

For a traditional English teashop head for **Badgers Tea House** (☎ 01323-871336; daily 9.30am-4.30pm, food until 3.30pm), housed in a building with a history dating back to 1510, and with a selection of home-made cakes, light lunches and cream teas.

Of a similar ilk is **The Singing Kettle** (☎ 01323-870723; daily 10am-5pm) which does tasty snacks such as buck rarebit (cheese on toast with a poached egg on top; £4.95) and ploughman's (£6.65).

For a large take-away baguette or sandwich you should try the **deli** in the post office and stores where they have a multitude of fillings for you to choose from.

The Star Inn (see Where to stay; food daily noon-3pm & 6-9pm, all day in holiday periods) has bar meals and a restaurant which is usually candlelit and in winter there is a roaring fire. The roast beef is £9.95 and they do a decent cream tea for £5.95.

Tudor House Restaurant (☎ 01323-870891, 🖳 www.tudorhouse-restaurant.co .uk; daily 10.30am-5pm, Wed-Sat 7-9pm) has excellent seabass (£14.95) and **Ye Olde Smugglers Inn** (aka The Market Inn; ☎ 01323-870241; food daily noon-9pm) has friendly staff and an attractive conservatory at the back. The Harvey's beer-battered cod (£8.95) is recommended; snacks such as sandwiches (£3) and jacket potatoes are served between 3 and 6pm. The name is derived from a famous gang of smugglers (see box p166) who once used the pub to plan smuggling ventures at Cuckmere Haven.

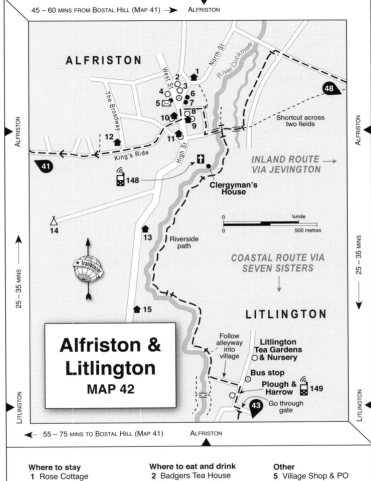

45 – 60 MINS FROM BOSTAL HILL (MAP 41) → ALFRISTON

ALFRISTON

North St

River Cuckmere

West St

The Broadway

King's Ride

High St

48

Shortcut across
two fields

ALFRISTON

ALFRISTON

1
2
3
4
5
6
7
8
9
10
11
12

148

INLAND ROUTE →
VIA JEVINGTON

Clergyman's
House

14

13

Riverside
path

★ trailblazer

COASTAL ROUTE VIA
SEVEN SISTERS
↓

0   ¼mile
0   500 metres

15

25 – 35 MINS

25 – 35 MINS

LITLINGTON

**Alfriston &
Litlington**
MAP 42

Follow
alleyway
into
village

Litlington
Tea Gardens
& Nursery

Bus stop

Plough &
Harrow

149

43

Go through
gate

LITLINGTON

LITLINGTON

← 55 – 75 MINS TO BOSTAL HILL (MAP 41)   ALFRISTON

Where to stay
1 Rose Cottage
9 The George Inn
10 The Star Inn
11 Chestnuts B&B
12 5 The Broadway
13 Deans Place Hotel
14 Pleasant Rise Farm
   Campsite
15 Alfriston Frog Firle YHA

Where to eat and drink
2 Badgers Tea House
3 The Singing Kettle
4 Ye Olde Smugglers Inn
   (Market Inn)
5 Deli (in village shop)
8 Tudor House Restaurant
9 The George Inn
10 The Star Inn
11 Chestnuts Tearoom

Other
5 Village Shop & PO
6 Apothecary
7 Not Just Chocolate

LITLINGTON   MAP 42, p157

Sitting on the eastern bank of the Cuckmere River, Litlington is yet another oh-so-charming little downland village complete with flint cottages. On the other side of the valley is a chalk-horse figure carved into the hillside by a certain James Pagden.

The local pub is the ***Plough and Harrow*** (☎ 01323-870632; food Mon-Thur noon-2.30pm & 6-8.30pm, Fri noon-2.30pm & 6.30-9pm, Sat noon-3pm & 6.30-9 pm, Sun noon-3pm & 6.30-8.30pm) which serves a variety of bar meals ranging from a ploughman's lunch to tiger prawns. The bar is open all day Saturday and Sunday but closes between 3 and 6pm during the week.

This village is also home to the very popular ***Litlington Tea Gardens & Nursery*** (☎ 01323-870222; Apr-Oct Tue-Sun & Bank Hols 11am-5.30pm). It's well worth leaving the path here to stop for a relaxing cup of tea and a scone in the lovely garden.

ALFRISTON TO EASTBOURNE (COASTAL ROUTE VIA CUCKMERE) MAPS 42-47

These **11 miles/17.5km** (plus another 1½ miles to Eastbourne; see town map p175) are arguably the highlight of the whole walk, including a stretch through the beautiful **Cuckmere Valley** (Map 43) which culminates in wide meanders leading to what is one of the few undeveloped river mouths in the South-East.

The final assault on Eastbourne is a spectacular roller-coaster ride over the **Seven Sisters** (or should that be eight; see Map 44 p161 & Map 45 p163), a line of chalk cliffs that are less famous than their Dover counterparts but far more spectacular.

If that was not enough the path continues to reach the final high point of the whole walk: **Beachy Head**, a spectacular chalk cliff jutting into the English Channel with 360° views (Map 47, p165). Even the sprawling mess of Eastbourne is well worth admiring from here.

The path finishes at the foot of the hill where it meets abruptly with Eastbourne's suburbs. There is accommodation and refreshments in the neighbourhood of **Meads Village** (see pp166-7) but if you want to go into Eastbourne there is a bus (see p166) or a rather tedious half-hour walk to the town centre. Alternatively, after walking one hundred miles there is no shame in calling a **taxi** to the town centre and Eastbourne Taxis (☎ 01323-720720) have a reliable fleet.

WEST DEAN & EXCEAT   MAP 43

On the north side of the small wooded ridge of chalk is the wonderfully secluded and secret **West Dean**, a tiny collection of beautiful cottages complete with duck pond, nestled in a wooded fold. On the other side of the ridge is **Exceat**, more a collection of tourist facilities than a village but with a very good information centre. This is the gateway to the **Seven Sisters Country Park** (see box p160) and the spectacular Cuckmere Valley and beach.

If Exceat is an overnight stop on your walk, try to arrive here as early in the day to give yourself time to enjoy the area around the beach.

Services

The excellent **information centre** (☎ 01323-870280; Apr to end Oct daily 10.30am-4.30pm), next to the path, has information on wildlife and conservation efforts in the Seven Sisters Country Park.

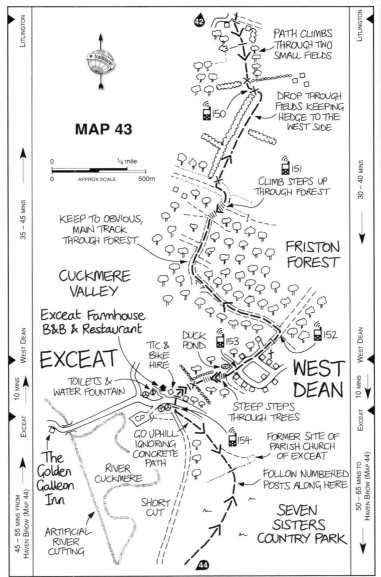

MAP 43

LITLINGTON

WEST DEAN

EXCEAT

45 – 55 MINS FROM HAVEN BROW (MAP 44)

35 – 45 MINS

10 MINS

LITLINGTON

30 – 40 MINS

WEST DEAN

10 MINS

50 – 65 MINS TO HAVEN BROW (MAP 44)

42

PATH CLIMBS THROUGH TWO SMALL FIELDS

150

DROP THROUGH FIELDS KEEPING HEDGE TO THE WEST SIDE

151

CLIMB STEPS UP THROUGH FOREST

KEEP TO OBVIOUS, MAIN TRACK THROUGH FOREST

FRISTON FOREST

CUCKMERE VALLEY

Exceat Farmhouse B&B & Restaurant

DUCK POND

153

152

TIC & BIKE HIRE

EXCEAT

WEST DEAN

TOILETS & WATER FOUNTAIN

STEEP STEPS THROUGH TREES

CP

GO UPHILL IGNORING CONCRETE PATH

154

FORMER SITE OF PARISH CHURCH OF EXCEAT

The Golden Galleon Inn

RIVER CUCKMERE

FOLLOW NUMBERED POSTS ALONG HERE

SHORT CUT

SEVEN SISTERS COUNTRY PARK

ARTIFICIAL RIVER CUTTING

44

0 ¼ mile
0 APPROX SCALE 500m

Bikes can be hired (£20 a day) next door at Cuckmere Cycle Co (aka Seven Sisters Cycle Co; ☎ 01323-870310, 🖳 www .cuckmere-cycle.co.uk; summer daily 10am-6pm, winter 10am to dusk). There's a **water fountain** behind the toilet block.

Brighton & Hove Buses' Nos 12 and 12a pass through Exceat and provide a regular service between Brighton and Eastbourne. Cuckmere Community Bus's No 47 service also stops here; see public transport map and table, pp38-40.

Where to stay and eat

Exceat Farmhouse (☎ 01323-870218; 1D/ 1T, both en suite) is a 17th-century farmhouse

with B&B from £75 per room; £50 for single occupancy. Their *restaurant (*Easter-Sep/Oct daily 10am-4pm, to 5pm in the main season) offers lunches, drinks and some delicious home-made cakes; they can also provide packed lunches.

By the bridge, the large *Golden Galleon Inn* (☎ 01323-892247; food Mon-Sat noon-10pm, Sun noon-9.30pm) has a big garden overlooking the River Cuckmere. Their menu includes bangers and mash at £6.75. It gets very busy during the summer due to its great location.

If staying at Exceat Farmhouse and visiting the pub in the evening, take a torch as the road between the two is unlit.

SEVEN SISTERS COUNTRY PARK

Halfway along the path between Exceat and Cuckmere Haven is the wonderful *Foxhole Campsite* (☎ 01323-870280, 🖳 www.seven sisters.org.uk/rte.asp?id=53; Easter-Oct)

MAP 44

situated in a fold in the Downs. It's £4.50 per person but if you don't have a tent there's always the large **camping barn** that sleeps 30 people for £6 each.

> ❏ **Seven Sisters Country Park**
>
> This extensive country park (☎ 01323-870280, 🖳 www.sevensisters.org.uk) of rolling coastal downland includes the spectacular Seven Sisters chalk cliffs over which the South Downs Way passes. There is an excellent visitor centre at Exceat where one can glean all sorts of information from the displays and exhibitions.
>
> Apart from the obvious attraction of the chalk cliffs and downland the park also includes Cuckmere Haven and estuary, one of the only river mouths in the south-east of England that has not been spoilt by development. That is not to say that the estuary is untouched. The natural meanders of the river, seen so spectacularly from the ridge above Exceat, have been left to sit as idle ponds thanks to the man-made channel that diverts the flow of the river more swiftly to the sea. Plans were underway to restore the Cuckmere Estuary to its natural state by filling in the man-made channel and allowing the blockade to gradually deteriorate. This would have restored the flow of the river through the meanders and encouraged the natural restoration of the saltmarsh and mudflats. However, by 2006 this plan had been suspended after a 'modelling miscalculation' by the project's environmental consultant was found.
>
> The country park covers an area steeped in history. Some of the most fascinating stories involve the numerous shipwrecks that litter the seabed below the Seven Sisters cliffs. The most significant of these is that of the Spanish ship *Nympha Americana* which, in 1747, ran aground halfway along the line of chalk cliffs, resulting in the deaths of thirty crewmen.

(Opposite) Top: An hour from Eastbourne on the spectacular white cliffs above Beachy Head Lighthouse. **Bottom**: Eastbourne (see p172), the finishing line (or the starting point).

(Overleaf) A hang-glider soaring high above Bo Peep. If you'd like to try paragliding or hang-gliding, the Downs make the perfect launch pad (see p146).

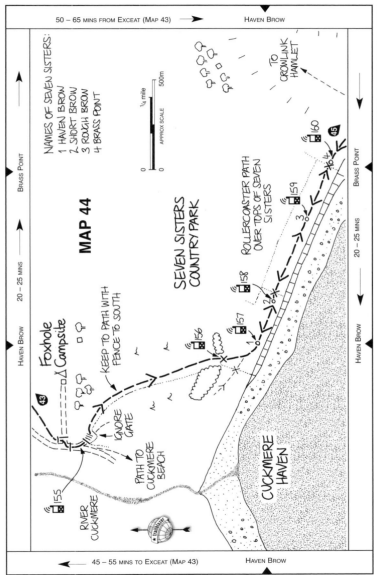

50 – 65 MINS FROM EXCEAT (MAP 43) →

HAVEN BROW

NAMES OF SEVEN SISTERS:
1 HAVEN BROW
2 SHORT BROW
3 ROUGH BROW
4 BRASS POINT

TO CROWLINK HAMLET

¼ mile
500m
APPROX SCALE
0

MAP 44

SEVEN SISTERS COUNTRY PARK

ROLLERCOASTER PATH OVER TOPS OF SEVEN SISTERS

160

159

158

Foxhole △ Campsite

KEEP TO PATH WITH FENCE TO SOUTH

157

156

155

IGNORE GATE

PATH TO CUCKMERE BEACH

RIVER CUCKMERE

CUCKMERE HAVEN

BRASS POINT

20 – 25 MINS

HAVEN BROW

20 – 25 MINS

HAVEN BROW

45 – 55 MINS TO EXCEAT (MAP 43) ←

HAVEN BROW

❏ The end of the Haven?

The coastline around Cuckmere Haven (see Map 44, p161) may look dramatically different in years to come. Proposals have been put forward by the Environment Agency to allow the Cuckmere Haven to flood and turn the valley into a 113-acre salt marsh.

The agency's reasons for doing so are simple. The embankments of a Victorian canal running along the bottom of the valley are disintegrating, and rather than spending £50,000 a year maintaining the sea defences in this area – largely by bulldozing shingle from the river mouth to the base of the cliffs – the agency has decided instead to allow the sea to reclaim the land, creating a natural marsh that should attract wading birds. The Environment Agency explains that it has been 'propping up' the river system in the area for the past 70 years, but with rising sea levels the task was becoming a hopeless one.

The proposal to flood the valley has met with stiff opposition, not least the signing of a 4000-strong petition. The biggest losers in the whole affair will be the owners of the three eighteenth-century clifftop cottages at Cuckmere Haven, built to give early warning of a Napoleonic invasion. The cottages became famous worldwide in 2007 when one of them was used for the final scene in *Atonement*, the Oscar-nominated movie based on the book by Ian McEwan and starring James McAvoy and Keira Knightley. The owners of the cottages even built defensive barricades in 1998 to prevent the sea encroaching, though these would become redundant if the plans go ahead.

Some estimates reckon that if the Environment Agency's proposals come into effect, the cottage in the film, which is closest to the end of the headland, will disappear within ten years as the sea engulfs it from both sides.

BIRLING GAP   MAP 45

Considering that Birling Gap is in such a beautiful position on a low saddle along the line of chalk cliffs, it is a shame that the few buildings here are so ugly and out of place.

There is a small line of terraced houses that are falling into the sea, a B&B and a hotel with a pub and restaurant. The ***Boathouse B&B*** (☎ 01323-423073; 2D/1S, all en suite) is the best option here with the friendly owner offering B&B for £45 for a double, or £30 for the single room.

Birling Gap Hotel (☎ 01323-423197, 🖥 www.birlinggaphotel.co.uk; 1S/5D/3F, all en suite; food Mon-Sat noon-2.30pm & 6-8.30pm, Sun 12.30-3.30pm) offers B&B for £65 or £75 for a room with a sea view, £35 for the single room. The pub, open all day, has inexpensive food such as two jumbo sausages, chips and peas for £7.95 and a carvery on Sundays. The adjoining coffee shop (daily 10am-5/6pm) also has cheap refreshments.

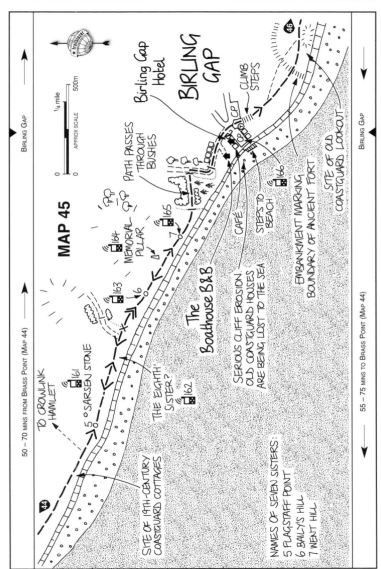

MAP 45

50 – 70 MINS FROM BRASS POINT (MAP 44)

BIRLING GAP

TO CROWLINK
HAMLET

SITE OF 19TH-CENTURY
COASTGUARD COTTAGES

5 ° SARSEN STONE

161

163 6

THE EIGHTH
SISTER?

162

MEMORIAL
PILLAR

164

165 7

PATH PASSES
THROUGH
BUSHES

Birling Gap
Hotel

BIRLING
GAP

CLIMB
STEPS

CP

46

The
Boathouse B&B

CAFÉ

STEPS TO
BEACH

166

SERIOUS CLIFF EROSION.
OLD COASTGUARD HOUSES
ARE BEING LOST TO THE SEA

EMBANKMENT MARKING
BOUNDARY OF ANCIENT FORT

SITE OF OLD
COASTGUARD LOOKOUT

NAMES OF SEVEN SISTERS:
5 FLAGSTAFF POINT
6 BAILY'S HILL
7 WENT HILL

BIRLING GAP

55 – 75 MINS TO BRASS POINT (MAP 44)

¼ mile
500m
APPROX SCALE

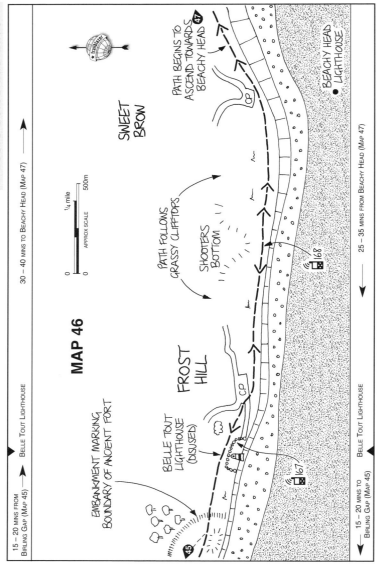

MAP 46

15 – 20 MINS FROM
BIRLING GAP (MAP 45) ➤ ➤ BELLE TOUT LIGHTHOUSE

30 – 40 MINS TO BEACHY HEAD (MAP 47) ➤

¼ mile
0 500m
0
APPROX SCALE

SWEET
BROW

PATH BEGINS TO
ASCEND TOWARDS
BEACHY HEAD 47

BEACHY HEAD
LIGHTHOUSE

PATH FOLLOWS
GRASSY CLIFFTOPS

SHOOTERS
BOTTOM

168

FROST
HILL

CP

CP

BELLE TOUT
LIGHTHOUSE
(DISUSED)

EMBANKMENT MARKING
BOUNDARY OF ANCIENT FORT

167

45

◀ BELLE TOUT LIGHTHOUSE

15 – 20 MINS TO
BIRLING GAP (MAP 45) ◀

25 – 35 MINS FROM BEACHY HEAD (MAP 47) ◀

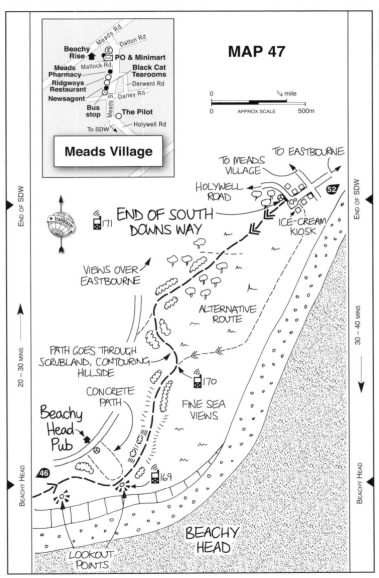

MAP 47

Meads Village

Meads Rd
Dalton Rd
Beachy Rise
PO & Minimart
Meads Pharmacy
Matlock Rd
Black Cat Tearooms
Ridgways Restaurant
Derwent Rd
Newsagent
Darley Rd
Bus stop
The Pilot
To SDW
Holywell Rd

0 — ¼ mile
APPROX SCALE
0 — 500m

TO EASTBOURNE
TO MEADS VILLAGE
HOLYWELL ROAD
CP
52
ICE-CREAM KIOSK

★ trailblazer

📱171

END OF SOUTH DOWNS WAY

VIEWS OVER EASTBOURNE

ALTERNATIVE ROUTE

PATH GOES THROUGH SCRUBLAND, CONTOURING HILLSIDE

📱170

CONCRETE PATH

FINE SEA VIEWS

Beachy Head Pub

46

📱169

LOOKOUT POINTS

BEACHY HEAD

END OF SDW

END OF SDW

30 – 40 MINS

20 – 30 MINS

BEACHY HEAD

BEACHY HEAD

❑ Smuggling

Smuggling of wool, brandy and gin was rife along the Sussex coast with Cuckmere Haven and Birling Gap being favourite places for gangs of smugglers to load and unload their contraband in the late 18th and early 19th centuries. One of the most infamous groups was the Alfriston Gang who would smuggle goods to and from Cuckmere Haven along the Cuckmere River.

The leader of the Alfriston Gang was Stanton Collins who owned the now aptly named Ye Olde Smugglers Inn from where the group plotted their exploits. These included a raid on a Dutch ship wrecked at Cuckmere Haven. The figurehead of the ship, a red lion's head, still stands next to the Star Inn in the village. Stanton Collins was eventually arrested in 1831 for sheep rustling and was shipped off to Australia.

BEACHY HEAD   MAP 47, p165

Beachy Head is, thankfully, relatively unspoilt with just one large chain pub near the top: *The Beachy Head* (☎ 01323-728060; food Mon-Sat noon-10pm, Sun noon-9.30pm). It's not the best place to celebrate the walk's end but could be useful if you need to shelter from the weather. Being a chain pub, the food is cheap but not particularly inspiring.

Brighton & Hove's No 12a **bus** service and Eastbourne Buses' No 3 service call here; see public transport map and table, pp38-40.

MEADS VILLAGE   MAP 47, p165

Meads Village is actually the most westerly suburb of Eastbourne. It is a quiet, well-to-do part of town with a genuine village feel. More importantly for South Downs Way walkers, it is positioned right at the official end of the walk, making a stop here a more appealing prospect than the half-hour walk into the hectic centre of Eastbourne.

To reach Meads Village head straight on where the South Downs Way reaches the ice-cream kiosk at the bottom of the hill and turn left at Holywell Rd.

Services

Everything one might need here is centred along one short stretch of Meads St. There is a **Minimart** (Mon-Sat 7.30am-9pm, Sun 8am-9pm) on the corner of Matlock Rd which also incorporates the **post office** (Mon-Fri 9am-5.30pm, Sat 9am-12.30pm) and an **ATM**.

Further down, next to the **newsagent**, is **Meads Pharmacy** (Mon-Fri 9am-1pm & 2-5.30pm, Sat 9am-1pm) for those requiring attention to blistered feet.

Eastbourne **Buses'** No 3 service is the one to catch into central Eastbourne; see public transport map and table, pp38-40. The bus leaves from the foot of the hill at the end of the path and also from here.

Where to stay and eat

The closest accommodation to the end of the walk – indeed the only option here – is *Beachy Rise* (☎ 01323-639171, 🖳 susanne 234@hotmail.co.uk; 3D/2D or T, all en suite) on Meads Rd with B&B at £25-40 per person.

The Pilot (☎ 01323-723440; food Mon-Fri noon-2.30pm & 6-9pm, Sat noon-9.30pm, Sun noon-9pm), on a bend on Meads St, is the first pub reached after leaving the end of the South Downs Way. The bar is open all day which makes it convenient for a celebration drink.

For something lighter try the *Black Cat Tearooms* (☎ 01323-646590; Mon, Tue, Thur & Fri 8.30am-4.30pm, Wed & Sat 8.30am-1.30pm), which serves both eat-in and takeaway food; the menu includes soups (£3.50) and sandwiches and they also have a specials board.

If, after 100 miles, you feel the need to treat yourself and push the boat out you can do no better than book a table at the exclusive *Ridgways Restaurant* (☎ 01323-726805; Wed-Sat noon-2pm & 7pm to late, Tue & Sun noon-2pm, booking strongly advised). They specialise in traditional English dishes. The 'smart/casual wear only' notice means that the hiking boots will have to be left behind.

ALFRISTON TO EASTBOURNE (INLAND ROUTE VIA JEVINGTON)
MAP 42 p157 & MAPS 48-51

This inland **alternative route** is geared towards horse-riders and cyclists but walkers are welcome to use the bridleway too.

Although these **7¹/₂ miles/12km** (plus another 1¹/₂ miles to Eastbourne centre) are not as spectacular as the coastal route there are still plenty of fine downland views to enjoy high up on **Windover Hill** (Map 48, p168) while a detour to see the famous **Long Man of Wilmington** (see box below) is strongly recommended.

It is a good idea to keep an extra day spare for this section even if you have already walked the coastal route.

MILTON STREET   MAP 48, p168
Milton Street is nothing more than a small collection of scattered houses. There is, however, a pub here, *The Sussex Ox* (☎ 01323-870840, 🖳 http://thesussexox.co.uk; food served daily noon-2pm & 6-9pm). Although it is open Mon-Sat 11.30am-3pm & 6-11pm and Sun noon-3pm & 6-10.30pm only, it is worth a visit. The varied menu changes daily but it might feature half a duck (£12.75), calf's liver (£10.75) or plaice (£12.75).

WILMINGTON   off MAP 48, p168
Wilmington is best known for the Long Man, a huge chalk figure adorning Windover Hill above the village.

A little way from the South Downs Way on the main road north of the village is *Crossways Hotel* (☎ 01323-482455, 🖳 www.crosswayshotel.co.uk; 1S/4D/2T, all en suite) with B&B from £115. The single room costs £75. From Tuesday to Saturday (7.30-8.30pm) they serve a four-course set meal including coffee for £35.95 .

❏ The Long Man of Wilmington
No-one is quite sure when or why this large chalk figure appeared on the side of Windover Hill above Wilmington (Map 48, p168). Best viewed from the lane leading out of the village, he stands 70m tall and holds a vertical rod in each hand. Although it was only in 1969 that the white blocks were placed along the lines of the figure, suggestions as to when the original was made range from the prehistoric era or the Roman age to just a few hundred years ago. As for the question of why, well that is even harder to answer. Some say he is a fertility symbol robbed of his genitalia; others claim he was carved out for fun by monks from the nearby Wilmington Priory. Or could it be that a real giant collapsed and died on that very spot?

ROUTE GUIDE AND MAPS

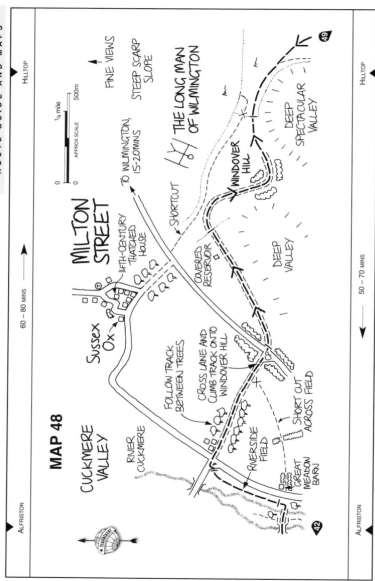

MAP 48

CUCKMERE VALLEY

Sussex Ox

MILTON STREET

14TH-CENTURY THATCHED HOUSE

FINE VIEWS

STEEP SCARP SLOPE

TO WILMINGTON, 15-20MINS

THE LONG MAN OF WILMINGTON

WINDOVER HILL

DEEP SPECTACULAR VALLEY

DEEP VALLEY

SHORTCUT

COVERED RESERVOIR

FOLLOW TRACK BETWEEN TREES

CROSS LANE AND CLIMB TRACK ONTO WINDOVER HILL

RIVER CUCKMERE

RIVERSIDE FIELD

SHORT CUT ACROSS FIELD

GREAT MEADOW BARN

¼ mile

APPROX SCALE   500m

0   0

42

49

60 – 80 MINS

50 – 70 MINS

ALFRISTON

HILLTOP

ALFRISTON

HILLTOP

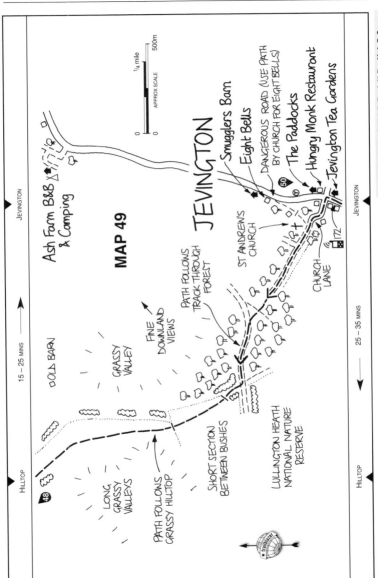

MAP 49

JEVINGTON

HILLTOP

15 – 25 MINS

JEVINGTON

Ash Farm B&B & Camping

OLD BARN

GRASSY VALLEY

FINE DOWNLAND VIEWS

PATH FOLLOWS TRACK THROUGH FOREST

ST ANDREW'S CHURCH

Smuggler's Barn

Eight Bells

DANGEROUS ROAD (USE PATH BY CHURCH FOR EIGHT BELLS)

The Paddocks

Hungry Monk Restaurant

Jevington Tea Gardens

50

CHURCH LANE

172

JEVINGTON

25 – 35 MINS

HILLTOP

48

LONG GRASSY VALLEYS

PATH FOLLOWS GRASSY HILLTOP

SHORT SECTION BETWEEN BUSHES

LULLINGTON HEATH NATIONAL NATURE RESERVE

¼ mile

APPROX SCALE

500m

0

0

trailblazer

❏ Lullington Heath

This hidden National Nature Reserve near Jevington (see Map 49, p169) is a short detour from the South Downs Way and is a good place to escape the crowds who tend to congregate around the tourist traps of Alfriston, Jevington and Wilmington.

The rough chalk grassland is a good place to see a variety of species of butterfly including the Chalkhill blue. In summer the shallow valley is often ablaze with the yellow flowers of gorse and broom. To the south of Lullington Heath is the expansive cover of **Friston Forest**, another good place to get lost and explore countless forest tracks.

JEVINGTON   MAP 49, p169

Jevington, sitting comfortably in the Cuckmere valley, is another beautiful village that provides a good alternative stop to the somewhat exploited streets of Alfriston.

Where to stay

For accommodation in the village there is *The Paddocks* (☎ 01323-482499, 🖳 www.thepaddockstables.co.uk; 1D/1T, both en suite), a comfortable B&B with rooms from £30 per person (£35 single occupancy) and the owner can provide packed lunches. They welcome dogs and there is also stabling to keep your horse, should you require it.

Another tempting option is *Smugglers Barn* (☎ 01323-483855, 🖳 www .smugglersbarn.co.uk; 1D private bathroom with Jacuzzi) which charges £30-35 per person for B&B in a very tastefully restored barn. They also have three self-contained cottages (sleeping 2-4 people) which cost £200-500 for a week but in the low season it may be possible to book them for shorter periods.

Cheap **camping** is available at the informal *Ash Farm* (☎ 01323-487335; 2D/1T/1F), where campers can pitch their tents for £5 per person per night. If it's raining you might prefer to take advantage of their B&B: two of the rooms have en suite facilities and the others share a bathroom. The rate is from £50 to £67 (£31.50 single occupancy). At the time of writing the owners were changing but the new owners are expected to continue with the B&B and camping.

Where to eat and drink

The village pub, the *Eight Bells* (☎ 01323-484442; food Mon-Sat noon-3pm & 6-9pm, Sun noon-9pm), is a five-minute walk up the lane (the blind bend on the road is very dangerous as there is no pavement for pedestrians – it is safer to use the path by the church). The bar is open all day, every day and they have a wide range of pub meals as well as a pleasant garden in which to eat them.

Jevington Tea Gardens (☎ 01323-489692; Mar (Mother's Day)-Oct, Wed-Sun, 10.30am-5pm) at Hawthorne Lodge sell cream teas and coffees indoors or in the garden and they also serve light lunches such as toasties and soups; everything is made on the premises.

In the centre of the village is the highly recommended *Hungry Monk Restaurant* (☎ 01323-482178, 🖳 www.hungrymonk.co.uk; food Tue-Fri noon-2pm & 6.45pm-9.30pm, Sat 6.45pm-9.30pm, Sun noon-2pm; booking is recommended), which claims to be the birthplace, in 1972, of banoffi pie.

Map 50   171

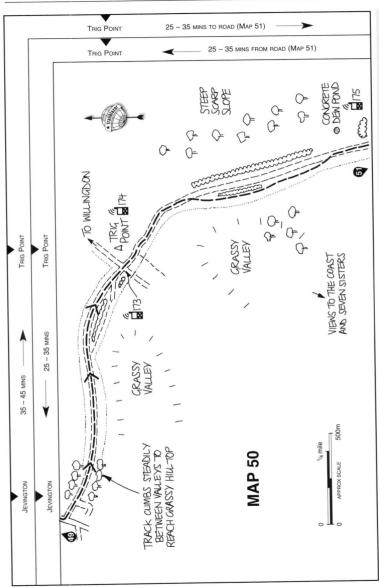

TRIG POINT   25 – 35 MINS TO ROAD (MAP 51) →

TRIG POINT   ← 25 – 35 MINS FROM ROAD (MAP 51)

STEEP
SCARP
SLOPE

CONCRETE
DEW POND

175

TO WILLINGDON

TRIG
POINT 174

173

GRASSY
VALLEY

GRASSY
VALLEY

VIEWS TO THE COAST
AND SEVEN SISTERS

51

TRIG POINT

TRIG POINT

JEVINGTON

JEVINGTON

35 – 45 MINS

25 – 35 MINS

MAP 50

TRACK CLIMBS STEADILY
BETWEEN VALLEYS TO
REACH GRASSY HILL-TOP

49

¼ mile

500m

APPROX SCALE

0

0

Whether you have it or not it will be £33.95 for a three-course dinner, while at lunchtimes it's £16.95 for two courses, £20.50 for three, and £29.95 for Sunday lunch. The menu is extraordinarily imaginative – indeed, they've even produced several books on cooking. There is also a vegetarian option. The cosy interior is very smart with polished tables in four separate dining rooms.

EASTBOURNE   MAP 52, p175

Eastbourne is a typical English seaside resort with something of a reputation as a retirement town.

Having received a lot of unfair criticism over the years as being one of the least adventurous resorts, particularly when compared to its upbeat neighbour Brighton, Eastbourne has recently undergone something of a revival. The signs on the edge of town shout out 'Welcome to the Sunshine Coast' and certainly this is one of the sunnier corners of the UK. However, whether this really is England's Costa del Sol is open to question.

Love it or hate it, Eastbourne, sprawled out below the hill and stretching along the coast, is a safe and friendly town. It may not have the history and charm of Winchester at the other end of the South Downs Way but Beachy Head, at least, makes for a fitting end to a long walk.

The **Wish Tower** is a Martello Tower, one of a number built along the coast to counter an invasion threat from Napoleon.

Services

The commercial centre is around Terminus Rd and the Arndale Shopping Centre, about 30 minutes' walk from the foot of the South Downs and the end of the Way.

The **tourist information centre** (TIC; ☎ 0871-663 0031, 🖳 www.visiteastbourne .com; summer Mon-Fri 9.30am-5.30pm, Sat 9.30am-5pm, winter Mon-Fri 9.30am-4.30pm, Sat 9.30am-1pm) is off the northern end of Terminus Rd on Cornfield Rd. There is plenty of free information here, not only for Eastbourne but also the rest of South-East England and London too. There is also an efficient accommodation-booking service.

The **post office** (Mon-Sat 9am-5.30pm) is not far away on the corner of Langney Rd and along the pedestrianised section of Terminus Rd there are also **chemists** and **banks**.

If you need to replace worn-out socks head to **Millets** or **Blacks**, both outdoor shops, on Terminus Rd (both open Mon-Sat 9am-5.30pm, Sun 10.30am-4.30pm).

Finally, there is a large Sainsbury's **supermarket** in the Arndale Shopping Centre which should cover all trekking food requirements, and another, smaller mini-market (Premier Supermarket) on Seaside Rd which has longer opening hours (daily 8am-11pm).

Regular **trains** (see box p36) from Eastbourne go to Lewes, Brighton, Hastings, Gatwick Airport and London Victoria.

Eastbourne Buses' **bus** No 3 runs to Meads Village at the end of the South Downs Way. Renown Coaches' No 126 goes via Alfriston to Seaford and Brighton & Hove Buses have several services to Brighton: the No 12 and 12a go via Seaford and Newhaven, (occasionally going via Birling Gap and Beachy Head, at least on Sundays). See the public transport map and table, pp38-40.

Try Eastbourne Taxis (☎ 01323-720720) if you need a **taxi**.

Where to stay

As a major seaside resort Eastbourne is overflowing with hotels and guesthouses. Listed here are just a few accommodation choices.

As you head into town from the coastal route you'll find the *Cherry Tree Guesthouse* (☎ 01323-722406, 🖳 www .cherrytree-eastbourne.co.uk; 3S/2T/3D/ 1D or F, all en suite) at 15 Silverdale Rd; it's an Edwardian townhouse with B&B from £42 per person low season to £55 in summer.

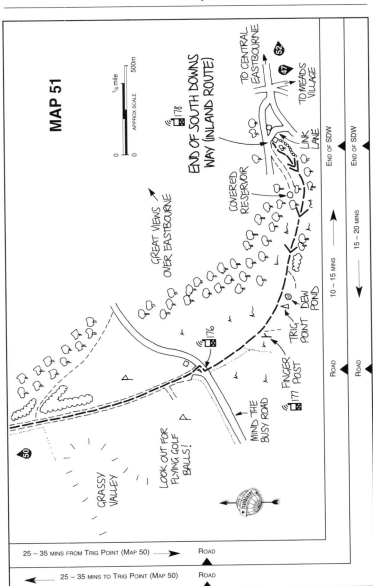

MAP 51

¼ mile

500m

0

0

APPROX SCALE

END OF SOUTH DOWNS WAY (INLAND ROUTE)

TO CENTRAL EASTBOURNE

52

47

TO MEADS VILLAGE

178

LINK LANE

COVERED RESERVOIR

END OF SDW

END OF SDW

GREAT VIEWS OVER EASTBOURNE

10 – 15 MINS

15 – 20 MINS

176

DEW POND

TRIG POINT

ROAD

ROAD

177 FINGER POST

MIND THE BUSY ROAD

50

LOOK OUT FOR FLYING GOLF BALLS!

GRASSY VALLEY

trailblazer

25 – 35 MINS FROM TRIG POINT (MAP 50)

ROAD

25 – 35 MINS TO TRIG POINT (MAP 50)

ROAD

Just around the corner is the slightly cheaper **Brayscroft Hotel** (☎ 01323-647005, 🖳 www.brayscrofthotel.co.uk; 1S/2T/3D, all en suite) at 13 South Cliff Ave, another Edwardian house with lots of antique furniture and beds for £36 per person; suppers available from £7.

Next door at number 15 is **Southcroft** (☎ 01323-729071, 🖳 www.southcrofthotel .co.uk; 2T/3D/1D or T, all en suite) which charges £68-80 depending on the time of year; single occupancy is from £44 to £50.

Along the seafront and King Edward's Parade there's **Alexandra Hotel** (☎ 01323-720131, 🖳 http://alexandrahotel.eastbour ne.biz; 11S/10D/17T, all en suite) where B&B is from £32. There's also **Oban Hotel** (☎ 01323-731581, 🖳 www.oban-hotel.co .uk; 7S/7D/13T/3F, all en suite), a large establishment with B&B from £32 per person.

Another good hotel is **The Gladwyn** (☎ 01323-733142, 🖳 www.gladwynhotel .com; 2S/3D or T/8D, all en suite), at 16 Blackwater Rd, where B&B starts at £30 per person in March, rising to £35 in August.

The following places are all on the north side of Terminus Rd which means a longer walk to get to them if coming from the end of the South Downs Way. Right opposite the pier is the appropriately named **The Pier** (☎ 01323 649544 or ☎ 0870-850 4508, 🖳 www.thepierhoteleastbourne.co .uk; 10S/10D/8T/1F, all en suite), a place that's not without its charms though it could do with a renovation as it's starting to look a little tired. Rooms, nevertheless, are good value at around £35 per person.

Also on the seafront are **Hotel Iverna** (☎ 01323-730768, 🖳 www.hotel-iverna.co .uk; 1S/2D/2T/1F, en suite or private facilities), 32 Marine Parade, with beds from £25 to £35 per person, and which claims to have 'probably the best breakfast in Eastbourne'; and the **Cromwell House** (☎ 01323-725288, 🖳 www.cromwell-house.co.uk; 2S/6D en suite), at 23 Cavendish Place, a Grade II listed Victorian townhouse with beds from £32 per person.

A particularly comfy place to stay is **Sea Beach House Hotel** (☎ 01323-410458, 🖳 www.seabeachhouse.co.uk; 1S/5D/4T, all en suite), at 40 Marine Parade. Most of the rooms have sea views and cost from £35 per person. Alfred, Lord Tennyson, the English poet (1809-92) who penned *The Charge of the Light Brigade*, once stayed in this attractive Georgian, listed building, as did Princess (later to become Queen) Victoria.

Finally, the **Lamb Inn** (☎ 01323-720545, 🖳 www.thelamb-eastbourne.co .uk; 4D/1F), on the High St in the Old Town (about ten minutes' walk north-west of the train station), Eastbourne's oldest pub, will be offering accommodation from summer 2009. New owners took over in January 2009 and the premises were undergoing a complete refurbishment. At the time of writing rates were not decided but were likely to be reasonable.

Where to eat and drink

You will find a surprisingly eclectic mix of restaurants and cafés, most of which are on or around Terminus Rd. On the pedestrianised section of this road are several rough-and-ready pubs with tables outside: **The Terminus** (☎ 01323-733964; food daily noon-3pm) is a bit scruffy but has cheap meals and bar food.

If you are looking for something a little classier there is plenty of choice. For food from across the pond try one of the numerous American-style diners such as the jazzy **Charlie Brown's Diner** (☎ 01323-726588; Tue-Sat 6-11pm), at 54 Seaside Rd, with wooden floors and pictures of New York skyscrapers all over the walls. There are burgers from £7.50 and steaks from £11.50.

Opposite at No 71 is **Mo Mambo's** (☎ 01323-732832; daily noon-10pm), an Italian restaurant with pasta dishes from £6.20 and a good-value lunch menu for just £4.95.

In a similar vein is **Rumble Bellys** (☎ 01323-728247; Mon-Thur 5.30-11pm, Fri 5.30-11.15pm, Sat noon-11.15pm, Sun noon-10.30pm), at 5-7 Seaside Rd, a sit-down diner with apache décor with sirloin for £14.95 and veggie burgers for £5.95.

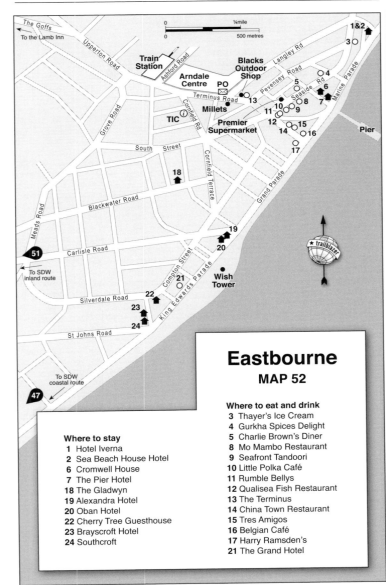

¼mile

500 metres

The Goffs
To the Lamb Inn

Upperton Road

Train Station

Ashford Road

Arndale Centre

PO

Blacks Outdoor Shop

Langley Rd

Pevensey Road

Seaside Rd

Marine Parade

1&2

3

4

5

6

7

Terminus Road

Millets

TIC

Cornfield Rd

Premier Supermarket

13

8

9

10

11

12

14

15

16

17

Pier

Grove Road

South   Street

Cornfield Terrace

18

Blackwater Road

Meads Road

Carlisle Road

51

To SDW inland route

Grand Parade

19

20

Silverdale Road

Compton Street

King Edwards Parade

21

Wish Tower

22

23

24

St Johns Road

To SDW coastal route

47

trailblazer

Eastbourne
MAP 52

Where to eat and drink
3 Thayer's Ice Cream
4 Gurkha Spices Delight
5 Charlie Brown's Diner
8 Mo Mambo Restaurant
9 Seafront Tandoori
10 Little Polka Café
11 Rumble Bellys
12 Qualisea Fish Restaurant
13 The Terminus
14 China Town Restaurant
15 Tres Amigos
16 Belgian Café
17 Harry Ramsden's
21 The Grand Hotel

Where to stay
1 Hotel Iverna
2 Sea Beach House Hotel
6 Cromwell House
7 The Pier Hotel
18 The Gladwyn
19 Alexandra Hotel
20 Oban Hotel
22 Cherry Tree Guesthouse
23 Brayscroft Hotel
24 Southcroft

On the same side of the road at No 55-61 is *Little Polka Café* (Tue-Sun noon-9pm), a Polish café serving such unusual delicacies as hunter's stew or *bigos* (meat, sausages and bacon all stewed with sauerkraut and served with mash) – a great dish if it's been a cold day out. You can also bring your own alcohol (£1 charge) and they do a takeout service too.

There are also a couple of good Mexican restaurants. Near the seafront on Terminus Rd is the cheerful *Tres Amigos* (☎ 01323-739944; Mon-Thur 5-10pm, Fri, Sat & Sun noon-10pm) with a range of tapas dishes from £3.10 and burritos from £8.95.

In a prime location by the seafront is *The Belgian Café* (☎ 01323-729967; food Mon-Fri 11am-3pm & 6-9pm, Sat 11am-10pm & Sun 11am-9pm) where they boast that they offer 50 different ways of eating mussels (including plain old *moules frites*); prices range from £5.95 to £20, and you can wash them down with any one of the 90 Belgian beers on offer here.

The best Indian restaurant is probably the *Seafront Tandoori* (☎ 01323-734608; daily 5.30-11pm), on Seaside Rd, where you can get good balti dishes from £5.95 eat-in or £4.50 take away. A decent rival is the Indian/Nepalese *Gurkha Spices Delight* (☎ 01323-640978; daily noon-2pm & 6-10pm), at 128 Seaside Rd, with a delicious *piro khasi* (spiced chilli hot lamb with ginger and garlic in a tomato-based sauce). Chinese food can be found at the *China Town Restaurant* (daily noon-2.30pm & 6-11.30pm), at 191-3 Terminus Rd. The lengthy menu includes Kung Po chicken (with chestnuts and ginger) for £4.20 and the always-popular crispy duck which is £7 for a quarter.

As a seaside town Eastbourne would not be complete without a few fish and chip outlets. Two of the best are the *Qualisea*

Fish Restaurant (☎ 01323-725203; daily 11am-10pm), at 189 Terminus Rd, which does cod and chips for £5 in the restaurant and £4 for takeaway, and opposite is the chain chippie *Harry Ramsden's* (☎ 01323-417454; daily 11am-10pm winter 11am-8pm), on the seafront at the end of Terminus Rd, where cod and chips costs £5.95-10.95. Another seaside tradition is ice cream; *Thayer's Ice Cream* (open daily 1-5pm) has 32 different flavours of the stuff, with one scoop for £1.40, or it's £3.20 for a Knickerbocker Glory.

The *Lamb Inn* (see Where to stay; food served daily noon-3pm & 6-9.30pm) is Eastbourne's oldest pub but was being refurbished at the time of writing. A selection of real ales should still be available but the menu was expected to change, though traditional fare such as ham, egg and chips should still be included. It is also possible that food will be served all day. An upstairs room is used by a dedicated folk club on Wednesday evenings.

If your walk ends at about tea time and you wish to celebrate in style there can be no better place for a top-of-the-range cream tea than *The Grand Hotel* (☎ 01323-412345, 🖥 www.grandeastbourne.com). It's served daily from 3pm to 6pm when for £21 you get a full spread including sandwiches, quiche and cakes. You can push the boat out even further and order the Grand Champagne Tea (£28). The tea varies slightly depending on the clocks: when they go forward for the summer the dessert is Eton Mess and when they go back for the winter it changes to a spiced-fruit purée. They also do a children's afternoon tea (£10.50) for children up to age 12 accompanied by an adult. The hotel is easy to find: it's on the seafront and you walk right past it on the way into Eastbourne from the end of the South Downs Way. Splash out – you deserve it!

APPENDIX A: MAP KEYS

Town plan key

🛏	Where to stay	ⓘ	Tourist Information	🕗	Bus stop
○	Where to eat	📖	Library/bookstore	ⓣ	Public telephone
△	Campsite	🛈	Internet	⊠	Public toilet
⊠	Post office	🏛	Museum/gallery	—◻—	Rail line & station
©	Bank/ATM	🏠	Church/cathedral		Park
		🕗	Bus station	●	Other

Trail map key

	Hedge		Trees		Boggy / Wet Ground
	Path		Trees	◻	Building
	Other Path		Fence	🠉	Accommodation
	4WD Track		Stone Wall	△	Campsite
	Tarmac Road		Water	†	Church
	Steps		Sand	◪	Public Toilet
	Stile		Boulders	ⓣ	Public Telephone
	Gate		Cliffs	⊗	Bus Stop
	Bridge		Stream	ⱷ	Golf Course
	Pylon / Mast		River	CP	Car Park

APPENDIX B: GPS WAYPOINTS

Each GPS waypoint was taken on the route at the reference number marked on the map as below.

MAP	REF	GPS WAYPOINT		DESCRIPTION
Map 2	001	N51° 03.228'	W01° 16.749'	Join road
Map 2	002	N51° 02.862'	W01° 16.146'	Turn left onto track
Map 2	003	N51° 03.006'	W01° 15.865'	Leave track
Map 3	004	N51° 02.813'	W01° 14.842'	Road crossing
Map 3	005	N51° 02.997'	W01° 14.437'	Through gate on track
Map 3	006	N51° 03.433'	W01° 14.089'	Track junction at farmyard
Map 3	007	N51° 02.955'	W01° 12.769'	Crossroads
Map 4	008	N51° 02.727'	W01° 12.399'	Gate into field
Map 4	009	N51° 02.346'	W01° 12.081'	Cross A272 road
Map 4	010	N51° 01.586'	W01° 11.793'	Join lane leading uphill
Map 5	011	N51° 01.041'	W01° 11.358'	The Milbury's
Map 5	012	N51° 00.821'	W01° 10.521'	Gate to Wind Farm
Map 5	013	N51° 00.580'	W01° 09.631'	Track past houses
Map 6	014	N51° 00.059'	W01° 08.913'	Beacon Hill car park
Map 6	015	N50° 59.555'	W01° 08.413'	Stile to cross fields
Map 6	016	N50° 59.342'	W01° 08.227'	Stile to cross track
Map 7a	017	N50° 59.040'	W01° 07.728'	The Shoe Inn, Exton
Map 7a	018	N50° 59.252'	W01° 07.208'	Bridge over stream
Map 7a	019	N50° 59.196'	W01° 06.725'	Cross disused railway
Map 7a	A	N51° 00.023'	W01° 07.920'	Join track at farm
Map 7a	B	N50° 59.882'	W01° 07.657'	Track junction
Map 7a	C	N50° 59.719'	W01° 07.100'	A32 road crossing
Map 7a	D	N50° 59.735'	W01° 07.047'	Old paper mill
Map 7b	E	N50° 59.484'	W01° 06.433'	Join disused railway
Map 7b	020	N50° 58.854'	W01° 05.328'	Hill fort, Old Winchester Hill
Map 8	021	N50° 59.009'	W01° 04.712'	Turn off track
Map 8	022	N50° 59.279'	W01° 04.827'	Car park
Map 8	023	N50° 59.443'	W01° 04.934'	Gate at fork in road
Map 8	024	N50° 59.238'	W01° 04.546'	Join track
Map 8	025	N50° 59.296'	W01° 04.200'	Left turn at farmyard
Map 8	026	N50° 59.446'	W01° 03.153'	Turn onto tree-lined avenue
Map 8	027	N50° 59.066'	W01° 03.085'	Crossroads
Map 9	028	N50° 58.079'	W01° 02.373'	Wetherdown Hostel
Map 9	029	N50° 57.939'	W01° 01.698'	Road junction
Map 10	030	N50° 58.051'	W01° 00.110'	Homelands Farm
Map 10	031	N50° 58.026'	W00° 59.794'	Junction with Hogs Lodge Lane
Map 10	032	N50° 58.465'	W00° 59.274'	Butser Hill car park
Map 10	033	N50° 57.891'	W00° 58.866'	Gate before A3 road crossing
Map 11	034	N50° 57.501'	W00° 58.639'	Car park, QE Country Park
Map 11	035	N50° 57.938'	W00° 58.020'	Benham Bushes BBQ site
Map 12	036	N50° 58.372'	W00° 57.375'	Car park and road crossing
Map 12	037	N50° 58.206'	W00° 56.456'	Track junction
Map 12	038	N50° 58.153'	W00° 55.787'	Road junction
Map 13	039	N50° 57.980'	W00° 54.137'	Road crossing
Map 13	040	N50° 57.611'	W00° 53.213'	Car park, B2146 road crossing

MAP	REF	GPS WAYPOINT		DESCRIPTION
Map 13	041	N50° 57.435'	W00° 52.672'	Car park, B2141 road crossing
Map 14	042	N50° 57.659'	W00° 51.469'	Turn-off to East Harting
Map 14	043	N50° 57.547'	W00° 51.119'	Trig point, Beacon Hill
Map 14	044	N50° 57.535'	W00° 50.447'	Path, not farm track!
Map 14	045	N50° 57.267'	W00° 49.981'	Track junction
Map 15	046	N50° 56.760'	W00° 49.665'	Track crossroads
Map 15	047	N50° 56.999'	W00° 48.587'	Track crossroads
Map 15	048	N50° 56.873'	W00° 47.494'	Path junction, Cocking Down
Map 16	049	N50° 56.759'	W00° 47.002'	Track crossroads
Map 16	050	N50° 56.660'	W00° 46.360'	Junction near ball of chalk
Map 16	051	N50° 56.571'	W00° 45.338'	Car park at A268 crossing
Map 16	052	N50° 56.544'	W00° 45.002'	Water tap
Map 17	053	N50° 56.440'	W00° 44.226'	Fork in track
Map 17	054	N50° 56.463'	W00° 43.706'	Path junction
Map 17	055	N50° 56.466'	W00° 43.258'	Turn-off to Heyshott
Map 18	056	N50° 56.457'	W00° 42.857'	Path junction
Map 18	057	N50° 56.378'	W00° 42.375'	Track junction
Map 18	058	N50° 56.353'	W00° 42.128'	Track junction
Map 18	059	N50° 56.239'	W00° 40.938'	Signpost with memorials
Map 18	060	N50° 56.016'	W00° 39.082'	Track junction
Map 19	061	N50° 55.902'	W00° 39.598'	Track crossroads
Map 19	062	N50° 55.307'	W00° 38.925'	Cross A285 road
Map 19	063	N50° 54.803'	W00° 38.488'	Track junction
Map 20	064	N50° 54.441'	W00° 37.926'	Track junction
Map 20	065	N50° 54.402'	W00° 37.319'	Track junction
Map 20	066	N50° 54.464'	W00° 36.968'	Bignor Hill car park
Map 20	067	N50° 54.587'	W00° 36.157'	Grave
Map 21	068	N50° 54.470'	W00° 35.814'	Track junction
Map 21	069	N50° 53.884'	W00° 34.403'	Cross A29 road
Map 21	070	N50° 53.837'	W00° 33.310'	Cross country lane
Map 22	071	N50° 53.952'	W00° 32.927'	Bridge over River Arun
Map 22	072	N50° 54.025'	W00° 32.358'	Leave B2139 road
Map 22	073	N50° 54.195'	W00° 31.927'	Road junction
Map 22	074	N50° 54.188'	W00° 31.839'	Leave road
Map 22	075	N50° 54.158'	W00° 31.215'	Gate & stile
Map 23	076	N50° 54.190'	W00° 30.413'	Join track
Map 23	077	N50° 54.145'	W00° 29.540'	Track junction
Map 23	078	N50° 54.111'	W00° 28.747'	Track junction
Map 23	079	N50° 54.051'	W00° 28.347'	Turn-off to Storrington
Map 25	080	N50° 53.656'	W00° 26.641'	New barn
Map 25	081	N50° 53.755'	W00° 26.032'	Gate on track
Map 25	082	N50° 53.791'	W00° 25.812'	Turn-off to Washington
Map 25	083	N50° 54.279'	W00° 25.030'	Join track
Map 25	084	N50° 54.251'	W00° 24.885'	Join road into Washington
Map 25	085	N50° 54.304'	W00° 24.306'	Frankland Arms, Washington
Map 25	086	N50° 54.189'	W00° 24.382'	Road junction, Washington
Map 25	087	N50° 53.807'	W00° 24.344'	Steep section of track
Map 26	088	N50° 53.617'	W00° 23.643'	Track junction
Map 26	089	N50° 53.757'	W00° 23.351'	Gate on track
Map 26	090	N50° 53.779'	W00° 22.928'	Chanctonbury Ring
Map 26	091	N50° 53.637'	W00° 22.612'	Gate on track

MAP	REF	GPS WAYPOINT		DESCRIPTION
Map 26	092	N50° 53.409'	W00° 22.421'	Track junction
Map 26	093	N50° 53.269'	W00° 22.001'	Track junction
Map 27	094	N50° 53.219'	W00° 21.675'	Turn-off to Steyning
Map 27	095	N50° 52.669'	W00° 20.972'	Track junction
Map 29	096	N50° 52.403'	W00° 17.958'	Turn-off A283 road
Map 29	097	N50° 52.430'	W00° 17.094'	Car park
Map 29	098	N50° 52.881'	W00° 15.991'	Join road to Truleigh Hill YH
Map 30	099	N50° 52.919'	W00° 15.461'	Truleigh Hill
Map 30	100	N50° 53.063'	W00° 13.763'	Turn-off to Fulking
Map 30	101	N50° 52.937'	W00° 13.213'	Gate
Map 31	102	N50° 53.092'	W00° 12.744'	Devil's Dyke Pub
Map 31	103	N50° 52.978'	W00° 12.254'	Gate on path
Map 31	104	N50° 53.309'	W00° 11.663'	Road crossing
Map 31	105	N50° 53.349'	W00° 11.466'	Gate into woodland
Map 31	106	N50° 53.410'	W00° 10.968'	Gate on path
Map 32	107	N50° 53.743'	W00° 10.001'	Join road
Map 32	108	N50° 53.923'	W00° 09.837'	Crossroads, Pyecombe
Map 32	109	N50° 54.056'	W00° 09.593'	Car park at golf club
Map 32	110	N50° 54.026'	W00° 08.687'	Track crossroads
Map 32	111	N50° 54.227'	W00° 08.718'	Track junction
Map 33	112	N50° 54.027'	W00° 07.845'	Turn-off to Dower Cottage
Map 33	113	N50° 54.146'	W00° 07.327'	Dew pond
Map 33	114	N50° 54.046'	W00° 06.278'	Car park, Ditchling Beacon
Map 33	115	N50° 53.940'	W00° 05.814'	Turn-off to Ditchling
Map 34	116	N50° 53.910'	W00° 04.709'	Road crossing
Map 34	117	N50° 53.876'	W00° 04.387'	Turn-off to Plumpton
Map 34	118	N50° 53.759'	W00° 03.198'	Turn-off to Lewes
Map 35	119	N50° 53.259'	W00° 03.666'	Gate at track junction
Map 35	120	N50° 53.000'	W00° 03.295'	Leave track through gate
Map 35	121	N50° 52.505'	W00° 02.808'	Through gate & stile
Map 35	122	N50° 52.426'	W00° 03.190'	Small hut and pylon
Map 35	123	N50° 51.977'	W00° 03.268'	Steps
Map 35	124	N50° 51.977'	W00° 03.487'	Bridge over A27 road
Map 35	125	N50° 51.872'	W00° 02.952'	Pass under railway
Map 36	126	N50° 51.548'	W00° 03.227'	Through gate
Map 36	127	N50° 51.224'	W00° 03.463'	Through gate
Map 36	128	N50° 51.025'	W00° 03.266'	Through gate, follow fence
Map 36	129	N50° 51.278'	W00° 02.526'	Through gate by dew pond
Map 36	130	N50° 51.032'	W00° 01.876'	Join track
Map 37	131	N50° 50.673'	W00° 01.557'	Track, Swanborough Hill
Map 37	132	N50° 50.086'	E00° 00.479'	Leave track through gate
Map 38	133	N50° 50.009'	E00° 00.149'	Through gate, cross track
Map 38	134	N50° 49.566'	E00° 00.315'	Through gate onto track
Map 38	135	N50° 49.795'	E00° 01.061'	Road junction, Southease
Map 38	136	N50° 49.805'	E00° 01.562'	Bridge over River Ouse
Map 38	137	N50° 49.888'	E00° 01.849'	Level crossing
Map 38	138	N50° 49.804'	E00° 02.228'	Bridge over A26
Map 39	139	N50° 49.875'	E00° 03.090'	Trig point & dew pond
Map 39	140	N50° 50.092'	E00° 03.667'	Gate onto track
Map 39	141	N50° 50.063'	E00° 04.114'	Masts, Beddingham Hill
Map 39	142	N50° 50.069'	E00° 04.468'	Gate on path

MAP	REF	GPS WAYPOINT		DESCRIPTION
Map 40	143	N50° 50.018'	E00° 04.987'	Car park, Firle Beacon
Map 40	144	N50° 50.029'	E00° 06.497'	Trig point, Firle Beacon
Map 40	145	N50° 49.527'	E00° 07.208'	Gate, Bo Peep
Map 41	146	N50° 49.108'	E00° 07.823'	Gate on path
Map 41	147	N50° 48.659'	E00° 08.550'	Track junction
Map 42	148	N50° 48.405'	E00° 09.581'	Church, Alfriston
Map 42	149	N50° 48.689'	E00° 09.581'	Plough & Harrow, Litlington
Map 43	150	N50° 47.440'	E00° 09.628'	Through stile on path
Map 43	151	N50° 47.098'	E00° 09.471'	Steps up through forest
Map 43	152	N50° 46.707'	E00° 09.699'	Track junction
Map 43	153	N50° 46.398'	E00° 09.559'	Crossroads, West Dean
Map 43	154	N50° 46.499'	E00° 09.244'	Road crossing, Exceat
Map 44	155	N50° 45.905'	E00° 09.085'	Turn off track
Map 44	156	N50° 45.909'	E00° 09.508'	Stile on path
Map 44	157	N50° 45.376'	E00° 09.578'	Haven Brow
Map 44	158	N50° 45.310'	E00° 09.793'	Short Brow
Map 44	159	N50° 45.198'	E00° 10.139'	Rough Brow
Map 44	160	N50° 45.143'	E00° 10.376'	Brass Point
Map 45	161	N50° 44.995'	E00° 10.792'	Sarsen stone
Map 45	162	N50° 44.957'	E00° 11.020'	The 'Eighth' Sister
Map 45	163	N50° 44.910'	E00° 11.284'	Baily's Hill
Map 45	164	N50° 44.570'	E00° 11.462'	Memorial pillar
Map 45	165	N50° 44.766'	E00° 11.667'	Went Hill
Map 45	166	N50° 44.585'	E00° 12.075'	Car park, Birling Gap
Map 46	167	N50° 44.302'	E00° 12.901'	Belle Tout Lighthouse
Map 46	168	N50° 44.112'	E00° 13.870'	Path near Shooters Bottom
Map 47	169	N50° 44.335'	E00° 15.220'	Lookout point
Map 47	170	N50° 44.634'	E00° 15.478'	Fork in path
Map 47	171	N50° 45.113'	E00° 16.027'	End of SDW coastal route
Map 49	172	N50° 47.518'	E00° 12.825'	Jevington Tea Gardens
Map 50	173	N50° 47.222'	E00° 14.083'	Turn-off to Willingdon
Map 50	174	N50° 47.196'	E00° 14.162'	Trig point
Map 50	175	N50° 46.658'	E00° 14.575'	Concrete dew pond
Map 51	176	N50° 45.901'	E00° 14.776'	Road crossing
Map 51	177	N50° 45.729'	E00° 15.000'	Finger post
Map 51	178	N50° 45.697'	E00° 15.830'	End of SDW inland route

INDEX

Page references in bold type refer to maps

188 Other walking guides from Trailblazer

TREKKING GUIDES
Europe
Corsica Trekking – GR20
Dolomites Trekking – AV1 & AV2
Scottish Highlands – The Hillwalking Guide
Tour du Mont Blanc
Trekking in the Pyrenees
Walker's Haute Route: Mt Blanc to Matterhorn

South America
Inca Trail, Cusco & Machu Picchu

Africa
Kilimanjaro
Moroccan Atlas – The Trekking Guide

Australasia
New Zealand – The Great Walks

Asia
Trekking in the Annapurna Region
Trekking in the Everest Region
Trekking in Ladakh

The Walker's Haute Route – Mt Blanc to the Matterhorn
Alexander Stewart 1st edn, 256pp, 60 maps, 30 colour photos
ISBN 978-1-905864-08-9, £12.99
From Mont Blanc to the Matterhorn, Chamonix to Zermatt, the 180km walkers' Haute Route traverses one of the finest stretches of the Pennine Alps – the range between Valais in Switzerland and Piedmont and Aosta Valley in Italy. Includes Chamonix and Zermatt guides.

Tour du Mont Blanc   *Jim Manthorpe*
1st edition, 208pp, 60 maps, 30 colour photos
ISBN 978-1-905864-12-6, £11.99
At 4810m (15,781ft), Mont Blanc is the highest mountain in western Europe, and one of the most famous mountains in the world. The snow-dome summit is the top of a spectacular massif stretching 60 miles by 20 miles, arguably the most magnificent mountain scenery in Europe. The trail (105 miles, 168km) that circumnavigates the massif, passing through France, Italy and Switzerland, is the most popular long distance walk in Europe. Includes Chamonix and Courmayeur guides.

Corsica Trekking – GR20   *David Abram*
1st edition, 208pp, 32 maps, 30 colour photos
ISBN 978-1-873756-98-0, £11.99
Slicing diagonally across Corsica's jagged spine, the legendary red-and-white waymarks of the GR20 guide trekkers across a succession of snow-streaked passes, Alpine meadows, massive boulder fields and pristine forests of pine and oak – often within sight of the sea. Physically demanding from start to finish, it's a superlative 170km, two-week trek. Includes guides to gateway towns: Ajaccio, Bastia, Calvi, Corte and Porte-Vecchio. *'Indispensible'. **The Independent*** *'Excellent guide'. **The Sunday Times***

New Zealand – The Great Walks   *Alexander Stewart*
2nd edition, 272pp, 60 maps, 40 colour photos
ISBN 978-1-905864-11-9, £12.99
New Zealand is a wilderness paradise of incredibly beautiful landscapes. There is no better way to experience it than on one of the nine designated Great Walks, the country's premier walking tracks which provide outstanding hiking opportunities for people at all levels of fitness. Also includes detailed guides to Auckland, Wellington, National Park Village, Taumaranui, Nelson, Queenstown, Te Anau and Oban.

Trekking in the Everest Region *Jamie McGuinness*
5th edition, 320pp, 30 maps, 30 colour photos
ISBN 978-1-873756-99-7, £12.99

New 5th edition of this popular guide to the Everest region, the world's most famous trekking region. Includes planning, preparation and getting to Nepal; detailed route guides – with 30 route maps and 50 village plans; Kathmandu city guide – where to stay, where to eat, what to see. Written by a professional trekking and mountaineering leader.

Trekking in the Annapurna Region *Bryn Thomas*
4th edition, 288pp, 55 maps, 28 colour photos
ISBN 978-1-873756-68-3, £11.99

Fully revised guide to the most popular walking region in the Himalaya. Includes route guides, Kathmandu and Pokhara city guides and getting to Nepal. *'Good guides read like a novel and have you packing in no time. Two from Trailblazer Publications which fall into this category are* 'Trekking in the Annapurna Region' *and* 'Silk Route by Rail' *'. Today*

Trekking in Ladakh *Charlie Loram*
3rd edition, 288pp, 75 maps, 24 colour photos
ISBN 978-1-873756-75-1, £12.99

Fully revised and extended 3rd edition of Charlie Loram's practical guide. Includes 75 detailed walking maps, guides to Leh, Manali and Delhi plus information on getting to Ladakh. *'Extensive...and well researched'.* **Climber Magazine** *'Were it not for this book we might still be blundering about...'* **The Independent on Sunday**

Scottish Highlands – The Hillwalking Guide
1st edition, Jim Manthorpe 312pp, 86 maps, 40 photos
ISBN 978-1-873756-84-3, £11.99

This guide covers 60 day-hikes in the following areas: ● Loch Lomond, the Trossachs and Southern Highlands ● Glen Coe and Ben Nevis ● Central Highlands ● Cairngorms and Eastern Highlands ● Western Highlands ● North-West Highlands ● The Far North ● The Islands. Plus: 3- to 4-day hikes linking some regions.

Dolomites Trekking Alta Via 1 & Alta Via 2 *Henry Stedman*
2nd edn, 192pp, 52 trail maps, 7 town plans, 38 colour photos
ISBN 978-1-873756-83-6, £11.99

AV1 (9-13 days) & AV2 (10-16 days) are the most popular long-distance hikes in the Dolomites. Numerous shorter walks also included. Places to stay, walking times and points of interest, plus detailed guides to Cortina and six other towns.

Kilimanjaro: the trekking guide to Africa's highest mountain
Henry Stedman, 2nd edition, 320pp, 40 maps, 30 photos
ISBN 978-1-873756-97-1, £11.99
At 19,340ft the world's tallest freestanding mountain, Kilimanjaro is one of the most popular destinations for hikers visiting Africa. It's possible to walk up to the summit: no technical skills are necessary. Includes town guides to Nairobi and Dar-Es-Salaam, excursions in the region and a detailed colour guide to flora and fauna. **Includes Mount Meru**. *'Stedman's wonderfully down-to-earth, practical guide to the mountain'.* **Longitude Books**

Himalaya by Bike – a route & planning guide
Laura Stone 368pp, 28 colour & 50 B&W photos, 60 maps
ISBN 978 1 905864 04 1, *1st edn*, £16.99
An all-in-one guide for Himalayan cycle-touring. Covers the Himalayan regions of Pakistan, Tibet, India, Nepal and Sikkim with detailed km-by-km guides to main routes including the Karakoram Highway and the Friendship Highway. Plus town and city guides.

Adventure Motorcycling Handbook – a route & planning guide
Chris Scott, 5th edn, 288pp, 28 colour & 100 B&W photos
ISBN 978 1 873756 80 5, £12.99
Every red-blooded motor-cyclist dreams of making the Big Trip – this book shows you how. Top ten overland machines, choosing a destination, bike preparation, documentation and shipping, route outlines. Plus – ten first-hand accounts of epic biking adventures worldwide.
'The first thing we did was buy the Adventure Motorcycling Handbook*'*
Ewan McGregor, *The Long Way Round*

Adventure Cycle-Touring Handbook – a route & planning guide
Stephen Lord, 320pp, 28 colour & 100 B&W photos
ISBN 978 1 873756 89 8, *1st edition*, £13.99
New guide for anyone planning (or dreaming) about taking a bicycle on a long-distance adventure. This comprehensive manual will make that dream a reality whether it's cycling in Tibet or pedalling from Patagonia to Alaska. Part 1 covers Practicalities; Part 2 includes Route outlines; and Part 3 has Tales from the Saddle. *'The definitive guide to how, where, why and what to do on a cycle expedition'* **Adventure Travel**

Tibet Overland – a route & planning guide
Kym McConnell
1st edition, 224pp, 16pp colour maps
ISBN 978 1 873756 41 6, £12.99
Featuring 16pp of full colour mapping based on satellite photographs, this is a guide for mountain bikers and other road users in Tibet. Includes detailed information on over 9000km of overland routes across the world's highest and largest plateau. Includes Lhasa–Kathmandu route and the route to Everest North Base Camp. '... *a wealth of advice...*' **HH The Dalai Lama**

Sahara Overland – a route & planning guide
Chris Scott
2nd edition, 640pp, 24 colour & 170 B&W photos
ISBN 978 1 873756 76 8 Hardback £19.99
Fully-updated 2nd edition covers all aspects Saharan, from acquiring documentation to vehicle choice and preparation; from descriptions of the prehistoric art sites of the Libyan Fezzan to the ancient caravan cities of southern Mauritania. How to 'read' sand surfaces, using GPS – it's all here along with detailed off-road itineraries covering 26,000kms in nine countries. *'THE essential desert companion for anyone planning a Saharan trip on either two wheels or four.'* **Trailbike Magazine**

Trans-Siberian Handbook
Bryn Thomas
7th edition, 448pp, 60 maps, 40 colour photos
ISBN 978 1 873756 94 2, £13.99
First edition short-listed for the **Thomas Cook Guidebook Awards**. New seventh edition of the most popular guide to the world's longest rail journey. How to arrange a trip, plus a km-by-km guide to the routes. Updated and expanded to include extra information on travelling independently in Russia. New mapping. *'The best guidebook is Bryn Thomas's "Trans-Siberian Handbook"'* **The Independent**

TRAILBLAZER GUIDES – TITLE LIST

Adventure Cycle-Touring Handbook	1st edn out now
Adventure Motorcycling Handbook	5th edn out now
Australia by Rail	5th edn out now
Azerbaijan	3rd edn out now
The Blues Highway – New Orleans to Chicago	2nd edn out now
China Rail Handbook	1st edn early 2010
Coast to Coast (British Walking Guide)	3rd edn out now
Cornwall Coast Path (British Walking Guide)	3rd edn Apr 2009
Corsica Trekking – GR20	1st edn out now
Cotswold Way (British Walking Guide)	1st edn out now
Dolomites Trekking – AV1 & AV2	2nd edn out now
Inca Trail, Cusco & Machu Picchu	3rd edn out now
Indian Rail Handbook	1st edn late 2009
Hadrian's Wall Path (British Walking Guide)	2nd edn out now
Himalaya by Bike – a route and planning guide	1st edn out now
Japan by Rail	2nd edn out now
Kilimanjaro – the trekking guide (includes Mt Meru)	2nd edn out now
Mediterranean Handbook	1st edn out now
Morocco Overland (4WD/motorcycling/cycling)	1st edn mid 2009
Moroccan Atlas – The Trekking Guide	1st edn mid 2009
Nepal Mountaineering Guide	1st edn late 2009
New Zealand – The Great Walks	2nd edn Apr 2009
North Downs Way (British Walking Guide)	1st edn out now
Norway's Arctic Highway	1st edn out now
Offa's Dyke Path (British Walking Guide)	2nd edn out now
Overlanders' Handbook – worldwide driving guide	1st edn Jan 2010
Pembrokeshire Coast Path (British Walking Guide)	2nd edn out now
Pennine Way (British Walking Guide)	2nd edn out now
The Ridgeway (British Walking Guide)	2nd edn out now
Siberian BAM Guide – rail, rivers & road	2nd edn out now
The Silk Roads – a route and planning guide	2nd edn out now
Sahara Overland – a route and planning guide	2nd edn out now
Sahara Abenteuerhandbuch (German edition)	1st edn out now
Scottish Highlands – The Hillwalking Guide	1st edn out now
South Downs Way (British Walking Guide)	3rd edn out now
South-East Asia – The Graphic Guide	1st edn out now
Tibet Overland – mountain biking & jeep touring	1st edn out now
Tour du Mont Blanc	1st edn out now
Trans-Canada Rail Guide	4th edn out now
Trans-Siberian Handbook	7th edn out now
Trekking in the Annapurna Region	4th edn out now
Trekking in the Everest Region	5th edn out now
Trekking in Ladakh	3rd edn out now
Trekking in the Pyrenees	3rd edn out now
The Walker's Haute Route – Mont Blanc to Matterhorn	1st edn out now
West Highland Way (British Walking Guide)	3rd edn out now

For more information about Trailblazer and our expanding range of guides, for guidebook updates or for credit card mail order sales visit our website:

www.trailblazer-guides.com

ROUTE GUIDES FOR THE ADVENTUROUS TRAVELLER

TRAILBLAZER'S LONG-DISTANCE PATH (LDP) WALKING GUIDES

We've applied to destinations which are closer to home Trailblazer's proven formula for publishing definitive route guides for adventurous travellers. Britain's network of long-distance trails enables the walker to explore some of the finest landscapes in the country's best walking areas and they are an obvious starting point for this series. These are guides that are user-friendly, practical, informative and environmentally sensitive.

● Unique mapping features

In many walking guidebooks the reader has to read a route description then try to relate it to the map. Our guides are much easier to use because walking directions, tricky junctions, places to stay and eat, points of interest and walking times are all written onto the maps themselves in the places to which they apply. With their uncluttered clarity, these are not general-purpose maps but fully edited maps drawn by walkers for walkers.

● Largest-scale walking maps

At a scale of just under 1:20,000 (8cm or 3^1/$_8$ inches to one mile) the maps in these guides are bigger than even the most detailed British walking maps currently available in the shops.

● Not just a trail guide – includes where to stay, where to eat and public transport
Our guidebooks are a complete guide, not just a trail guide. They include: what to see, where to stay (pubs, hotels, B&Bs, campsites, bunkhouses, hostels), where to eat. There is detailed public transport information for all access points to each trail so there are itineraries for all walkers, both for hiking the route in its entirety and for day walks.

West Highland Way *Charlie Loram* ISBN 978-1-905864-13-3, £9.99
3rd edition, 192pp, 53 maps, 10 town plans, 40 colour photos

Pennine Way *Keith Carter & Chris Scott* ISBN 978-1-905864-02-7, £11.99
2nd edition, 272pp, 135 maps & town plans, 40 colour photos

Coast to Coast *Henry Stedman* ISBN 978-1-905864-09-6, £9.99
3rd edition, 240pp, 109 maps & town plans, 40 colour photos

Pembrokeshire Coast Path *Jim Manthorpe* ISBN 978-1-905864-03-4, £9.99
2nd edition, 208pp, 96 maps & town plans, 40 colour photos

Offa's Dyke Path *Keith Carter* ISBN 978-1-905864-06-5, £9.99
2nd edition, 208pp, 88 maps & town plans, 40 colour photos

South Downs Way *Jim Manthorpe* ISBN 978-1-905864-18-8, £9.99
3rd edition, 192pp, 60 maps & town plans, 40 colour photos

Hadrian's Wall Path *Henry Stedman* ISBN 978-1-905864-14-0, £9.99
2nd edition, 208pp, 60 maps & town plans, 40 colour photos

North Downs Way *John Curtin* ISBN 978-1-873756-96-6, £9.99
1st edition, 192pp, 60 maps & town plans, 40 colour photos

The Ridgeway *Nick Hill* ISBN 978-1-905864-17-1, £9.99
2nd edition, 192pp, 53 maps & town plans, 40 colour photos

Cotswold Way *Tricia & Bob Hayne* ISBN 978-1-905864-16-4, £9.99
1st edition, 192pp, 60 maps & town plans, 40 colour photos

Cornwall Coast Path *Edith Schofield* ISBN 978-1-873756-93-5, £9.99
2nd edition, 224pp, 112 maps & town plans, 40 colour photos

> '*The same attention to detail that distinguishes its other guides*
> *has been brought to bear here*'. **The Sunday Times**